International Perspectives on Theorizing Aspirations

Social Theory and Methodology in Education Research series

Edited by Mark Murphy

The Bloomsbury *Social Theory and Methodology in Education Research* series brings together books exploring various applications of social theory in educational research design. Each book provides a detailed account of how theory and method influence each other in specific educational research settings, such as schools, early childhood education, community education, further education colleges and universities. Books in the series represent the richness of topics explored in theory-driven education research, including leadership and governance, equity, teacher education, assessment, curriculum and policy studies. This innovative series provides a timely platform for highlighting the wealth of international work carried out in the field of social theory and education research, a field that has grown considerably in recent years and has made the likes of Pierre Bourdieu and Michel Foucault familiar names in educational discourse. Books in the *Social Theory and Methodology in Education Research* series offer an excellent resource for those who wish to use theoretical concepts in their research but are not sure how to do so, and who want to better understand how theory can be effectively applied in research contexts, in practically realisable ways.

Also available in the series

Education Governance and Social Theory, edited by
Andrew Wilkins and Antonio Olmedo
Foucault and School Leadership Research, Denise Mifsud

Forthcoming in the series

Education Research with Bourdieu, Julie Rowlands and Shaun Rawolle
Norbert Elias and the Sociology of Education, Eric Lybeck
Poststructuralist Theory and Educational Research, Tim Jay
Social Theory for Teacher Education Research, edited by
Kathleen Nolan and Jennifer Tupper
The Future of Qualitative Research, edited by
Matthew Thomas and Robin Bellingham

International Perspectives on Theorizing Aspirations

Applying Bourdieu's Tools

Edited by
Garth Stahl, Derron Wallace,
Ciaran Burke and Steven Threadgold

BLOOMSBURY ACADEMIC
LONDON • NEW YORK • OXFORD • NEW DELHI • SYDNEY

BLOOMSBURY ACADEMIC
Bloomsbury Publishing Plc
50 Bedford Square, London, WC1B 3DP, UK
1385 Broadway, New York, NY 10018, USA

BLOOMSBURY, BLOOMSBURY ACADEMIC and the Diana logo are trademarks
of Bloomsbury Publishing Plc

First published in Great Britain 2019

Cover design: Anna Berzovan
Cover image © Nanette Hoogslag / GettyImages

A catalogue record for this book is available from the British Library.

A catalog record for this book is available from the Library of Congress.

ISBN: HB: 978-1-3500-4033-5
ePDF: 978-1-3500-4117-2
eBook: 978-1-3500-4034-2

Series: Social Theory and Methodology in Education Research

Typeset by Deanta Global Publishing Services, Chennai, India
Printed and bound in Great Britain

To find out more about our authors and books visit www.bloomsbury.com
and sign up for our newsletters.

Contents

List of Figures and Tables

Figures

Tables

Notes on Contributors

Barbara Adewumi is a lecturer in sociology and social research methods at the University of Canterbury. She currently teaches sociology and social research methods across sociology, criminology and social work disciplines for undergraduates. Prior to her academic career she was a research consultant for the Work Foundation. Her research and scholarly interests include the aspirations of the black middle class in Britain, critical race theory, Bourdieu's forms of capital, lived experiences of Caribbean and African diaspora, and more recently how culturally contextualized ethnic minority groups shape their identity, engage and navigate through higher education and in the workplace.

Jim Albright is a professor in the School of Education at the University of Newcastle and Editor-in-Chief for *Educational Science*. Jim's interests range from literacy education and curriculum theory and design to professional learning and school reform. Recently, his work has focused on developing teacher capacity across subject areas through the building of conditions needed in schools for innovative teaching and improved student performance.

Pere Ayling is a lecturer and a researcher at the University of Suffolk, Ipswich, United Kingdom. Her areas of specialization include consumption, (in)equality, race, elite education and class (re)production strategies. She is particularly interested in how social class, gender and race as well as (dis)ability intersect to (re)produce 'privilege' and 'inequality' in education and society in general. Her latest publications include 'The Three Rs: Parental Risk Management Strategies in the International Secondary Education Market' (*Journal of Curriculum Inquiry*, 2017); 'Diversity, Equality and Rights' in *(Dis)abled Childhood?* (Palgrave Macmillan, 2018) and *Distinction, Exclusivity and Whiteness: Elite Nigerian Parents and the International Education Market* (Springer, forthcoming).

Tamsin Bowers-Brown is learning, teaching and student experience lead in the Centre for Excellence in Learning and Teaching, University of Derby. As a sociologist of education, her research focuses on inequalities in education, pedagogy and student experience. She has a strong interest in creating inclusive learning experiences that encourage critical thinking and reflection. Her scholarship has shown how policies and practice can reduce or entrench disadvantage. Her recent research relates to the aspirations of girls in secondary education in England. Recent publications include "'It's Like If You Don't Go to Uni, You Fail in Life": Bourdieu, Decision Making and the Forms of Capital', in J. Thatcher, N. Ingram, C. Burke and J. Abrahams (eds), *Bourdieu: The Next Generation*, London: Routledge, 2016.

Ciaran Burke is an associate professor of higher education at the University of Derby, UK. His research focuses on issues of access to higher education and entry into the graduate labour market. His work has applied and extended Bourdieusian social theory and in particular developed the application of inverted symbolic violence and institutional habitus. He is a founding member of the British Sociological Association Bourdieu Study Group and an executive member of the Sociological Association of Ireland.

Kristin Cipollone is an assistant professor of curriculum and instruction in elementary education at Ball State University, Indiana. Her two strands of research focus on the intersections of race and class in the transition from high school to college and their influence on the (re)production and maintenance of inequality, and the preparation of culturally responsive teachers. She is co-author of the recent book *Class Warfare: Class, Race, and College Admission in Top-Tier Secondary Schools* (University of Chicago, 2014) and has recently published in *Sociology of Education, Urban Education*, the *British Journal of Sociology of Education, American Education Research Journal* and has a forthcoming co-authored piece in the *Journal of Teacher Education*.

Russell Cross is an associate professor in language and literacy education within the Melbourne Graduate School of Education, where he leads their teaching and research initiatives in bilingual education and content and language integrated learning (CLIL). His research focuses on teachers' work, with particular attention to the social, cultural and political dimensions of professional teacher knowledge and practice from a Vygotskian sociocultural perspective. His work has appeared widely in *Modern Language Journal, Teachers & Teaching, Language & Education, Journal of Curriculum Studies, British Journal of Sociology of Education* and the *Journal of Teacher Education* among others.

Marta Curran has a PhD in sociology from the Autonomous University of Barcelona and is a member of the globalization, education and social policies and interdisciplinary group on education policies research groups. Her main research areas are education inequalities related to class and gender, and educational policies and programmes. Her doctoral thesis deals with how gender and class shape educational experiences, expectations and decisions.

Joan Forbes is an honorary professor in education at the Centre for Child Wellbeing and Protection, Faculty of Social Sciences, University of Stirling. Her research interests include social theory, questions of knowledge and power, and policy sociology. Her empirical and theoretical research on elite independent schooling is published in several international journals including *British Journal of Sociology of Education, Gender and Education, International Journal of Qualitative Studies in Education* and *Research Papers in Education*; and in edited collections including *Privilege, Agency and Affect* (Palgrave Macmillan, 2013), *Elite Education: International Perspectives* (Routledge, 2016), and *New Sociologies of Elite Schooling* (Routledge, 2017).

Trevor Gale is a professor of education policy and social justice at the University of Glasgow. His research is focused on the reproduction of inequalities in and through practices in formal education systems, particularly in schools and in higher education. His most recent publications include *Policy and Inequality in Education* (Springer, 2017), *Practice Theory and Education* (Routledge, 2017), and articles in the *Journal of Education*, the *British Journal of Sociology of Education* and the *Journal of Teacher Education*. He is the founding editor of *Critical Studies in Education* and of the Springer book series 'Education Policy and Social Inequality'.

Sol Gamsu is a postdoctoral researcher at the University of Bath. His PhD (geography, King's College London) examined the contemporary and historical geography of elite schooling across the UK. He works on an ESRC-funded research project led by Michael Donnelly exploring spatial and social mobility on entry to and graduation from UK universities. His interests lie at the intersection of sociology, geography and history, with a focus on the formation of educational inequalities over time and in space. His work on elite schooling was published in *Urban Studies* and another paper forms part of a forthcoming special issue of the *British Journal of Sociology*.

Jennifer Gore is a laureate professor in the School of Education at the University of Newcastle. Jenny is Director of the Teachers and Teaching Research Centre at the university and is Co-Editor of the international journal *Teaching and Teacher Education*. Her educational and research interests have consistently centred on quality and equity, including studies of teacher socialization, power relations in teaching, reform of teaching and teacher education, and teacher development.

Kathryn Holmes is a professor of education (science, mathematics and technology) and Director of Research in the School of Education at Western Sydney University. Her research interests focus on the application of technology in education, increasing participation in STEM disciplines, and improving quality, equity and access in schools and higher education.

Claire Maxwell is a reader in sociology of education at UCL Institute of Education, University College London. She has published widely on elite and private education focusing on the English system, theorizing the intersections between agency, privilege and affect in young women, and considering how processes of internationalization are reconfiguring how elite education is defined. Her recent work can be found in *Elite Education and Internationalisation: From the Early Years into Higher Education* (Palgrave Macmillan, 2018), *Elite Education: International Perspectives* (Routledge, 2016), *Sociology, L'Année sociologique, British Journal of Sociology of Education* and *Sociological Review*.

Carmen Mills is a senior lecturer in teaching, learning and classroom pedagogy in the School of Education at the University of Queensland, Australia, where she is the director of secondary pre-service programmes. Her research interests are informed broadly by the sociology of education and specifically by issues of social justice in education, schooling in disadvantaged communities and teacher education for the development of socially just dispositions. Her work has appeared in a range of journals including *British Journal of Sociology of Education, Journal of Teacher Education, Educational Philosophy and Theory* and *Asia-Pacific Journal of Teacher Education*.

Maxwell Smith is a professor in the School of Education at the University of Newcastle where he is a core member of the Teachers and Teaching Research Centre. With particular emphasis on quality and equity, Max's research interests extend from child development and pedagogy in the twenty-first century to measurement and evaluation in education.

Garth Stahl is a senior lecturer at the School of Education at the University of South Australia and research fellow, Australian Research Council (DECRA). His research interests lie on the nexus of neoliberalism and sociocultural studies of education, identity, equity/inequality and social change. Currently, his research projects and publications encompass theoretical and empirical studies of learner identities, gender and youth, sociology of schooling in a neoliberal age, gendered subjectivities, equity and difference, and educational reform.

Amy E. Stich is an assistant professor of higher education at the Institute of Higher Education, University of Georgia, and a 2016 National Academy of Education/Spencer postdoctoral fellow. Stich is a sociologist of education and qualitative researcher whose work focuses on social class and inequality of access, opportunity and outcome at various levels of education. Her current work examines the structure and social consequences of post-secondary tracking. Stich has published widely in academic journals, including *Sociology of Education, British Journal of Sociology of Education, American Educational Research Journal, Urban Education* and *Review of Educational Research*. Stich is also the author of *Access to Inequality: Reconsidering Class, Knowledge, and Capital in Higher Education* (Lexington Books, 2012) and is co-editor of *The Working Classes and Higher Education: Inequality of Access, Opportunity, and Outcome* (Routledge, 2015).

Aina Tarabini has a PhD in sociology from the Autonomous University of Barcelona, and is a senior lecturer in sociology of education at the same university and a member of the Globalization, Education and Social Policies and Interdisciplinary Group on Education Policies research groups. Her research is concerned with the educational effects of social inequalities at three main levels: actors' subjectivities, schools' practices and educational policies. She is currently the principal researcher of a three-year competitive project on young people's educational choices and transitions in Spain (EDUPOST16).

Steven Threadgold is a senior lecturer in sociology at the University of Newcastle. His research focuses on youth and class, with particular interests in unequal and alternate career trajectories; underground and independent creative scenes; and cultural formations of taste. Steve is convenor of the Newcastle Youth Studies

Group and an associate editor of the *Journal of Youth Studies*. His latest book is *Youth, Class and Everyday Struggles* (Routledge, 2017).

Derron Wallace is an assistant professor of education and sociology at Brandeis University with joint affiliations in African and Afro-American Studies and Social Justice & Social Policy. He is a sociologist of race, ethnicity and education who specializes in cross-national studies of inequalities and identities in urban schools and neighborhoods, focusing specifically on the experiences of young people of African descent. His work has appeared in journals such as *Sociology: The Journal of the British Sociological Association*, the *British Journal of Sociology of Education*, and *Disability & Society*. His research has been supported by the Andrew W. Mellon Foundation, the Gates Cambridge Trust, the Marion & Jasper Whiting Foundation and the Hutchins Center for African and African American Research. Prior to joining the Brandeis faculty, he served as a professional community organizer in London, working on youth safety, living wage, fair housing and immigrant rights campaigns.

Series Editor's Foreword

Education research has a long history of adapting ideas from social theory. While this has always been the case when it comes to educational foundations, in recent years there has been an enormous growth in the adoption of social theory in the field of educational research. The names of theorists such as Pierre Bourdieu, Jürgen Habermas, Judith Butler and Michel Foucault have become commonplace in the field, making social theory increasingly familiar to those who both conduct education research and utilize it in their teaching.

As its familiarity increases, so too does the desire to engage with social theory in more thoughtful and effective ways. There is currently a strong desire for applying social theory in educational research contexts, which makes sense, as without theory, much education research can be overly descriptive and/or restricted by narrow definitions of professional practice. Social theory can assist in efforts to transcend the everyday taken-for-granted understandings of education, while also reflecting erstwhile concerns around power, control, social justice and transformation.

The issue then becomes one of applying theory to method, with the focus shifting to a growing interest in the art of application itself. This interest comes with a set of key questions given below:

- How best to apply concepts such as habitus, subjectivation and performativity in educational research contexts?
- What are the ways in which methodological concerns meet theoretical ones?
- In what ways does social theory shape the quality of research outcomes?

These questions require thoughtful responses and the purpose of this book series is to help provide solutions to these issues, while also helping to develop the capacity, in particular, of postgraduate and early career researchers, to successfully put social theory to work in research. This is especially important as theory application in method is a challenging and daunting enterprise. The set of theories developed by the likes of Foucault, Jacques Derrida, Bourdieu and others could never be described as 'simple' or easy to navigate. On top of that there are a variety of issues faced when applying such ideas in research contexts, a field of complex interwoven imperatives and practices in its own right.

These challenges – epistemological, operational, analytical – inevitably impact on researchers and our attempts to make sense of research questions, whether these be questions of governance and political regulation, social reproduction, power, cultural or professional identities (among others). So care needs to be taken when applying a challenging set of ideas onto a challenging set of practices, incorporating a strong consideration for both intellectual arguments alongside the concerns of the professional researcher.

The series should hold a strong appeal to the growing numbers of researchers who are keen to apply social theory in their research, as evidenced by the growing audience for the editor's own website, www.socialtheoryapplied.com. It will offer an excellent resource for those who wish to begin using theoretical concepts in their research, and will also appeal to readers who have a strong interest in better understanding how theory can be effectively applied in research contexts, in practically realizable ways.

In terms of output, this series is designed to provide a collection of books exploring various applications of social theory in educational research design. Each book provides a detailed account of how theory and method influence each other in specific educational research settings, such as schools, early years, community education, further education colleges and universities. The series represents the richness of topics explored in theory-driven education research, including leadership and governance, equity, teacher education, assessment, curriculum and policy studies. It also provides a timely platform for highlighting the wealth of work done in the field of social theory and education research, a field that has grown considerably in recent years and has made the likes of Pierre Bourdieu and Michel Foucault familiar names in educational discourse.

Embedded in the design of the series is a strong pedagogical component, with a focus on the 'how' of applying theory in research methodology and an emphasis on operationalizing theory in research. This pedagogical remit is addressed explicitly in the texts in different ways – the responsibility of addressing this falls to the authors and editors, but can take the form of case studies, learning activities, 'focus' sections and glossaries detailing the key theoretical concepts utilized in the research.

International Perspectives on Theorizing Aspiration: Applying Bourdieu's Tools, co-edited by Garth Stahl, Derron Wallace, Ciaran Burke and Steven Threadgold, is a very welcome and timely addition to the series, given the strength of interest in Pierre Bourdieu's work and the influence of his ideas in applied education research. Bourdieu is arguably the most prominent social theorist in education and well cited in the literature, but this is the first book of its kind that explicitly focuses on Bourdieu in relation to aspirations, a subject that has wide appeal. The focus of this edited collection centres on four structuring questions: (1) In contemporary sociology, how do Bourdieu's conceptual tools assist in theorizing aspiration?; (2) In the study of aspirations, what can we learn from the study of the different applications of Bourdieusian theory?; (3) How is applying theory to method positioned in this context?; and (4) How can we better understand the connections between Bourdieu and intersectional categories such as race, class and gender, in relation to aspiration research?

Drawing on a diverse range of topics, including widening participation, migration, race, gender, elites and curriculum, the contributors included in the book reflect on how they have applied Bourdieu's tools to transcend the everyday taken-for-granted understandings of educational aspirations as well as the relevancy of Bourdieu's conceptual tools. I particularly like the fact that the authors have sought to draw on the breadth of Bourdieu's conceptual toolkit, so alongside habitus, capital and field, there is also substantial engagement with habitus clivé, illusio, misrecognition and doxa.

The book offers readers an important vantage point from which to understand and engage with the field of Bourdieu and aspiration research. As a 'go to' text for postgraduate, early career researchers and also more experienced Bourdieu scholars, it is written and designed specifically to support and guide those researchers interested in putting Bourdieu's ideas to work in aspiration research. It delivers a text that can be used to make sense of a key figure in social theory while also allowing aspiration researchers to make effective links between social theory and research method.

Mark Murphy, Series Editor,
Social Theory and Methodology in Education Research

Foreword

The unequal opportunity structures of society 'determine aspirations by determining the extent to which they can be satisfied'. (Bourdieu 1973: 83)

When Pierre Bourdieu died in 2002, along with great sadness I felt an overwhelming sense of loss not only in relation to the man but in relation to his scholarship – those many wonderful publications that not only helped me understand the world I live in but also enabled me to think and to reason better. In relation to the scholarship, that sense of loss has been tempered by books like this one which are infused with Bourdieusian insights, and take his theory in new and exciting directions. The reader is able to gain a strong sense of the ways in which Bourdieu's intellectual project and powerful theory live on in the chapters that follow.

This book is teeming with elective affinities. The authors are not simply thinking with Bourdieu but also feeling with him about a research area that is underpinned by powerful inequalities and misrecognitions. Garth Stahl, the lead editor, has a strong track record of working and researching with Bourdieu, and that expertise is evident in the way he and the other contributors tackle the thorny subject of aspirations. And there has never been a more important issue to scrutinize through a reflexive Bourdieusian lens. Aspirations are one of the most misunderstood concerns of our era. As Stefan Collini (2016) perceptively points out, it will serve early-twenty-first-century Britain right if this becomes known as 'the Aspirational Age'. The babble around aspirations, particularly in the northern hemisphere, has reached fever pitch just at a historical point when social mobility is stagnating or going into decline. In the UK, in particular, growing numbers of highly aspirational working-class students are graduating from university and ending up in poorly paid, casualized, non-graduate jobs with on average £60,000 worth of loans. Aspiration has been puffed up over the last two decades and now the aspiration bubble has begun to burst! But, rather like the emperor with no clothes, no one seems to have noticed. Too often the popular and political discourses on aspirations are accepted at face value. Because political and policy leaders are telling us aspirations are straightforwardly positive, are lacking in the working classes, and abundant in the upper and middle classes, most of us seem to have accepted that more aspiration, especially among the working classes, is unreservedly a good thing. This book then is a powerful wake up call to start taking aspirations seriously as a topic of academic scrutiny.

While the dominant neoliberal discourse on aspirations individualizes aspirations as a set of desired personality traits, Bourdieu has long shown us that dispositions such as aspirations cannot be divorced from their political, economic and social contexts. The chapters in this book meticulously lay out the historical, institutional and wider social contexts that shape aspirations, and the myriad ways in which they meld with individual trajectories. One of the most powerful injunctions that comes through Bourdieu's work is how crucial it is for all of us to be aware of, and to scrutinize, the fields in which we are located, and all the chapters pay meticulous attention to institutional and, beyond that, wider political and economic contexts. But the critical point about reflexivity for Bourdieu is that we need to recognize and articulate the relationship between the researcher and the object of study, and crucially how this relationship shapes research, and this is what all the authors in this book have been constantly vigilant about. They excavate with painstaking probity the micro details of the production of aspirations, and the objective conditions of that production.

Refreshingly, unlike the remorseless policy focus on the aspirations of the disadvantaged, *International Perspectives on Theorizing Aspiration: Applying Bourdieu's Tools* adopts a wide brief, ranging across groups as diverse as graduates from working-class backgrounds, elite Nigerian families and upper-middle-class girls. It becomes very clear that aspirations mean very different things, and constitute very different bodies of intellectual and psychic work, depending on where the individual is positioned in both the economic and the educational fields. As Tarabini and Curran make clear in their chapter, aspirations are always framed by an individual's social circumstances and their imagined place in the world. Historical context is also crucial for a Bourdieusian understanding of aspirations. Neoliberalism has changed the rules of the educational game, making aspirations to be middle-class 'obligatory' for those from disadvantaged backgrounds. Yet, as Bourdieu has signalled in his own work, for young people in elite private schools with parents with abundant economic and cultural capital, aspirations constitute the highly probable while, for working-class young people in poorly performing under-funded state schooling, aspirations are essentially about the impossible. And it is this illusory nature of aspirations for some groups, and the predictability of achievement for others, that emerges powerfully through the chapters in the book.

Aspirations then are not all of a piece. The amount of work that needs to go into achieving them, and the often powerful emotions that underpin aspirations, differ widely according to context. We can see this in relation to Bourdieu's own trajectory. He wrote of his own social mobility as a miracle but what the reader also sees in his account of 'reaching for the sky' are powerful emotions of anger, indignation and resentment at the way the world was for those from his rural peasant background, and the powerful barriers that stood in their way. The contrast with the relatively easy confident entitlement of the already privileged as they move through social space is salutary.

The contemporary orthodoxy is to see aspirations as individualized, yet what we also learn from the book is that they can be collective as well as individual. They can be both about striving for the remote and unattainable and aspiring to what is commonplace and normative for 'people like us'.

They can be richly resourced and nourished or they can entail difficult and arduous struggle that is largely unsupported. What we learn is that aspirations are far from being all of a piece, and their realization has very different benefits and costs for individuals, requiring very different levels of effort and personal transformation. This complexity is too often overlooked and *International Perspectives on Theorizing Aspiration: Applying Bourdieu's Tools* reminds us not just that aspirations are multifaceted but that the best way of dealing with the multidimensional nature of aspirations is to apply conceptual tools that are both incisive and discerning, and engage with rather than skim over the complexity of the concept. Bourdieu argues that the habitus not only 'engender[s] *aspirations* and practices objectively compatible with the objective requirements' (Bourdieu and Passeron 1977: 77), it also 'generates strategies which can be objectively consistent with the objective interests of their authors without having been expressly designed to that end' (Bourdieu 1993: 76). In order to understand aspirations in any rigorous and reflective way, we need to first understand the dispositions of habitus that generate those aspirations, and the extent to which they are shaped or not by social class, gender and race.

The unreflexive orthodoxy that aspirations are normative, uniform and universal is rarely challenged directly in the chapters but it is powerfully undermined by the forensic analyses that excavate the conditions of possibility of aspirations for different social groups, and pay rigorous attention to historical, geographical, cultural and institutional contexts. In ways that demonstrate beautifully the subtleties of Bourdieu's understandings of the universal and the particular, local and global, individual and collective, subjectivity and objectivity, the chapters approach aspirations as a complex amalgam of all these things. In the twenty-first century, while the aspirations of the advantaged are part of 'effective demand', what Bourdieu calls 'a realistic relationship to what is possible' (1990: 65), the aspirations of the disadvantaged are cut from a very different cloth. They are 'demands without effect based on need and desire' (Bourdieu 1990: 65), and rarely realized. From very different perspectives, and focusing on very different cultural and economic groups, the chapters in *International Perspectives on Theorizing Aspiration: Applying Bourdieu's Tools* direct the reader's attention to this injustice, as they lay bare the inequalities that always constitute aspirations under neoliberal capitalism.

Diane Reay
Visiting Professor of Sociology, LSE

References

Bourdieu, P. (1973), 'Cultural Reproduction and Social Reproduction', in R. K. Brown (ed.), *Knowledge, Education, and Cultural Change: Papers in the Sociology of Education*, 71–112, London: Tavistock.

Bourdieu, P. (1990), *In Other Words: Essays Towards a Reflexive Sociology*, Cambridge: Polity Press.

Bourdieu, P. (1993), *Sociology in Question*, London: Sage.

Bourdieu, P., and J. C. Passeron (1977), *Reproduction in Education, Society, and Culture*, London: Sage.

Collini, S. (2016), *Common Writing: Essays on Literary Culture and Public Debate*, Oxford: Oxford University Press.

Introduction: Using Bourdieu to Theorize Aspirations

Garth Stahl, Derron Wallace, Ciaran Burke and Steven Threadgold

In contemporary times, aspirations matter. Although aspirations have long been deemed valuable resources across a range of national contexts, public declarations on increasing or improving aspirations are of growing significance. Aspiration, as typically defined, is the hope or ambition of achieving a goal or setting oneself on a particular pathway. There is general consensus in social theory that aspirations are constituted in the social world through an amalgamation of different sources (family, schooling, etc.) as well as through intersecting identities (gender, ethnicity, class, etc.). Furthermore, dominant moral discourses in the social imaginary heavily influence aspirations as orientations towards one's future (Baker 2017). The future is an intangible absent presence in one's life. As with the past, the future haunts the present. Within an era of neoliberal governance, people's aspirations are often linked primarily to acquiring material goods and financial or career advancement. The rhetoric of neoliberalism can be ambiguous, mask assumptions and fail to reveal the complexities of the competing and overlapping life worlds experienced by students (Spohrer, Stahl and Bowers-Brown 2017). As aspirations manifest, they are negotiated in affective economies that both inform and reform class dynamics (Threadgold, this volume). There are significant and problematic language games concerning aspirations, where they can be referred to as 'high' or 'low' and conceived as either 'raised' or 'lowered', depending on resources, and existing within either bolstered or limited opportunity structures. Furthermore, as aspiration 'deficits' are increasingly regarded as personal character traits (Spohrer 2011), individuals are depicted as lacking value (and morals) unless they present an identity that adheres to a very specific aspirational discourse as agents contend with narrowing criteria for 'success' and 'failure' (Sellar and Gale 2011; Stahl 2015). Although aspirations are often 'presented as an active capacity of the self' (Zipin, Sellar and Hattam 2012: 186), we must conceive of aspirations as deeply social, where the process of 'aspiring' is a 'relational, felt, embodied process, replete with classed desires and fantasies, defences and aversions, feelings of fear, shame and guilt, excitement and desire' (Allen 2013). As scholars, we consider *how people aspire* to be an important topic of study requiring adept tools applied skilfully. Drawing on empirical research from diverse contexts, the scholars in this collection consider what Bourdieu lends to the study of aspirations.

A Bourdieusian theoretical approach

Bourdieu rose to become an esteemed chair of Sociology at the Collège de France and his life represents a dramatic rise in social status, an exception that proves the rule. Perhaps interrelated to his biography, Bourdieusian sociologists, especially those interested in the study of aspiration and social mobility, have been particularly fascinated by how one aspires beyond one's habitus of origin. In his progression from a working-class background in a local, provincial lycée (in Pau, in the Béarn, in south-west France) to the esteemed École Normale Supérieure in Paris, Bourdieu sought to conduct research that would consistently juxtapose the perceptions of analysts with those of the subjects of their analyses. However, Bourdieu's breadth of scholarship is wide, from his early work in Algiers to his later work on social suffering in contemporary Paris. With class and class positioning as his central focus, he wrote on a range of topics including media, politics, the arts, academia and taste. Methodologically he worked with qualitative, quantitative and mixed methods, as well as did pioneering work in the use of visual methods.

Throughout his oeuvre, Bourdieu's theory of human action, his conception of praxeology, stressed that dispositions are generated through the internalization of structures, institutions and overlapping fields. Dispositions are (re)produced in relation and in response to the social, economic and cultural structures with which agents identify and from which they distance themselves (Murphy and Costa 2016: 5). As a critical departure from other sociological theories, Bourdieu's theoretical approach foregrounds human practice. Despite Bourdieu's efforts to construct theoretical tools that are not devoid of agency and do not preclude agency, critics have attacked his theory of practice as being overly deterministic (Sullivan 2002) or unreflexive (McRobbie 2002).

In order to reconcile agency and structure, Bourdieu refers to his method as 'constructivist structuralism' or 'structural constructivism', with 'constructivist' pertaining to 'the dynamic reproduction of human activity' in changing contexts and 'structuralist' referring to the relations of those involved. Bourdieu's 'structuralist constructionist' approach includes perceptions of objective reality and objective measures of aggregate behaviour (Swartz 1997: 146). In contrast to structuralist objectivism, the subjectivist – or constructivist – point of view asserts that our social realities are an ongoing accomplishment of competent social actors. Through this lens

> society appears as the emergent product of the decisions, actions, and cognitions of conscious, alert individuals to whom the world is given as immediately familiar and meaningful. Its value lies in recognizing the part that mundane knowledge, subjective meaning, and practical competence play in the continual production of society. (Bourdieu and Wacquant 1992: 9)

As Bourdieu sought to introduce new ways of thinking about social class, he held to his principal belief that society cannot be analysed simply in terms of economic classes and ideologies. Bourdieu believed that, in order to gain a more accurate representation of social classes, we must understand the educational, social and cultural factors that foster classed subjectivities and reaffirm the symbolic power attached to capital(s). He posited a symbiotic relationship between structures and practices; specifically, he considered how 'objective structures tend to produce structured subjective dispositions that produce structured actions which, in turn, tend to reproduce objective structure' (MacLeod 2009: 15). For Bourdieu, structural disadvantages are internalized through socialization to varying degrees, producing certain forms of behaviour.

Foundational to his approach, Bourdieu refused to 'establish sharp demarcations between the external and internal, the conscious and the unconscious, the bodily and the discursive', where 'social structures and cognitive structures are recursively and structurally linked, and the correspondence between them provides one of the most solid props of social domination' (Bourdieu and Wacquant 1992: 19, 14). Bourdieu set out to develop an approach to investigating how 'social and cultural differences are inseparable and that, through time, the social, which is synonymous with natural or indigenous culture, is modified by degrees of initiation into artificial, acquired culture' (Robbins 2005: 23). As a result, Bourdieu composed theoretical *tools to think with*, which he refined and adapted over the course of his career. This 'tools in a toolbox' approach is central to this edited collection, as the authors take up the call to work with Bourdieu in exploring how inequalities shape aspirations, they engage in an ongoing reflexive process that is integral to *doing Bourdieu justice* (Stahl 2016).

Bourdieusian theory and the study of aspirations

A variety of different theoretical frameworks exist to consider aspirations, from scholars such as Appadurai (2004), Boudon's social opportunity model (1974), Bauman (1998), Goldthorpe (1998), and Giddens (1991), each with their strengths and weaknesses. Bourdieusians, on a whole, typically conceptualize aspirations as future-focused, 'habituated' (Zipin et al. 2015), embedded in the social imaginary – but also informed by history and constrained through current contexts. Highlighting how aspirations are structured in the social world, and often aligned with the prerogatives of the dominant classes, we see how, in Bourdieu's view, aspirations can often be dreams not fully realized where individuals are often 'obliged to live out the contradiction between their messianic aspirations and the reality of their practice, to cultivate uncertainty as to their social identity in order to be able to accept it' (Bourdieu 1984: 366).

Furthermore, Bourdieu highlights how agents can experience disjuncture between 'aspirations and real probabilities' producing 'misfirings of the dialectic of aspirations and probabilities which led their predecessors to accept their social destiny, almost always unquestioningly, and sometimes with positive eagerness (like the miners' sons who used to identify their entry into manhood with their first descent into the mine)' (1984: 144). For studying the formation of aspirations through a Bourdieusian approach, this disjuncture is incredibly important. In *Sketch for Self-Analysis* (2007), Bourdieu discusses how he sees his own success as a disloyalty to his roots, highlighting how the uneasiness he experiences through his upward mobility leads to negative psychic implications, a habitus clivé. This notion of 'psychic costs' as has resonated greatly with the Bourdieusian community interested in question of aspiration and social mobility (Reay 2013; Stahl 2015; Burke 2016; Friedman 2016).

In *Distinction* (1984), Bourdieu discusses how the onset of mass education in the French educational system and the expanding secondary and tertiary sector meant that aspirations had to be realigned. He writes where previously, agents 'aspirations were perfectly realistic, since they corresponded to objective probabilities' these aspirations were often context-dependent, 'deflated by the verdicts of the scholastic market or the labour market' (143). This brings about what Bourdieu calls 'collective disillusionment' which

> results from the structural mismatch between aspirations and real probabilities,
> between the social identity the school system seems to promise, or the one it
> offers on a temporary basis, and the social identity that the labour market in fact

offers is the source of the disaffection towards work, that *refusal of social finitude*, which generates all the refusals and negations of the adolescent counter-culture. (1984: 144, emphasis in original)

Furthermore, Bourdieu highlights, academic qualifications consecrate the cultural elite, and through this process the educational system structures aspirations by 'channelling pupils towards prestigious or devalued positions implying or excluding legitimate practice' which inscribes a 'certain type of cultural accumulation and a certain image of cultural accomplishment' (25).

As aspirations are negotiated, some individuals may experience disjuncture and others may not. To complicate this, throughout his oeuvre, Bourdieu describes aspirations using words like 'imagined', 'real', 'blurred' and 'fuzzy', highlighting how aspirations are always in formation, continually contested, being formed 'based on an earlier structure of objective opportunities' (Bourdieu 1984: 150) as well as present circumstances. However, what is clear for Bourdieu is that aspirations and probabilities are always working in tandem where 'aspirations of successive generations, parents and children, are formed in relation to different states of the distribution of goods and of the chances of obtaining the different goods' (Bourdieu 1993: 98).

To study how aspirations are formed and maintained, the scholars in this edited collection carefully illustrate how they have adhered to Bourdieu's theory of practice, his 'constructivist structuralism' or 'structural constructivism', and operationalized Bourdieu's conceptual toolkit in order to explore how aspirations are a process on ongoing negotiation and strategy. For Bourdieu, aspirations are (re)produced through the interaction of habitus, a matrix of dispositions that shape how the individual operates in the social world; capital, which is economic, cultural, social and symbolic; and field, that is, social contexts. Bourdieu's theory of practice was focused on 'strategies', where the social action of individuals is guided by a practical sense, by what he called a 'feel for the game' (1988: 782). Game, considered here as a provocative metaphor, assists researchers in understanding the dialectical relationship between the 'nexus of habitus, capital and field' (Wacquant 2011: 86). Bourdieu reminds us that

people are not fools; they are much less bizarre or deluded than we would spontaneously believe precisely because they have internalized, through a protracted and multisided process of conditioning, the objective chances they face. They know how to 'read' the future that fits them, which is made for them and for which they are made (by opposition to everything that the expression 'this is not for the likes of us' designates), through practical anticipations that grasp, at the very surface of the present, what unquestionably imposes itself as that which 'has' to be done or said (and which will retrospectively appear as the 'only' thing to do or say). (Bourdieu and Wacquant 1992: 130)

Therefore, for Bourdieu, while aspirations are socially embedded, his tools allow researchers to emphasize individual strategies and struggles (Threadgold 2018), and the ways one may come to understand the 'future that fits them' or is 'not for the likes of us'.

Aims of the collection

In sociology, there has been a revival of interest in Bourdieu's work (Adkins, Brosnan and Threadgold 2016; Albright, Hartman and Widin 2017; Costa and Murphy 2015; Murphy and Costa 2016; Thatcher et al. 2016). It has become, at times, difficult to keep up with the scholars interested in Bourdieu to explore social phenomena. In theorizing processes of capital acquisition and mobilization, Bourdieu's framework has been used to show how students make sense of their capitals in an increasingly competitive and global educational environment (Bathmaker, Ingram and Waller 2013; Burke 2015; Fuller 2009; Gale and Parker 2015; Gore et al. 2015; Hart 2013; Stahl 2015; Threadgold and Nilan 2009; Wallace 2016; Zipin et al. 2015). In line with Bourdieu's original intent, we see many scholars adapting Bourdieu's tools, blending or bridging them with other theoretical approaches.

Furthermore, Bourdieusian theorizing has not been confined to edited collections, monographs and peer-reviewed journals. We increasingly see his concepts employed beyond academia where concepts like cultural capital permeate policy documents and *The Guardian*. Social media has become an interdisciplinary space connecting scholars interested in Bourdieu in new ways. The British Sociological Association Bourdieu Study Group has adeptly used social media (i.e. Twitter feed @BSABourdieu) to converse about his tools, exchange information, generate debate and also draw on Bourdieu's ideas to advocate against inequality in reference to current events.

In our experience, the application of Bourdieu tends to bring forth strong opinions. He resonates intensely with people who have moved through fields and experienced class practices and prejudices in full operation. For Bourdieusian scholars, his conceptual tools (habitus, capital, field and practice) provide both a language to articulate experiences and a theoretical orientation in research. However, on the whole, Bourdieu scholars have deep, enduring respect for his efforts to devise a conceptual toolbox which aims to bridge the theory–method divide. Bourdieu's key concepts are malleable, designed to be adapted, and therefore 'receptive to multiple and original applications' (Murphy and Costa 2016: 4). Naturally, as scholars pursue extensions, modifications and theoretical innovations, there have been ongoing turf wars within the Bourdieusian community regarding different 'styles' of application. Clearly, how best to apply Bourdieu can mean different things for different people. In this collection, it is worth noting the scholars fully acknowledge the debates regarding whether we are employing his tools properly, how far his tools can be extended, and what is beyond the remit of a Bourdieusian lens.

The application of Bourdieu's theoretical tools has a long-standing history in the study of social reproduction, educational inequality, social mobility and aspirations. The aim of this collection is to allow scholars to demonstrate the diverse ways in which they have applied Bourdieu's tools to empirical research documenting how aspirations are (re)formed. Aspirations, realized and enacted within social spheres, are both a 'subjective and intersubjective process' of 'multiple socio-cultural resources including policy and populist ideologics but also family and community histories and the lived-cultural agency of people in the present' (Zipin et al. 2015: 228).

In considering the way social theory shapes research, the collection centres on four key questions:

1. In contemporary social research, how do Bourdieu's conceptual tools and theory of practice assist in theorizing aspiration?
2. In the study of aspirations, what can we learn from the different applications of Bourdieusian theory?
3. In comparing different applications, how is the application of theory to method positioned?
4. In the study of aspirations, to what extent does Bourdieu's conceptual tools problematize or reaffirm theories of aspiration in reference to intersectional categories (race, class and gender) which are in operation during the ongoing formation of aspiration?

What is particularly compelling about the collection is the varied ways in which scholars apply Bourdieu's conceptual toolkit to recent international empirical research from a wide range of areas (i.e. widening participation, migration, middle classes and elites). Moving beyond the tools of habitus, capital and field, the scholars seek to draw on the breadth of Bourdieu's conceptual toolkit (habitus clivé, illusio, misrecognition, doxa) as well as recent theoretical innovations in the application of Bourdieu's tools (institutional habitus, black cultural capital, etc.). The vibrant mix of scholars we have assembled explore political issues of inequality, identity and Bourdieu's legacy, each in their own way, representing new *theories of application*. What excites us is how these Bourdieusians grapple with putting his tools to work in reference to cutting-edge research, while also ensuring Bourdieu's original intentions are respected. The contributors actively reflect on how they apply Bourdieu's tools to transcend the everyday taken-for-granted understandings of education when researching how the aspirations of their participants are formed. These chapters represent an almost sub-genre of Bourdieusian sociological studies focused on the strengths and weaknesses of applying Bourdieu's conceptual toolbox (Adkins, Brosnan and Threadgold 2016; Costa and Murphy 2015; Thatcher et al. 2016).

Outline of chapters

The scholars in this collection confront the question of how researchers can put Bourdieu's conceptual tools to work in their own research and what they negotiate when translating theory into method and vice versa. After all, as Murphy and Costa note, Bourdieu's ideas in educational research are 'both an object and means of investigation' (2016: 12). Each chapter grapples with how Bourdieu attempted to overcome the theory–method dichotomy, the ways in which he operationalized and developed his own concepts in research, how Bourdieu's tools have been adapted and what this means for the authors' own research on aspirations.

As these Bourdieusian scholars apply his theories to underexplored and under-theorized areas ('race'/ethnicity, gender, elites, migration, etc.) and adapt his tools (combining with intersectionality, affect, Fanon, Skeggs, critical race theory, etc.), it is integral to their project to identify and reflect upon the strengths and weaknesses of applying a Bourdieusian approach. The thirteen chapters which comprise *International Perspectives on Theorizing Aspiration: Applying Bourdieu's Tools* are varied; however, each chapter involves extensive reflexivity, where scholars highlight the adaptability of the tools as well as the dangers of cherry-picking Bourdieu's concepts.

Advancing Bourdieu's conceptual tools

In the first chapter, Ciaran Burke uses Bourdieu's theory of practice to investigate individuals' habitus and the composite effect of capitals within their 'field of the possibles'. In using the biographical narrative interview method (BNIM), Burke draws on empirical research to examine the stark contrasts between the working-class respondents' life histories and what is expected of them as they move from the field of higher education to that of graduate employment. Using the well-known Bourdieusian phrase 'that's not for the likes of us' as a provocation, Burke considers how class effects self-exclusion, where education functions as a thinly veiled cover for middle-class inheritance and the reproduction of the dominant group's position and power.

As previously noted, Bourdieu is subject to different styling and rendering which has led to certain critiques. In the second chapter, Steven Threadgold defends Bourdieu against the critique that he is a determinist. He argues that, in understanding facets of aspiration, Bourdieu's concepts of illusio, struggle, strategy and social gravity remain neglected. To explore this in depth, Threadgold demonstrates how aspirations manifest in affective economies that make and remake class. Building on Hage (1994) and others, Threadgold shows how Bourdieu's theories need to be used as a way of *doing* sociology that welds theoretical concerns with methodological imperatives.

Using and developing habitus

In using habitus to explore the nexus of institutions, educational aspirations and post-school destination choices, Aina Tarabini and Marta Curran draw upon the ABJOVES project, which documented the aspirations of Catalan young people attending five public secondary schools in Barcelona at the end of their compulsory schooling. Using Bourdieu's theory of action, they analyse students' aspirations and choices from a threefold perspective: first, the influence of working-class habitus on students' dispositions and subjectivities and, secondly, how gender contributes to configuring students' learner identities beyond the impact of social class. Finally, bringing this together, they draw on their scholarly work on institutional habitus (Tarabini, Curran and Fontdevila 2017) to explore the role different schools play in fostering certain student identities. Tarabini and Curran use Bourdieu's toolkit to show that aspirations are a negotiation. They find that student subjectivities fall mainly into five main types: internalized incapacity and sense of futility, resistant dispositions, lack of control over the rules of the game, low levels of self-esteem and the feeling of 'not fitting in' to the school.

In continuing work on habitus as generative of student identities, the chapter by Garth Stahl focuses on extending Bourdieu's (1993: 383) conception of habitus clivé, where the habitus lacks a certain unity, or cohesiveness, accepting the particular messages within the new field while simultaneously maintaining the key dispositions of the habitus of origin. Reflecting on previous research which worked with habitus to explore the aspirations of working-class boys in education (Stahl 2015), he argues for taking habitus clivé one step further through theorizing a counter-habitus as a safeguard. This approach provides insight into the potential of habitus to actively construct counter-narratives to the cultures of institutions, in this case neoliberal forms of schooling. Stahl emphasizes how the habitus can resist and rebuff a clivé, which, in turn, can lend considerable weight to how his participants come to aspire.

Using and developing theoretical approaches to capital

The next chapter by Jim Albright, Jenny Gore, Maxwell Smith and Kathryn Holmes draws on the large-scale four-year aspirations longitudinal study in New South Wales, Australia, documenting how educational and career aspirations become instrumental in students' decisions regarding participation in post-secondary education. In their approach to Bourdieu, the scholars employ a 'composite capital construct', which works across both Bourdieu as well as Becker and Tomes. Central to this chapter is how they contend with methodological and theoretical dilemmas. In using Bourdieu to study of students' aspirations, they highlight the difficulties involved in measuring capitals.

Continuing to explore how capital is best put to work, Amy E. Stich and Kristin Cipollone draw on a three-year longitudinal ethnographic study in the United States of non-dominant students' college-going aspirations. In this chapter, they continue their work on the development of 'shadow capital' as a new and distinct form of cultural capital (Stich and Cipollone 2017). Shadow capital outwardly resembles dominant cultural capital, but when activated it fails to yield the same exchange value promised by its dominant façade. Therefore, through drawing upon but also critiquing Bourdieu's original conception of cultural capital, Stich and Cipollone are able to better theorize existing inequalities, the realization of aspirations, as well as the many unmet promises of US educational reform.

Advancing Bourdieu's concepts in the field of education

In broadening critical work on how institutions inform aspirations, Sol Gamsu's study of student aspirations in two elite public schools in London draws on an under-utilized Bourdieusian approach to history, specifically the coming together of institution and individual, the structural history which shapes the rules of the field and the processes associated with the accumulation of symbolic capital which all dominant institutions must master. He demonstrates that it is imperative to consider how student aspirations are formed by a dynamic coming together of institutional and personal history. Furthermore, Gamsu extends Bourdieu by also drawing on Ball's concept of 'circuits of education', which he asserts aides in theorizing institutional positions, and their influence on aspirations, within the wider field of education.

In contrast to Gamsu's work on elite schooling in the UK, the chapter by Russell Cross, Carmen Mills and Trevor Gale relays findings from recent research in a disadvantaged school context in Australia. The scholars focus specifically on Bourdieu's understanding of *dispositions* (collectively, the habitus), and their application to a study of teachers' pedagogies and commitment to social justice. Their research interrogates the otherwise taken-for-granted recurring and enduring patterns of teachers' work that unfold in everyday schooling and the implications for the formation of student aspirations. Presenting a case study on Caitlyn, an experienced health and physical education teacher working in challenging conditions, they explain how they used Bourdieu's tools to show why socially just outcomes are so hard to achieve in schools, even when the aspirations that teachers and school leaders claim for their students are high.

Bourdieusian perspectives on aspirations and gender

In the next chapter, '"It Was Noticeable So I Changed": Supergirls, Aspirations and Bourdieu', Tamsin Bowers-Brown uses Bourdieu's concepts, alongside an intersectional approach, to assist in exploring how girls in secondary education negotiate a web of practices in order to achieve their aspirations. Bowers-Brown demonstrates how Bourdieu's theory and intersectionality can be used to demonstrate how aspirations are constructed in a way that rewards and misrecognizes privilege. As the young women in her study accumulate valued capitals, it is clear that not all aspirations are equally accessible. Therefore, in exploring how these young women aspire, Bowers-Brown focuses on how girls' engagement with school can involve an adherence to symbolically violent requirements that necessitate an adaptation of the self in order to become the 'supergirl' that the dominant discourse purports them to be.

In continuing work on the intersection of gender and institutional cultures, Joan Forbes and Claire Maxwell use Bourdieu's concept of habitus as both a focus of analysis and an analytical method in examining how one elite girls' secondary school in Scotland actively shapes its students' aspirations. Forbes and Maxwell term their approach a hybrid, 'Bourdieu plus', and they use this blended approach to uncover the interworkings of a specific institutional culture. Drawing upon habitus and institutional habitus, they show how certain moments are created where school and family intertwine, structuring social–emotional affect norms where young women are discursively and affectively produced as intellectually able, socially connected and self-reflective.

Ethnic inequalities and identities: Assessing Bourdieu's tools

Focusing on the relationship between ethnic identities and aspiration, Derron Wallace explores the utility of a Bourdieusian approach to doxa in order to understand the aspirations of second-generation black Caribbean youth in Britain. His chapter documents the application of deficit perspectives on black and ethnic minority communities through misappropriation and misrecognition that is not simply an epistemological shortcoming, but a political act that reifies and reinforces whiteness as the norm. By interrogating such doxic deficit depictions, Wallace suggests that another future becomes possible through a renewed articulation and application of Bourdieu's work.

Continuing work on elites and elite identity practices concerning aspirations (see Forbes and Maxwell and Gamsu, this volume), Pere Ayling's chapter draws on recent research conducted with elite Nigerian parents on how they acquire what they perceive as 'attributes of excellence' for their children in mainly white international schools located outside Nigeria. Thinking *with* and *beyond* Bourdieu, Ayling bridges the two conceptual approaches of Bourdieu (class) and Fanon (race). She argues that combining the respective theories engenders a more nuanced understanding of how colonialism has permeated and reconfigured the habitus of highly educated Nigerian elites.

In keeping with the focus of these studies of the African and Caribbean diaspora, Barbara Adewumi presents research on the role of race and racial identity among black middle-class parents in the UK who operationalize their capitals, moving geographical locations to attend better schools. Through this process they maintain advantage for themselves and their children. Adewumi couples Bourdieu's concepts with critical race theory (CRT) in order to understand the complex interrelations of race, class, capitals and aspirations. By working across these two approaches she investigates the parenting strategies of the black middle class and how such approaches (re)shape their children's aspirations.

Conclusion

As he sought to introduce new ways of thinking about the relationship between social class and aspirations, Bourdieu maintained that sociologists needed richer conceptual tools and these tools needed to be employed skilfully across a range of contexts. As evidenced in this collection, we see that Bourdieu's tools, by their very composition, are beneficial for the study of aspirations, as they require scholars to consider aspirations as embedded in the social milieu. It should be acknowledged that recent critics of Bourdieu have highlighted a certain irony; where Bourdieu's theoretical framework was developed to assist in our critique of the so-called tyranny of meta-narratives, the Bourdieusian toolbox has arguably become a metanarrative unto itself (Stahl 2016). This is certainly an intriguing criticism but one to be viewed with scepticism. We see in this edited collection, the versatility of Bourdieusians applying his toolbox to new areas where they are consistently adapting and combining his tools. Such adaptations are an integral to their project as they identify and contend with the strengths and weaknesses of applying a Bourdieusian approach. What is particularly insightful about this collection is how the contributors apply a Bourdieusian toolbox to empirical research in underexplored areas (e.g. Nigerian elites, the work of Australian teachers, the Caribbean diaspora, etc.), which have led them to reflect and think anew about the applicability of Bourdieusian theory. Therefore, we see each scholar as reflexive, highlighting the flexibility of the tools, the limitations of Bourdieu's concepts, and how they grapple not only with the concepts but also their 'styles' of operationalization (Stahl, Perkins and Burnard 2017).

Interestingly, in using Bourdieu to analyse aspiration many of the authors have highlighted a more nuanced understanding of intersectional categories, drawing attention to how aspirations have been 'strongly inflected, shaped, and constrained by identities and inequalities of gender, social class, [and] "race"/ ethnicity' (Archer, Hollingworth and Mendick 2010: 80). Furthermore, more intersectional analyses has meant that in many cases a Bourdieusian theoretical approach has become infused with other theories (Hart 2013; Thatcher et al. 2016; Murphy and Costa 2016; Webb et al. 2017).

As the contributors to this edited collection often note, Bourdieu's tools remain contested and subject to extensive critiques (cf. Jenkins 1992; Throop and Murphy 2002; Mouzelis 2007). There exists no singular reading of Bourdieu, but rather many ways of putting his 'theory into action' (cf. Stahl 2016). It is our hope that this collection makes a contribution to the reflexive project Bourdieu held in high esteem, where, as sociologists, we can consider the 'intellectual unconscious embedded in analytical operations surrounding research' (Bourdieu and Wacquant 1992: 37). What unites the chapters in this volume is the demonstration of how Bourdieu's tools are applied and the insights that can be gained from working with Bourdieu to study aspiration in diverse contexts. All the scholars critically interrogate the various gaps in Bourdieu's theoretical tools but they also point to the capacity of the toolkit to help us understand how aspirations are formed, negotiated and problematized in an ever-changing empirical world. Each chapter shows that through critically engaging with Bourdieu's concepts, and combining them with other social theories, his framework continues to be enriching.

References

Adkins, L., C. Brosnan and S. Threadgold (2016), *Bourdieusian Prospects*, New York, Oxon: Routledge.

Albright, J., D. Hartman and J. Widin (2017), *Bourdieu's Field Theory and the Social Sciences*, London: Palgrave Macmillan.

Allen, K. (2013), 'Coalition Policy and "Aspiration Raising" in a Psychic Landscape of Class', paper presented at Journal of Youth Studies Conference, Glasgow, 7 April.

Appadurai, A. (2004), 'The Capacity to Aspire: Culture and the Terms of Recognition', in V. Rao and M. Walton (eds), *Culture and Public Action*, 59–84, Stanford, CA: Stanford University Press.

Archer, L., S. Hollingworth and H. Mendick (2010), *Urban Youth and Schooling: The Experiences and Identities of Educationally 'At Risk' Young People*, Berkshire: Open University Press.

Baker, W. (2017), 'Aspirations: The Moral of the Story', *British Journal of Sociology of Education*, 38 (8): 1203–16.

Bathmaker, A. M., N. Ingram and R. Waller (2013), 'Higher Education, Social Class, and the Mobilisation of Capitals: Recognising and Playing the Game', *British Journal of Sociology of Education*, 34 (5–6): 723–43.

Bauman, Z. (1998), *Globalization: The Human Consequences*, New York: Columbia University Press.

Boudon, R. (1974), *Education, Opportunity and Social Inequality: Changing Prospects in Western Society*, London: John Wiley.

Bourdieu, P. (1984), *Distinction: A Social Critique of the Judgement of Taste*, Oxon: Routledge.

Bourdieu, P. (1988), 'Vive la Crise! For Heterodoxy in Social Science', *Theory and Society*, 17 (5): 773–87.

Bourdieu, P. (1993), 'A Life Lost', in P. Bourdieu et al. (eds), *The Weight of the World: Social Suffering in Contemporary Society*, 381–91, Stanford, CA: Stanford University Press.

Bourdieu, P. (1993), *Sociology In Question*, London: Sage.

Bourdieu, P. (2007), *Sketch for a Self-analysis*, Cambridge: Polity Press.

Bourdieu, P., and L. Wacquant (1992), *An Invitation to Reflexive Sociology*, Cambridge: Polity Press.

Burke, C. (2015), *Culture, Capitals and Graduate Futures: Degrees of Class*, London: Routledge.

Burke, C. (2016), 'Bourdieu's Theory of Practice: Maintaining the Role of Capital', in J. Thatcher, N. Ingram, C. Burke and J. Abrahams (eds), *Bourdieu: The Next Generation*, Oxon, New York, Routledge: 2–25.

Costa, C., and M. Murphy (2015), *Bourdieu, Habitus and Social Research: The Art of Application*, London: Palgrave Macmillan.

Friedman, S. (2016), 'The Limits of Capital Gains: Using Bourdieu to Understand Social Mobility in Elite Occupations', in J. Thatcher, N. Ingram, C. Burke and J. Abrahams (eds), *Bourdieu: The Next Generation*, 107–22, Oxon, New York, Routledge.

Fuller, C. (2009), *Sociology, Gender, and Educational Aspirations: Girls and Their Ambitions*, London: Continuum.

Gale, T., and S. Parker (2015), 'Calculating Student Aspiration: Bourdieu, Spatiality and the Politics of Recognition', *Cambridge Journal of Education*, 45 (1): 81–96.

Giddens, A. (1991), *Modernity and Self-Identity: Self and Society in the Late Modern Age*, Cambridge: Polity.

Goldthorpe, J. H. (1998), 'Rational Action Theory for Sociology', *British Journal of Sociology*, 49 (2): 167–92.

Gore, J., K. Holmes, M. Smith, E. Southgate and J. Albright (2015), 'Socioeconomic Status and the Career Aspirations of Australian School Students: Testing Enduring Assumptions', *Australian Educational Researcher*, 42: 155–77.

Hage, G. (1994), 'Pierre Bourdieu in the Nineties: Between the Church and the Atelier', *Theory and Society*, 23: 419–40.

Hart, C. S. (2013), *Aspirations, Education and Social Justice: Applying Sen and Bourdieu*, London: Bloomsbury.

Jenkins, R. (1992), *Pierre Bourdieu*, London: Routledge.

MacLeod, J. (2009), *Ain't No Makin' It: Aspirations and Attainment in a Low-Income Neighbourhood*, Boulder, CO: Westview Press.

McRobbie, A. (2002), 'A Mixed Bag of Misfortunes? Bourdieu's Weight of the World', *Theory, Culture & Society*, 19 (3): 129–38.

Mouzelis, N. (2007), 'Habitus and Reflexivity: Restructuring Bourdieu's Theory of Practice', *Sociological Research Online*, 12 (6). Available online: www.socresonline. org.uk/12/6/9.html

Murphy, M., and C. Costa (2016), *Theory as Method in Research: On Bourdieu, Social Theory and Education*, London: Routledge.

Reay, D., 2013. 'Social Mobility, a Panacea for Austere Times: Tales of Emperors, Frogs, and Tadpoles', *British Journal of Sociology of Education* 34 (5–6): 660–77.

Robbins, D. (2005), 'The Origins, Early Development and Status of Bourdieu's Concept of "Cultural Capital"', *British Journal of Sociology*, 56 (1): 13–30.

Sellar, S., and T. Gale (2011), 'Mobility, Aspiration, Voice: A New Structure of Feeling for Student Equity in Higher Education', *Critical Studies in Education*, 52 (2): 115–34.

Spohrer, K. (2011), 'Deconstructing "Aspiration": UK Policy Debates and European Policy Trends', *European Educational Research Journal*, 10 (1): 53–62.

Spohrer, K., G. Stahl and T. Bowers-Brown (2017), 'Constituting Neoliberal Subjects? "Aspiration" as Technology of Government in UK Policy Discourse', *Journal of Education Policy*, online before print 15 June. doi:10.1080/02680939.2017.1336573

Stahl, G. (2015), *Aspiration, Identity and Neoliberalism: Educating White Working-Class Boys*, London: Routledge.

Stahl, G. (2016), 'Doing Bourdieu Justice: Thinking with and beyond Bourdieu', *British Journal of Sociology of Education*, 37 (7): 1091–103.

Stahl, G., R. Perkins and P. Burnard (2017), 'Critical Reflections on the Use of Bourdieu's Tools "In Concert" to Understand the Practices of Learning in Three Musical Sites', *Sociological Research Online* 22 (3): 57–77.

Stich, A., and K. Cipollone (2017), 'Shadow Capital: The Democratization of College Preparatory Education', *Sociology of Education*, 90 (4): 333–54.

Sullivan, A. (2002), 'Bourdieu and Education: How Useful is Bourdieu's Theory for Researchers?', *Netherlands Journal of Social Sciences*, 38 (2): 144–66.

Swartz, D. (1997), *Culture and Power: The Sociology of Pierre Bourdieu*, Chicago, IL: Chicago University Press.

Tarabini, A., M. Curran and C. Fontdevila (2017), 'Institutional Habitus in Context: Implementation, Development and Impacts in Two Compulsory Secondary Schools in Barcelona', *British Journal of Sociology of Education*, 38 (8): 1177–89.

Thatcher, J., N. Ingram, C. Burke and J. Abrahams (eds) (2016), *Bourdieu: The Next Generation*, Oxon: Routledge.

Threadgold, S. (2018), *Youth, Class and Everyday Struggles*, Abington: Routledge.

Threadgold, S., and P. Nilan (2009), 'Reflexivity of Contemporary Youth, Risk and Cultural Capital', *Current Sociology*, 57 (1): 47–68.

Throop, J. C., and K. M. Murphy (2002), 'Bourdieu and Phenomenology: A Critical Assessment', *Anthropological Theory*, 2 (2): 185–207.

Wacquant, L. (2011), 'Habitus as Topic and Tool: Reflections on Becoming a Prizefighter', *Qualitative Research in Psychology*, 8: 81–92.

Wallace, D. (2016), 'Reading "Race" in Bourdieu? Examining Black Cultural Capital Among Black Caribbean Youth in South London', *Sociology*, 51 (5): 907–23.

Webb, S., P. J. Burke, S. Nichols, S. Roberts, G. Stahl, S. Threadgold and J. Wilkinson (2017), 'Thinking with and Beyond Bourdieu in Widening Higher Education Participation', *Studies in Continuing Education* online: 1–23.

Zipin, L., S. Sellar and R. Hattam (2012), 'Countering and Exceeding "Capital": A "Funds of Knowledge" Approach to Re-imagining Community', *Discourse: Studies in the Cultural Politics of Education*, 33 (2): 179–92.

Zipin, L., S. Sellar, M. Brennan and T. Gale (2015), 'Educating for Futures in Marginalized Regions: A Sociological Framework for Rethinking and Researching Aspirations', *Educational Philosophy and Theory*, 47 (3): 227–46.

Part One

Advancing Bourdieu's Conceptual Tools

1

Maybe It Is for the Likes of Us: Reconsidering Classed Higher Education and Graduate Employment Trajectories

Ciaran Burke

Introduction

To say that Bourdieu has been an influential voice in contemporary sociology would be an understatement. He is one of the most referenced, applied and debated figures within sociology and its sister fields, the subject of editorials, symposiums and conferences, leading some to bemoan that we have reached peak Bourdieu. We need to ask ourselves why this French peasant–turned professor is so relevant, especially as he died before many of the events which now shape post-industrial society, in particular the 'war on terror' and the 2007 global financial crisis. One account (and certainly an argument I support) is that, despite Beck's assertion that we have entered a period of 'capitalism without the class' (1992: 88), we very much live in a society of increasing inequalities, violence and enduring privilege, all thinly veiled behind the concept of the individual and freedom. This social reproduction of power and the playing out of one's 'place' is perhaps no more clearly expressed than in the higher education system and, by extension, the graduate labour market.

There have been a number of significant moments in the UK higher education system starting with the Robbins Report in 1963, which led to the amalgamation of vocationally oriented technical schools into polytechnics, and began the democratization of post-compulsory education and the opening up of the sector. These new polytechnics, with degree-awarding powers, would increase the level of participation in higher education, in particular by those groups who, until then, were not represented in the higher education system: women, ethnic minority and non-traditional/working-class students. Over time, these polytechnics emerged as universities. This movement culminated in the 1992 *Higher Education Act*, which further reduced barriers to access, put all degree-awarding institutions on an equal level and addressed the binary system which had emerged through the establishment of polytechnics. Until the late 1990s, university courses were not subject to tuition fees, and grants and student loans were also available. While the introduction of university tuition fees was seen to close the door on those very students the Robbins Report intended to support, the policy of deferred fees, introduced alongside the raising of tuition fees in the 2004 *Higher Education Act*, was in part a move to alleviate this criticism. Further increases in tuition fees in 2010 were mediated through widening participation policies such as access agreements or the now-defunct educational maintenance allowance (Mountford-Zimdars, Sullivan and Heath 2009), a small bursary for students at the end of compulsory education intended to balance income lost as a result of continuing their education.

What this quite brief tour through UK higher education policy has demonstrated is that there has been an opening up of higher education in terms of places, fees and attitudes of institutions. Access to education is a key facet of Ulrich Beck's model of reflexive modernity (Beck and Beck-Gernsheim 2002) and of reducing the shackles of industrial Britain – in particular, social class (Beck 1992). Diane Reay characterizes this context of increased choice and opportunities as the 'triumph of individualisation' (2000: 995), in which the successes of the individual are considered theirs to enjoy and praise is offered to the individual and the individual alone. Blame for failures is also levelled at the individual and the individual alone, without considering enduring structural influences on attitudes and practice.

These attitudes dull what C. Wright Mills (1959) described as the sociological imagination, the position that to understand an individual or society we must account for both. Blurring the sociological gaze prevents us from observing how structure and agency interact, leading to such agentic arguments offered by Beck. There are two central issues when considering the continuing structural influences in UK higher education: structural mechanisms which advantage elite/middle-class students (Jones 2013) and issues of self-regulation limiting/ rejecting levels of aspirations and expectations. It is the latter which this chapter – indeed, this collection – intends to unpack. The source and influence of aspirations and expectations of higher education and graduate employment will be critically examined through Bourdieu's theory of practice.

The research which this chapter discusses has been extensively discussed elsewhere (Burke 2015a); however, a brief overview is now supplied. The research asked: *To what extent are strategies that graduates use to secure employment influenced by social class?* The research sample comprised twenty-seven university graduates who had graduated between two and ten years before the research was carried out. Respondents had all attended a Northern Irish university for their undergraduate degree, and the degrees the respondents completed were categorized as non-vocational. The sample was stratified in terms of gender, institution attended and social class, which was measured using the NS-SEC self-completion questionnaire. The primary form of data collection was the Biographical Narrative Interview Method (BNIM).

Thinking with Bourdieu: Habitus, capital and field

The central components of Bourdieu's theory of practice – habitus, capital and field – have been discussed in numerous texts, monographs (Bathmaker et al. 2016; Atkinson 2010; Reay, David and Ball 2005) and other guides/introductions (Webb, Schirato and Danaher 2002; Grenfell 2008); indeed, this collection begins with a summation or clarification of these conceptual tools. What makes these tools so robust and relevant today is that there is still a requirement for the researcher to account for how they used them; the fundamental position that these are tools to be used, not commandments to be adored, is what gives Bourdieu's work longevity and relevance in different contexts in both time and space. For this chapter and the research which informs it, the application of Bourdieu's theory is similar to Bourdieu's epistemic position: a combination of history/structure and creativity/agency.

Despite the criticisms against Bourdieu, in particular charges of structural determinism (Jenkins 2002; Archer 1996, 2003), Bourdieu's theoretical project was concerned with bridging structure and agency. Writing at a time of competition between structural anthropology and phenomenology, Bourdieu (with Wacquant 1992) attempted to provide a middle ground characterized as 'structural constructivism'. In other words, Bourdieu's theoretical project was concerned with understanding and accounting for the social world through an appreciation of both structure and agency, in the case of my research social class and higher education/graduate employment trajectories. To assist in this theoretical project, Bourdieu developed thinking tools; three central tools for this research were habitus, capital and field. Before I unpacked and conceptually stretch each tool, it is important to note Bourdieu's position that these three tools should be used in unison, expressed as the formula: [(habitus) (capital)] + field = practice (1984: 101).

Habitus, arguably one of Bourdieu's most applied concepts (at times to the point of saturation) (Reay 2004), is a central facet of Bourdieu's structural constructivism. Habitus – our way of seeing the world, sense of place, dispositions and values – is both structured and set but also open to choices within certain limits. Formed through institutions including family, school, peers and environment (Bourdieu 1977), there are boundaries to an individual's sense of what is appropriate/suitable and their understanding of how various environments and institutions operate and how to successfully navigate such spaces. Within these boundaries, there are choices to be made; this almost contradictory understanding of choice and constraint was described by Bourdieu as 'regulated improvisations' (Bourdieu 1977: 78). The particular nature of variables which engender habitus means that, at its most basic level, habitus is unique to each individual; however, shared environment, culture and norms mean that those in close proximity, socially, geographically and so on, are likely to share a significant number of characteristics, leading to a group habitus or class habitus (Bourdieu and Wacquant 1992). Among other qualities, the group/collective habitus reinforces each individual member through providing a shared identity and actively rejecting divergent identities and practices (Bourdieu 1974).

Turning specifically to educational aspirations and expectations, Bourdieu and Passeron (1977) apply the concept of habitus to theorize why educational dropout rates (essentially self-exclusion) are concentrated within one social class rather than randomly distributed. The authors discuss 'subjective expectations of objective probabilities' – in other words, the level of (honest) expectation a working-class student has of successfully entering and graduating from the education system and becoming socially mobile. This arrangement all but condemns working-class/dominated students. As Bourdieu (1974) illustrates, the education system benefits the middle class through architecture, language, tacit expectations and application of resources. Diane Reay comments that habitus is a combination of 'products of opportunities and constraints framing the individual's earlier life experiences' (2004: 433); it is these constraints, coming from the education system in particular, that help frame the often referenced 'that's not for the likes of us' (Bourdieu 1984: 380). Through such processes, becoming socially mobile via education is an untenable goal, allowing the education system to perform its primary function: to act as an acceptable form of inheritance for the dominant social group (Bourdieu and Passeron 1979). As I have said, the 'not for the likes of us' line in Bourdieu is one of his most referenced, but, if we continue reading, we are afforded not only a succinct articulation of the relationship between habitus and aspiration but also a lesson in its durability. Bourdieu comments: 'Objective conditions also contain a warning against the ambition to distinguish oneself by identifying with other groups, that is, they are a reminder of the needs of class solidarity' (1984: 381).

It is the sense of solidarity and the reassurance that stems from belonging to a group, and indeed the group/collective habitus, that supports the durability of the individual habitus, aligning an individual's norms, attitudes, aspirations and expectations closely to those of the larger group and reducing opportunity for divergence. While habitus has considerable influence over actions and attitudes, which seemingly grows stronger over time, Bourdieu is careful to explain that habitus is not some sort of inescapable prison, arguing that '[habitus] is durable but not eternal!' (1992: 133). To return to the main components that form the habitus – family, school and environment – none of these can claim immortality; moreover, some of the components (in particular environment) are more likely to change as we move into a liquid modern period of history (Bauman 2000). Characterizing such a shift in environment as an 'out-of-environment experience' (Burke 2016), I have demonstrated instances of an altered habitus in the context of an increasingly fluid graduate labour market. Importantly, these experiences did not render habitus powerless or inapplicable but changed the core elements of habitus, particularly levels of understanding of how to navigate the graduate labour market.

I have previously argued (Burke 2016) that capital operates in the shadow of habitus, but, in Bourdieu's theoretical formula, capital is as directive and influential as habitus on the outcome of practice. Within his theoretical project, Bourdieu (2004) outlines three main forms of capital. First, there is economic capital, which is essentially economic resources, including savings, property, stocks and so on. This form of capital was a way to acknowledge the Marxist position on class conflict while also forestalling comparisons between the two theorists. Second, there is social capital, which is comprised of access to social networks and whether these networks can be used in an advantageous manner. Third and finally, there is cultural capital, best described as cultural competency. Capital carries a number of different functions; an immediate role is to demonstrate the transactional nature of resources. Thinking about resources such as social networks or cultural know-how as capital provides us with the language to describe what is happening: a transaction between a resource and goods and services – in the case of my research, an ability to navigate higher education and the graduate labour market in a way that has a direct impact on the realization of aspirations and expectations. Very often, pathways to success were 'bought' with these forms of capital. Levels of success were decided by the buying power of the capital.

Another key function capital provides is to allow us to plot individuals' and groups' positions within social space. Through comparing relational access and use of resources and capitals, we can begin to build heuristic groups and classes. Alongside habitus providing an understanding of how to navigate institutions, capital provides or denies the individual/group the resources required to put this understanding into practice. When specifically considering issues of aspirations and expectations, we need to return to arguments about 'subjective expectations of objective probabilities' and 'that's not for the likes of us'. While both of these statements are often related to habitus, I argue capital plays a significant role in framing objective probabilities and impacting on what is for the 'likes of them'. In other words, the levels of capital that an individual possesses frame objective probabilities; they inform what individuals feel is possible or what is reasonable to expect (Tarabini and Curran, this volume; Stahl, this volume). As Bourdieu comments: 'To a given volume of inherited capital there corresponds a band of more or less equally probable trajectories leading to more or less equivalent positions (this is the field of the possibles objectively offered to a given agent)' (1984: 110).

In the context of the UK higher education system, characterized by increased opportunity for entry and a reduced/limited financial burden, I argue educational capital has a significant buying power. As such, the 'probable trajectories' that are offered through high levels of scholastic capital include access to higher education. While there are processes that reproduce social inequality and maintain a level of distinction for the dominant group, such as the influence of institutional habitus (Reay, David and Ball 2001; Burke, Emmerich and Ingram 2013; Tarabini and Curran, this volume) or non-academic capitals and admissions selection, these are mediated through the strong human capital narrative that runs through the majority of UK education policy from New Labour onwards (Burke 2015a). Examining educational aspirations and expectations through the concept of the 'field of the possibles' provides a theoretical account of shifts in levels of aspirations. The same application of capital can also be used to theorize the disconnect or contrast between high levels of aspiration and expectation concerning higher education and comparatively low levels concerning graduate employment. Unlike the higher education system, which does reward scholastic capital, the subsequent graduate labour market, characterized by an over-supply of graduates, does not recognize the buying power of scholastic capital in the same way and rewards *a priori* capital, therefore limiting the 'field of the possibles' for working-class students. In other words, what is reasonable to expect before entry into higher education and after graduation is quite different; this contrast is based on the different objective probabilities afforded by capital and capital's relationship to habitus.

The final piece of Bourdieu's theoretical puzzle is field. Field is much more than a passive arena in which habitus and capital interact and influence various practices. The field has particular laws, rules and expectations which must be adhered to in order to successfully 'play the game'. Thomson (2008) observes that the French term Bourdieu uses for field is *le champ*, more accurately translated as 'battlefield'; this translation is much more helpful to think through. Rather than habitus and capital equipping the players with resources in order to win or lose a game, with inconsequential or short-term effects, the field is a site of aggression and competition in which winning and losing have long-term, deeply rooted consequences. The taken-for-granted and accepted rules of the field, or doxa, are often tacitly applied, rewarding those who possess a habitus which allows the individual to both identify and understand the rules and meet the field's requirements. In the field of (higher) education, the tacit rules and expectations are most compatible with those with familial experience of (higher) education and, in particular, those from the middle class. What Bourdieu and Passeron termed 'unexamined exclusion' (1977: 152) includes cultural competency, associated with capitals, and dispositions and sense of belonging, associated with habitus. I argue that levels of fit and ability to get on in the education system, in part, frame the aspirations/expectations which individuals 'allow' themselves to develop and pursue. In other words, losing on this particular battlefield leads to 'educational death rates' (Bourdieu and Passeron 1979: 2).

An empirical approach to a theoretical question

I now discuss how I applied Bourdieu's theoretical tools, as I understand them, to my research examining social class, aspirations and higher educational/ graduate pathways. In an effort to protect my research from charges that theory resided only on the surface and was applied at the last minute, social theory and, in particular, Bourdieusian social theory played a role in each of the substantive stages of my research. I focus on the application of Bourdieu's thinking tools in the preparation for the research, data collection, and analysis and construction of findings.

As briefly mentioned above, the main form of data collection employed for this research was the BNIM. While this approach does fall under the more generic life history approach, it is quite a specific method with strict rules and guidelines (Miller 2000; Rosenthal 2005; Schütze 2008). I have previously discussed the productive relationship between the BNIM and Bourdieusian social theory (Burke 2011, 2015a, 2015b); in summation: in the context of Bourdieu's (1987) assertion that habitus is best observed through repetition of actions and attitudes, a longitudinal ethnographic study appears to be the form of data collection that is best suited to observing and charting the subtle expressions of habitus and transactions of capitals in various fields, including development, regulations and manifestation of aspirations and expectations. Opportunities for longitudinal ethnographic studies are few, so, as researchers, we must improvise and creatively approach the research question in order to gain useful and comparable data. The specific mechanisms within the BNIM – most notably, asking a respondent to 'tell me about your life' and then sitting in relative silence while a respondent discusses the significant moments of their lives at length and in no particular order – provide an opportunity to chart the effect of both habitus and capitals on aspirations in different combinations and different contexts in order to examine the outcome, the type of practice they engender. Importantly, the collection of biographical information concerning a respondent, rather than an auto-ethnographic study, provides protection from Bourdieu's quite hostile comments concerning autobiography, describing it as 'both conventional and illusory' (2007: 1).

For my analysis (Figure 1.1), I adopted the two models of analysis suggested by Angrosino (2007: 67–8). He suggests descriptive analysis – essentially, breaking down the data into themes to appreciate patterns. The second form was theoretical analysis, employing theory to make sense of these themes or regularities. To supplement my thematic analysis and offer a thicker interpretation of my respondents' life stories, I employed narrative analysis. Narrative analysis is an extremely useful and proficient checking device for the more general thematic analysis. My main reason for employing this form of analysis is the richness and the depth of data a researcher can observe through narrative analysis. Of particular interest to me was how narratives of aspirations

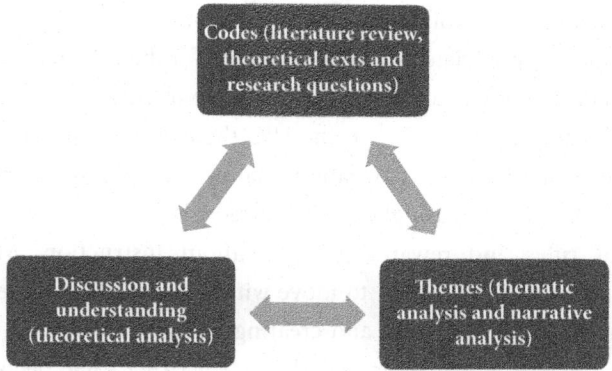

Figure 1.1 Summary of analysis process

and expectations were mediated by social structures and the level in which these could be seen as durable. Returning to the 'that's not for the likes of us' refrain, I operationalized aspirations/expectations through a sense of belonging or self-regulation/dismissal. Appreciating habitus as the repetition of practices/attitudes over the life course and charting aspirations/expectations against the composition of an individual's capital at any given time allowed me to consider aspirations within the Bourdieusian theoretical framework.

Reflections on findings: Putting Bourdieu to work

Applying Bourdieusian social theory throughout the research process, in terms of design, collection and analysis, provided theoretically robust and empirically grounded findings concerning aspirations and development of aspirations. In particular, using the BNIM provided an opportunity to observe both the manifestation of habitus and the transaction/influence of capitals. Despite some trajectories that illustrated a level of social mobility (Burke 2015b) or a reduction in privilege (Burke 2017), the findings from the research presented a clear binary model in which middle-class graduates were quite successful in entering the graduate labour market in stark contrast to their working-class counterparts, who often entered long-term, non-graduate positions in retail and hospitality.

Through charting actions and attitudes of graduates as they negotiated the labour market (what we would call habitus), clear patterns emerged demarcating the middle-class and working-class samples. Two key themes emerged concerning the levels of understanding and the ability to navigate a situation/institution. Middle-class respondents demonstrated a strong understanding of the higher education system in terms of the most effective combination of A-level subjects to study, the most appropriate university to attend for their degree, and the most beneficial balance between academic studies and extracurricular activities.

In the graduate labour market in the UK, the data indicated these durable levels of understanding and navigation manifested themselves through an ability to negotiate an increasingly de-structured labour market which operates through tacit rules and rewards ability without instruction. Middle-class respondents knew how and when to move within the market, appreciating the internal structures of institutions and creating a bespoke pathway. This ability to play the game – or practical mastery (Bourdieu 1977) – had been developed throughout the respondents' lives via the family and education system. The almost pre-reflexive ability to navigate a number of related fields, the strong sense of belonging, and the durability of both understanding and practical mastery point to the role of habitus. The presence of a group habitus reinforces among other things a sense of what is for the likes of them; it reassures members of this conceptual group of their expected path and the likelihood of them reaching their goals.

In contrast, the vast majority of the respondents from the working-class sample demonstrated quite low levels of understanding and navigational success. Many indicators of habitus could be seen as mirror images of the middle-class respondents' dispositions and practices. A number of respondents found it quite difficult to choose appropriate subjects to study at secondary and higher level; some respondents were required to spend an extra year completing their studies due to incompatible combinations or subject choices which were unsuitable. In addition, the vast majority of the working-class sample prioritized academic studies over extracurricular activities, understanding the latter as an optional pastime and not related to their university profile or future career. When entering the graduate labour market, working-class respondents found it very difficult, with some relying exclusively on the buying power of their degree. These respondents found it difficult to apply their undergraduate degrees beyond the narrow remit of their studies and often criticized the lack of guidance provided during their time in higher education.

Alongside habitus, the BNIM provided an excellent opportunity to understand the role of capital in the realization of aspirations. Within the research findings, capital had two main roles: articulating the transaction of resources and influencing aspirations. Between the two main classed groups of respondents, there were clear differences in access to resources. Middle-class respondents were able to exchange their high levels of economic, social and cultural capital for ease of trajectory through the various stages of education and for preferential positions in the labour market. Middle-class respondents acquired quite detailed information about their particular area within the graduate labour market from their social networks; in addition, they were able to rely on economic capital to buoy their lifestyles and consumption until they located an opening in the labour market and, finally, through high levels of cultural capital, they possessed the soft skills required for the majority of post-industrial professions. In contrast, working-class respondents had very little *a priori* capitals; that is, capitals which are inherited rather than earned and cultivated, such as educational capital. Working-class graduates, too, availed themselves of social contacts to gain insights into the labour market, but these contacts led to non-graduate positions; there was, however, a great deal of pressure to take these positions due to financial constraints, and limited levels of cultural capital meant entering the graduate labour market was much less likely.

In terms of aspirations and expectations, there were, again, marked differences between the two main classed groups of respondents. Middle-class respondents very much expected to study at an academically focused grammar school[1] and continue on to university and then a graduate profession. In contrast, working-class respondents were, at times, quite unsure of their suitability for secondary and higher level education; these attitudes were directed by previous education achievements, and they had quite low levels of aspirations and expectations concerning the graduate labour market, often being willing to settle for non-graduate jobs. The contrast in aspirations between groups of respondents and, in particular, the contrast between working-class respondents' aspirations concerning higher education and the graduate labour market can be accounted for through Bourdieu's concept of the 'field of the possibles'. A sense of what an individual perceives she or he can achieve is crucial in determining their trajectory:

> The subjective expectation which leads an individual to drop out depends directly on the conditions determining the objective chances of success proper to his category, so that it must be counted among the mechanisms which contribute to the actualisation of objective probabilities. (Bourdieu and Passeron 1977: 156)

In the context of this particular study, for the middle-class respondents who possess both high levels of *a priori* capital and educational capital, their field of the possibles is quite vast and set within a field which rewards high levels of capital and a middle-class habitus. What is perhaps more interesting, as suggested above, is the disconnect between working-class aspirations before attending university and after graduating. Working-class respondents were apprehensive about their suitability for university and questioned whether they belonged in such a place – 'that's not for the likes of us'; however, very often, a sense of belonging came through achieving the required entry grades for admission to their preferred course. There was a temporary validation via educational capital – while they resided within an institution which rewarded educational capital, their field of the possibles, their aspirations and expectations, was quite vast. However, on graduating and returning to a context where *a priori* capitals were rewarded, their field of the possibles shrunk, narrowing their aspirations, and leading the working-class respondents to over-represent what we could term 'graduate employment death rates'. While this method does come with limitations (Burke 2015b), it is only through the close ethnographic detail of the BNIM that the subtle transaction of capitals and the exchange rate within different fields (which leads to an inflated or decreased field of the possibles) is acknowledged, allowing us to theorize contrasting levels of aspirations and expectations between social groups along the life course.

Conclusion

The primary purpose of this chapter was to unpack my particular understanding of Bourdieu's key thinking tools, provide a theoretical account of the impact of habitus and capital on higher educational and graduate employment aspirations and outline the role of Bourdieusian social theory within the research process. In the UK policy context of an increasingly marketized higher education system built on the principle of choice and of savvy students forging their own trajectory, it is the responsibility of social science to remind policy makers and the public that structural barriers exist and that dispositions and attitudes run deep. Through focusing particularly on the role of capital in forming aspirations as the 'field of the possibles', this chapter has provided a theoretical point of departure to think beyond habitus. In addition, this chapter has provided empirical blueprints to observe the transaction of capital and its formation/ curtailment of 'the field of the possibles'. Bourdieusian sociology, like any good sociology, is meant to be taken and used; these ideas and debates are meant for more than academic symposia or special editions of journals – hopefully, this chapter, and this collection as a whole, will play a role in putting these theories to work.

Note

1   Northern Ireland still operates on a grammar and secondary school system.
Grammar schools are more academically focused, and entry into a grammar school
is based on passing an entry exam often referred to as the 11+.

Recommended further reading

Abrahams, J. (2017), 'Honourable Mobility or Shameless Entitlement? Habitus and
Graduate Employment', *British Journal of Sociology of Education*, 38 (5): 625–40.
Ingram, N. and A. Tarabini (eds) (2018), *Educational Choices, Aspirations and
Transitions in Europe: Systemic, Institutional and Subjective Challenges*, London:
Routledge.
Bourdieu, P. and J-C. Passeron (1979), *The Inheritors*, Chicago: Chicago Press.

References

Angrosino, M. (2007), *Doing Ethnographic and Observational Research*, London: Sage.
Archer, M. S. (1996), *Culture and Agency*, revised edn, Cambridge: Cambridge
University Press.
Archer, M. S. (2003), *Structure, Agency and the Internal Conversation*, Cambridge:
Cambridge University Press.
Atkinson, W. (2010), *Class, Individualisation and Late Modernity: In Search of the
Reflexive Worker*, Hampshire: Palgrave Macmillan.
Bathmaker, A.-M., N. Ingram, J. Abrahams, T. Hoare, R. Waller and H. Bradley (2016),
Higher Education, Social Class and Social Mobility: The Degree Generation, London:
Palgrave.
Bauman, Z. (2000), *Liquid Modernity*, Cambridge: Polity Press
Beck, U. (1992), *Risk Society*, London: Sage.
Beck, U., and E. Beck-Gernsheim (2002), *Individualisation*, London: Sage.
Bourdieu, P. (1974), 'The School as a Conservative Force: Scholastic and Cultural
Inequalities', in J. Eggleston (ed.), *Contemporary Research in the Sociology of
Education*, 32–47, London: Methuen and Co.
Bourdieu, P. (1977), *Outline of a Theory of Practice*, Cambridge: Cambridge University
Press.
Bourdieu, P. (1984), *Distinction: A Social Critique of the Judgement of Taste*, London:
Routledge and Kegan Paul.

Bourdieu, P. (1987), 'The Biographical Illusion', *Working Papers and Proceedings of the Centre for Psychosocial Studies*, 14: 1–7.

Bourdieu, P. (2004), 'The Forms of Capital', in S. J. Ball (ed.), *The RoutledgeFalmer Reader in Sociology of Education*, 15–29, London: RoutledgeFalmer.

Bourdieu, P. (2007), *Sketch for a Self-Analysis*, Cambridge: Polity Press.

Bourdieu, P., and J.-C. Passeron (1977), *Reproduction in Education Society and Culture*, 2nd edn, London: Sage.

Bourdieu, P., and J.-C. Passeron (1979), *The Inheritors: French Students and their Relation to Culture*, Chicago: University of Chicago Press.

Bourdieu, P., and L. Wacquant (eds) (1992), *An Invitation to Reflexive Sociology*, Cambridge: Polity Press.

Burke, C. T. (2011), 'The Biographical Illumination: A Bourdieusian Analysis of the Role of Theory in Educational Research', *Sociological Research Online*, 16 (2). Available online: http://www.socresonline.org.uk/16/2/9.html

Burke, C. (2015a), *Culture, Capitals and Graduate Futures: Degrees of Class*, London: Routledge.

Burke, C. (2015b), 'Habitus and Graduate Employment: A Re/structured Structure and the Role of Biographical Research', in C. Costa and M. Murphy (eds), *The Art of Application: Bourdieu, Habitus and Social Research*, 55–73, London: Palgrave.

Burke, C. (2016), 'Bourdieu's Theory of Practice: Maintaining the Role of Capital', in J. Thatcher, N. Ingram, C. Burke and J. Abrahams (eds), *Bourdieu: The Next Generation*, 8–24, London: Routledge.

Burke, C. (2017), 'Graduate Blues: Considering the Effects of Inverted Symbolic Violence on Underemployed Middle-Class Graduates', *Sociology*, 51 (2): 393–409.

Burke, C. T., N. Emmerich and N. Ingram (2013), 'Well-Founded Social Fictions: A Defense of the Concepts of Institutional and Familial Habitus', *British Journal of Sociology of Education*, 34 (2): 165–82.

Grenfell, M. J. (ed.) (2008), *Pierre Bourdieu: Key Concepts*, Durham, UK: Acumen.

Jenkins, R. (2002), *Pierre Bourdieu*, revised edn, London: Routledge.

Jones, S. (2013), '"Ensure That You Stand Out from the Crowd": A Corpus-Based Analysis of Personal Statements According to Applicants' School Type', *Comparative Education Review*, 57 (3): 397–423.

Miller, R. L. (2000), *Researching Life Stories and Family Histories*, London: Sage.

Mills, C. W. (1959), *The Sociological Imagination*, Oxford: Oxford University Press.

Mountford-Zimdars, A., A. Sullivan and A. Heath (2009), 'Elite Higher Education Admissions in the Arts and Sciences: Is Cultural Capital the Key?', *Sociology*, 43 (4): 648–66.

Reay, D. (2000), 'Rethinking Social Class: Qualitative Perspectives on Class and Gender', in S. J. Ball (ed.), *Sociology of Education: Major Themes Vol. 2*, 990–1008, London: Routledge.

Reay, D. (2004), 'It's All Becoming a Habitus: Beyond the Habitual Use of Habitus in Educational Research', *British Journal of Sociology of Education*, 25 (4): 431–44.

Reay, D., M. David and S. Ball (2001), 'Making a Difference? Institutional Habituses and Higher Education Choice', *Sociological Research Online*, 4 (5). Available online: http://www.socresonline.org.uk/5/4/reay.html

Reay, D., M. E. David and S. Ball (2005), *Degrees of Choice: Social Class, Race and Gender in Higher Education*, Stoke on Trent: Trentham Books.

Robbins, L. (1963), *Higher Education: Report of a Committee* (Robbins Report), London: HMSO.

Rosenthal, G. (2005), 'Biographical Research', in R. L. Miller (ed.), *Biographical Research Methods Volume III*, 25–58, London: Sage.

Schütze, F. (2008), 'Biography Analysis on the Empirical Base of Autobiographical Narratives: How to Analyse Autobiographical Narrative Interviews Part I', EU Leonardo da Vinci Programme. Available online: http://www.biographical counselling.com/download/B2.1.pdf

Thomson, P. (2008), 'Field', in M. Grenfell (ed.), *Pierre Bourdieu: Key Concepts*, 67–81, Durham, UK: Acumen.

Webb, J., T. Schirato and G. Danaher (2002), *Understanding Bourdieu*, London: Sage.

2

Bourdieu is Not a Determinist: Illusio, Aspiration, Reflexivity and Affect

Steven Threadgold

Introduction

When I started reading social theory as an undergraduate in 1999, I had no real idea why I was going to university other than the realization that I had to do something, anything, other than what I was doing beforehand. In terms of aspirations, to be discussed below regarding illusio, I thought university study would allow me to get a better job after shifting through about twenty of them in the years since I left school, but I was not sure what specific job: maybe a music or sports journalist? Starting an arts degree with the thought of changing to communications, I began as a politics major and was quickly enamoured by Baudrillard, then Foucault, and to a lesser extent Deleuze and Guattari. Like many others, discovering Bourdieu provoked an instant emotional connection (see Reay 2015; Thatcher et al. 2015), especially as a first-in-family university student, having completed an electrical apprenticeship sometime before, followed by a few years of casual, under- and unemployment and a stint in the UK to play cricket. Once I realized I was more into sociology than politics, it was too late to change majors, but I was hooked nonetheless. I personally identified with the symbolic violence of attending university as a person who had failed their Higher School Certificate and as a (relatively young) mature-aged student.

Bourdieu has sometimes been treated poorly by both 'servile disciples' and 'opponents or even enemies' wishing to relegate him to the past or downplay his utility (Lahire 2011: viii). His concepts need to be approached as 'thinking tools' that can be used to create a methodological apparatus for doing research (Thatcher et al. 2015). Therefore, it is useful to consider Bourdieu's tools more along the lines of 'theory as method' (Murphy and Costa 2015) to construct a 'sociological practice' (Hage 1994). Bourdieu's conceptual toolkit contains heuristics or devices; instruments to be used to think with, not to be thought of as sociological rules or laws. That is not to say that Bourdieu does not 'do' theory, but from a researcher's point of view work needs to be done to separate his theory from method.

I argue here that Bourdieu's conceptual toolbox needs to be used as a way of doing sociology that welds theoretical concerns with methodological imperatives, with the concept of illusio being particularly vital for thinking through the formation of aspirations. Bourdieu's practical craft (Bourdieu, Chamboredon and Passeron 1991) for doing empirical research, the methodological construction of relational social space, with its objective and subjective social orders, is well equipped to interrogate aspects of situational affect, reflexivity and social change, in relation to broader concerns with social reproduction. This is especially important as affective economies are central to the ways class is made and remade, and how the borders between classes are fuzzy and policed.

'Determinism' and Bourdieu's underutilized concepts

If the accusation of determinism simply means that individuals are constrained by the realistic possibilities available to them, *à la* Marx's famous quotation (1978: 595), then that would be appropriate. Realistic probabilities would allude to Bourdieu's central object of study: social struggles. Bourdieu's conception of emotional individuals investing themselves in an array of social struggles is a deliberate move away from the existential agent, the false consciousness dupe or the rational actor. That is to say, Bourdieu's model of the actor is less deterministic than this. However, the determinist tag is used as a form of dismissal as it characterizes his oeuvre as too simplistic, structural, functional or classical. Importantly, Bourdieu was not above these kinds of casual dismissals himself, for instance, his caustic critique of Latour and Callon in *Science of Science and Reflexivity* (2004). Certainly, there are parts of Bourdieu's work that are more functional or deterministic than others, and there are inconsistencies throughout where sometimes he does not follow his own argument, talks in generalist terms, or is too polemical. Bourdieu's work and life were full of such tensions, fundamentally interrogating long-held dichotomies of object–subject, agency–structure and theory–method. In his life he described his habitus clivé, feeling uncomfortable in French academia because of his humble background (Bourdieu 2008), all the while occupying one of its most prestigious chairs.

Furthermore, he openly criticized the position of public intellectuals, all the while becoming one (*Sociology is a Martial Art* 2002).

The ever-expanding introductory and secondary texts about Bourdieu often focus their attention on the famous habitus-field-capital triad and often position Bourdieu as a determinist or structural functionalist. Which is to say, those presentations of Bourdieu's 'theories' are themselves an act of misrecognition. This seems to have developed from the time and place these first introductions were being produced, where 'post-structuralism' was the relatively new dominant paradigm, and where much of the writing about French theory as it came to be translated into English was writing under the spectre of Marxism and existentialism (see Milchman and Rosenberg 2002, for instance, on Foucault in this regard). For our purposes here, I think I have always read Bourdieu from a 'post-structuralist' perspective, rather than in the tradition of a previous generation's interlocutors' more structuralist reading, especially the authors of the first introductions to Bourdieu in English (Robbins 2004, 2005). Importantly though, it must be acknowledged that there exist more and less 'deterministic' versions of Bourdieu. Clearly, the Bourdieu writing *Reproduction in Education, Society and Culture* (Bourdieu and Passeron 1990) can be read as more 'determinist' than the Bourdieu of *Pascalian Meditations* (2000).

Nevertheless, I find it difficult to recognize the Bourdieu of his own words in the representations in some of the texts that introduced his work in English. Where was the elucidation of language such as improvisation, immanence, blips, indeterminacy, fuzziness, dangling, plurality and trajectory? To be fair, these secondary texts seemed to present Bourdieu's theories through the empirical work he and his colleagues published, which do mostly illustrate forms of reproduction. However, the 'glass half empty' determinist reading of Bourdieu by some interlocutors, and the focus on the habitus-field-capital triad, seems to downplay concepts that emphasize social *relations* – illusio, doxa, social gravity, symbolic violence, hysteresis, misrecognition, struggle, strategy and trajectory – all of which are fertile for understanding ever-present tensions between social change and social reproduction.

These concepts have much to offer for understanding social phenomena and for developing a lexicon of the relations between inequality, experiences and emotions. They are also useful for grasping how those same experiences and emotions are put to work to reinforce inequalities or transform them. In terms of the study of aspirations, young people generate their own everyday reality – their 'practical sense' – but they do so contingent upon their accumulated history, their position in social space, using the very tools that constitute that position, and their conception of what may come in the future. With this in mind, the following will outline the utility of illusio for thinking about the trajectory of aspirations.

Using illusio to think about aspiration, motivation, commitment and reward

If we understand the Bourdieusian social subject as one that accumulates being, a cumulative self (Noble 2004) that gathers things, relations and experiences in the constant struggle for meaning and recognition, illusio provides a path into how this process unfolds. Illusio, therefore, is a concept for thinking about how meaning is created, maintained and transformed (see Bourdieu 1990: 195). If someone is invested in the illusio of a field, they are motivated by its stakes as something worth struggling over; they see the investment of their own time, effort and emotion as a valuable endeavour; and they are committed to reaping the rewards of the field, that is, they see something worth aspiring towards. Once an illusio is personally invested in, a trajectory is formed where one is 'taken in and by the game' (Bourdieu and Wacquant 1992: 116).

Investment and trajectory form what Bourdieu, in passing, has called social gravity (see Hage 2011), where the momentum of previous investment in a field pushes and pulls an actor in the general doxic direction, while instilling the 'gravity' of the situation in their dispositional armoury. That is, once one has invested through a commitment of time, effort and emotion struggling in a field, these practices become 'serious' and there is an array of consequences if one loses commitment or takes up the wrong strategies. This way of thinking about how one practices in a particular field, or across an array of fields, troubles the very idea of 'choice'. The concept of trajectory is particularly relevant to the point above about Bourdieu and determinism: 'To see people on a trajectory is to also see them as capable of acting strategically within their class position' (Hage 2011: 85).

Research on aspirations usually considers its object discursively: 'I want to go to the University of Sydney'; 'I would really like to be a high school teacher'; 'If I get a good job, hopefully I can travel and meet someone to start a family with.' This approach sheds valuable light on what young people think about their intentions, motivations and possible outcomes, which can then be linked to how class, gender, race and ethnicity, location, disability and so on both mediate what they aspire to and whether they can realistically achieve their goals. But the discursive is only one ontological aspect of how aspiration works. There are affective elements that play a role in how aspirations are present in specific situations and where one's trajectory meets moments of desire that do not match expectations or even possibilities. To be clear here, I am not downplaying the importance of discourse as per non-representational affect theorists. Instead, I am advocating a 'more-than-representational' position (Lorimer 2005), where affective encounters are simultaneously sensed, recognized, categorized and communicated, all of which rely upon habitus, which is one's history rolled up into an affective reservoir of immanent dispositions (Threadgold 2017). As Wetherell argues: 'We cannot stop the clock, start it from just from some constructed moment of initial impingement and ignore the meaning-making contexts and histories that so decisively shape the encounters between bodies and events' (2013: 355).

One's orientation towards illusio *affects* processes of social homology and social closure. Symbolic violence, therefore, is a form of affect or, more specifically, an affecting force that mediates feeling rules (Hochschild 1983), cruel optimisms (Berlant 2011), and sticky subjectivities (Ahmed 2004). There are nods to these kinds of affective economies in Bourdieu's oeuvre – phrasing like 'blighted hope' and 'frustrated promise' (Bourdieu 1984: 150) – but they are left as descriptors of symbolic violence without going any deeper into how it may work, that is, as an affective force producing specific emotions and future practice. Bourdieu's notion of habitus has a vague understanding of emotion and affect (Probyn 2005; Reay 2004), although he did begin to refer to affect throughout *Pascalian Meditations* (2000).

Bourdieu theorized illusio to engage two distinct aspects of social life (Aarseth 2016). First, he used the concept to help disclose the 'hidden profits' that guide individual action. This aspect relates to the discursive aspects of aspirations mentioned above, where motivations to go to a particular university or to get a better job are not only about attaining ontological security, but also relate to forms of economic gain, recognition and status distinction. Secondly, illusio is formulated to show how individuals are moved by stimuli in certain fields and not others. Possessed by what he called social libido (Bourdieu 2000), forms of social gravity hail individuals out of a state of indifference towards fulfilling their desires (Wacquant 1992: 26).

> Read this way, Bourdieu's notion of illusio offers a tool for grasping the different formations of anxieties and desire that emerge in and in turn incite particular engagements with the world, an affective dynamic underlying the enchantment with the game. (Aarseth 2017: 12)

Bourdieu's conception of illusio is useful for unpacking the other elements of aspirations beyond the discursive. To begin with, I suggest that there are three ways in which illusio is useful for thinking about aspirations in higher education, the labour market and beyond.

Illusio speaks to different motivations and aspirations

Illusio is quite commonly used in aspirations research, especially in education studies (see Bowers-Brown 2016), even if the term itself is not used explicitly. These studies investigate how the different motivations and goals of students are inflected by modalities of inequality (Bathmaker et al. 2016). While the broad illusio of attending university may be getting a good job, and achieving material and ontological security, these processes and goals will look very different for students from different classes.

For instance, my PhD research (Threadgold and Nilan 2009) explored how students at a 'working-class' high school in Australia were either deciding whether or not to *try* to go to university, or had aspirations just to get to university, any university they could. In contrast, students at the academically selective school and the expensive private school in my research were not even considering whether to go to university or not; they were deciding which university to attend, often based on its status, and which professional degree they would undertake. Therefore, the very aspiration of university attendance has obvious class implications, where the entering of university is seen as an achievement in and of itself for some young people, while others see it just as a taken-for-granted stepping stone on the trajectory to something else. Importantly, the value of attending university in a time of degree inflation and mass attendance is not questioned; it is seen as an intrinsic good, even if the very experience of pursuing this illusio may have detrimental effects on individual well-being. In this sense, university attendance exists as a common-sense given, a doxa which

> does not belong to the order of explicit principles, theses that are put forward and defended, but of action, routine, things that are done, and that are done because they are things that one does and that have always been done that way. (Bourdieu 2000: 102)

Investigating illusio in terms of these motivations uncovers the hidden profits of individual actions by showing how they are entrenched in an affective economy, where one's aspirations will be in relationship to possible fulfilment through relations of social homology and social closure. Further, using illusio as a way of thinking about how some aspirations – such as the benefit of attending university – are held up as beyond dispute or discussion can afford education scholars an opportunity to ask reflexive questions about the principles of belief, including their own, which may jeopardize the very illusio of their own field (Bourdieu 2000: 102).

Different commitments, orientations and intensity towards illusio

Considering 'modalities and intensities of consciousness' (Noble and Watkins 2003) also provides an important insight into the relations between illusio, capitals and the very possibility of achieving aspirations. 'Along with class position one needs to examine the strategies of "position-taking" … that social subjects engage in' (Hage 2011: 85). There are two aspects to this.

First, there is one's commitment towards the illusio: just how much time, effort and emotion is one willing to spend to achieve one's aspirations in a particular field, just how much one is willing to 'buy in'. This includes 'whether one is inclined to "furiously" accumulate capital or to "take it easy". This [aspect of] disposition is an important component of what Bourdieu calls habitus' (Hage 2011: 86). While intensity may point to aspects of individual psychology or personality traits, it can also shed light on the strategies one uses to overcome barriers to achievement. For example, if a student is doing a university degree that requires regular face-to-face attendance, but lacks a car and lives in an area with poor public transport options, their commitment to the illusio may be drained by very real material barriers. You can be as committed to study and as motivated as anyone to do well, but the *affects* of material barriers can have deleterious consequences on your aspirations and motivations. A student may begin with all the intensity that is humanly possible, but if there is no support to help overcome this kind of classed material obstacle, it will be experienced as a form of symbolic violence. It may also be experienced reflexively, the reflexive experience of inequality, aspects of which will be discussed further below.

Secondly, and following on from thinking about intensities in relation to illusio, there are 'levels of awareness' that play a role in how people strategize and network towards achieving their goals. Developing Bourdieu's games metaphor, specifically using tennis, Noble and Watkins argue:

> Our ability to play requires different uses of these intensities for different things: when we play tennis, we can simply 'go with the flow' and 'forget' our bodily movements in terms of shot execution; or we can check our stroke when

we realize it isn't working; or we can reflect upon our strategy and alter it as we see fit. (2003: 533)

'Check our stroke' here describes a reflexive moment. In research I have been conducting with colleagues about the struggles faced and the strategies used in transitions from higher education to the labour market, we are finding different orientations towards what students think a degree will provide and what extracurricular activities are needed to lubricate success. In very broad terms, we are finding that social science degree students, who tend to be the first in their family to attend university and from relatively low socio-economic backgrounds, often think that a degree will be enough to get them a job. In comparison, business degree students, who tend to come from more middle-class backgrounds, are often furiously networking while studying, trying to make connections to set themselves up post-university (Bathmaker, Ingram and Waller 2013). Social science students seem to be going more with the flow; business students seem to realize that a degree is not enough (Bathmaker et al. 2016: 96), and adjust their strategy to a precarious labour market that sees free internships and volunteering as a given. Of course, their very knowledge and ability to network with the right people relates to their family's position in social space (Forbes and Maxwell, this volume), putting their social capital to work.

'The form and degree of the urgencies with which the necessities of the world impose themselves' (Bourdieu 2000: 226) affects relations to time and therefore relations to the future (see Adkins 2011). 'The more power one has over the world, the more one has aspirations that are adjusted to their chances of realization, and [are] also stable and little affected by symbolic manipulation' (Bourdieu 2000: 226). For those with less 'power over the world', that is, in less possession of forms of capital, aspirations may 'burgeon', feel a little off, and instil a dispositional sense of 'lack of a future' (ibid).

Considering illusio through intensities and awareness brings forth affective and temporal elements of aspirations, where one may perceive and understand the illusio of the field, but lack realistic strategies and time to be able to pursue the rewards. This formulates an affective economy that has implications for the trajectory towards one's aspirations.

Illusio may transfer across fields to change dispositions

Bourdieu conceived of illusio as field specific, a shared sense of purpose within a field, a collusio (Bourdieu 2000: 145), but it becomes an individual's own sense of purpose once they begin to invest themselves. Aspirations in education research tend to focus on aspirations in that field only, or on labour market outcomes, and more rarely on a wider sense of general well-being. By invoking illusio and thinking about aspirations more generally, we may be able to see how this thinking tool works across an array of fields and how some aspirations, motivations and rewards may take priority over others. While in Bourdieu's work an illusio is field specific, the concept maintains scope to consider how the experience of aspirations, motivations, commitments and rewards from one field may come to influence the strategies and struggles in another.

For instance, in my research with young people in a DIY music scene in Australia (Threadgold 2017), there were instances where it seemed that some were using the values developed in the punk scene, with its DIY doxa, to pursue what they perceived as an authentic life and to bring a moral sensibility into their career decisions. Mirroring the 'downshifters', 'seachange' and 'treechange' movements of older, comfortable, middle-class professionals (Hamilton and Denniss 2006), participants who had done the 'right' thing in terms of the doxic norms taught from school onwards – finished university, got a good paying professional job in a global city – were downsizing their careers to concentrate on their artistic and creative passions. This is a reflexive reconfiguring of aspirations. Why were they doing this? As participants in an underground music scene, often since their mid-teens, they developed what I describe as a punk and DIY illusio: a broad commitment to attitudes, ethics and aesthetics that align with the notion of 'self-design' (Mankowski 2013) while at the same time creating an alternative space where like-minded people can work outside of the 'mainstream' to foster a relatively autonomous space for artistic creativity, community building and identity work (McKay 1998; O'Connor 2016 Woods 2017). This investment became an integral part of fostering their more general disposition. The illusio to which they have invested their most passionate time, energy and emotion from their cultural practices is smuggled into more legitimized fields to make decisions about career and lifestyle in general. Therefore, the affectivity of the punk illusio is constituted with more social gravity than the more normative/mainstream illusio. That is to say, they become motivated by what they see as creative, ethical and moral rewards more than the material. The punk illusio begins to formulate their dispositional orientation towards making broader life decisions, which can look nothing like the cultural dupe or the rational actor. Illusio from different fields interact and are imbued with more or less intense social gravity to form an affective economy of aspirations within and between fields.

Reimagining illusio through the problem of reflexivity

Some researchers have considered the implications of reflexivity for Bourdieu's conceptual armoury, especially as the original conception of habitus relied on sub- or pre-conscious conceptions of practice. Some authors (Archer 2012; Atkinson 2010) are critical of the possibility of bringing a concept like reflexivity into a Bourdieusian perspective, while others have theorized that it is useful, even necessary (Sweetman 2003; Threadgold and Nilan 2009; Farrugia and Woodman 2015). Drawing upon Aarseth and colleague's (Aarseth 2016, 2017; Aarseth, Layton and Nielsen 2016) work, which considers affective elements of illusio, the emotionally intensive work of 'becoming modern' means that 'conflicts in the habitus' (Aarseth, Layton and Nielsen 2016) are at the fore of contemporary subjectivity formation. Conflicts in the habitus form a spectrum from everyday reflexivity to moments of hysteresis (see Strand and Lizardo 2017). Facing the contradictory demands of a wide array of fields, there is an increasing call on individuals for a 'labour of integration' as social life is more differentiated (Silva 2016). While Bourdieu created a delineation between consciousness and habitus, recent work has brought conscious deliberation into the notion of habitus, which makes the concept less mechanistic (Mead 2016).

In relation to Bourdieu and the criticisms of determinism, illusio is not a proxy for ideology. While it can and often does play a socially reproductive role, an illusio can function in anti-dominant ideological ways, in the sense that the doxa of some fields or sub-fields are committed to resisting and subverting dominant norms in all manner of ways, from everyday practices that 'make do' (De Certeau 1984), to criminal activity (McRobbie 2002), to protesting on the street and even terrorist acts. So, while illusio captures the ways that individuals are taken in by social games, as a conceptual tool it is meant to function as ideologically neutral. Illusio is not illusion or self-delusion per se. Bourdieusian sociological practice uncovers how one is captured by social games and struggles for their rewards through forms of self-investment. From the outside of fields, illusio may appear absurd or irrational: a priest's belief in god; the collector's search for that rare item; the edgeworker's dance with death; the sociologist's endless quest for funding. But illusio does not always work to reproduce social relations; sometimes it transforms them.

The last example is not just meant to be a self-conscious bon mot. A productive way to illustrate how illusio works, and to consider what I propose is its concurrent burgeoning relationship to reflexivity, is the very situation of sociologists in academia. We are writing chapters like this; building our CVs;

applying for grants with tiny success rates; self-promoting on 'Academic Twitter'; writing blogs; and creating profiles on Academia.edu and ResearchGate. These practices seem to indicate a deep commitment to the game, and are evidence of commitment to career-based aspirations. But at the same time, we are likely to be well aware of what we may refer to as 'whackademia' (Hil 2012) and the 'toxic university' (Smyth 2017): the wasted time and money going into applications with a 12 per cent success rate; the endless KPIs, REFs, ERAs, and other quantitative measures of our ever-increasing 'outputs'; the managerial bullying; the publish or perish culture that now sees PhD scholarship applications needing publications to be competitive; the university at the vanguard of asserting labour market precarity; the consumption and sharing of online academic satire such as Academic Obscura, Shit Academics Say and PhD Comics. As sociologists, we are particularly well equipped to understand and to *feel* these dismal phenomena. Notice at conferences we spend a lot of time complaining about this stuff over post-seminar drinks. We are aware of the absurd demands of our own field. We know that academics are over-represented in terms of depression and anxiety (Guthrie et al 2017). But we do it anyway; we struggle on. We 'come to know what we know', which is central to the very possibility of labouring to overcome deleterious social forces or, relenting to necessity, where we 'lucidly know [what] extends beyond [our] capacity to amend' (Mead 2017). Reflexively speaking, I think that my own habitus clivé in academia makes me particularly sensitive to these phenomena, where 'the emotional pull of class loyalties can entangle subjects in the affinities of the past' (Friedman 2016: 129), which affords a relative ironic distance from these varieties of symbolic violence.

To be clear, I am aware that academics are a relatively privileged lot, and I am not arguing that academics or sociologists are alone in experiencing an increasingly reflexive, ironic or even an outright hostile disposition towards aspects of the illusio of their own field. There is no reason those outside the social sciences cannot have the same reflexive relation to their own aspirations, motivations and rewards, which Bourdieu (2000) enjoyed pointing out in his critique of scholastic reason. My suspicion is that this ironic disposition is increasingly the norm and the resultant affects are the insecure and anxious subject position sketched out by theorists of reflexive modernity (Beck and Beck-Gernsheim 2002), where it seems mental health problems are the new alienation of late capitalism (Fisher 2009). The rewards of the doxic promises we are immersed in from an early age – be good, be disciplined, study, work hard, make the right choices, buy the right stuff and you will be happy – are becoming a form of cruel optimism, except for the very privileged. There are costs and benefits for the upwardly mobile (Friedman 2014), and even the very privileged are not very happy (Hamilton and Denniss 2006). If this is the case, I suspect more and more people across the class spectrum will begin to reflexively question the very utility of investing in those illusio so intensely. In this sense, I am arguing that the ambivalent nature of illusio, that is, illusio can work towards social reproduction, social change or may even be relatively benign, can offer space for emancipatory social change.

The rejection of illusio has been implicit in youth transitions research, especially in instances where young people are seen to 'fail': for instance, an anti-school culture where 'working-class kids get working-class jobs' (Willis 1977). But reimagining illusio with the rise of the reflexive subject and ironic culture is a newer development that has implications for the very possibility of considering what aspirations are, as well as who can achieve them, and how.

Conclusion

As Wark points out in regard to Marx, 'The mark of a major body of work is that it will support more than one interpretation, all of which are coherent and persuasive, and each of which is open-ended enough for further elaboration' (2017: 15). Bourdieu's conceptual armoury fits this bill well: it has supported numerous interpretations and provides an architecture for not just further elaboration, but to be imagined through and with different ontological paradigms (Hage 2015). In this chapter I have made a case for illusio to do just that. Consideration of intensity and temporality in terms of investment in illusio can bring an affective layer to research on aspirations that utilize a Bourdieusian approach. Irony and reflexivity pose problems to illusio as unquestioned, but open it up as a tool for thinking about social change, despite Bourdieu's continual association with social reproduction (which is appropriate) and determinism (which is misplaced).

Recommended further reading

Hage, G. (1994), 'Pierre Bourdieu in the Nineties: Between the Church and the Atelier', *Theory and Society*, 23: 419–40.

Threadgold, S. (2017), *Youth, Class and Everyday Struggle*, London: Routledge.

Threadgold, S. (2018), 'Creativity, Precarity and Illusio: DIY Cultures and "Choosing Poverty"', *Cultural Sociology*, 12 (2): 156–73.

References

Aarseth, H. (2016), 'Eros in the Field? Bourdieu's Double Account of Socialized Desire', *Sociological Review*, 64: 93–109.

Aarseth, H. (2017), 'Fear of Falling – Fear of Fading: The Emotional Dynamics of Positional and Personalised Individualism', *Sociology*, online ahead of print 2 October. doi:10.1177/0038038517730219

Aarseth, H., L. Layton and H. B. Nielsen (2016), 'Conflicts in the Habitus: The Emotional Work of Becoming Modern', *Sociological Review*, 64 (1): 148–65.

Adkins, L. (2011), 'Practice as Temporalisation: Bourdieu and Economic Crisis', in S. Sussen and B. S. Turner (eds), *The Legacy of Pierre Bourdieu: Critical Essays*, 347–65, London: Anthem Press.

Ahmed, S. (2004), 'Affective Economies', *Social Text*, 22 (2): 117–39.

Archer, M. (2012), *The Reflexive Imperative in Late Modernity*, Cambridge: Cambridge University Press.

Atkinson, W. (2010), *Class, Individualization, and Late Modernity*, New York: Palgrave Macmillan.

Bathmaker, A.-M., N. Ingram, J. Abrahams, A. Hoare, R. Waller and H. Bradley (2016), *Higher Education, Social Class and Social Mobility*, London: Palgrave Macmillan.

Bathmaker, A.-M., N. Ingram and R. Waller (2013), 'Higher Education, Social Class and the Mobilisation of Capitals: Recognising and Playing the Game', *British Journal of Sociology of Education*, 34 (5–6): 723–43.

Beck, U., and E. Beck-Gernsheim (2002), *Individualization*, London: Sage.

Berlant, L. (2011), *Cruel Optimism*, Durham, NC: Duke University Press.

Bourdieu, P. (1984), *Distinction: A Social Critique of the Judgement of Taste*, Cambridge, MA: Harvard University Press.

Bourdieu, P. (1990), *The Logic of Practice*, Cambridge: Polity.

Bourdieu, P. (2000), *Pascalian Meditations*, Cambridge: Polity.

Bourdieu, P. (2004), *Science of Science and Reflexivity*, Cambridge: Polity.

Bourdieu, P. (2008), *Sketch for a Self-Analysis*, Chicago: Chicago University Press.

Bourdieu, P., and J.-C. Passeron (1990), *Reproduction in Education, Society and Culture*, trans. R. Nice, London: Sage.

Bourdieu, P., and L. Wacquant (1992), *An Invitation to Reflexive Sociology*, Cambridge: Polity.

Bourdieu, P., J.-C. Chamboredon and J.-C. Passeron (1991), *The Craft of Sociology*, New York: Walter de Gruyter.

Bowers-Brown, T. (2016), '"It's Like If You Don't Go to Uni, You Fail in Life": Bourdieu, Decision Making and the Forms of Capital', in J. Thatcher, N. Ingram, C. Burke and J. Abrahams (eds), *Bourdieu: The Next Generation*, 55–72, London: Routledge.

de Certeau, M. (1984), *The Practice of Everyday Life*, Berkeley, CA: University of California Press.

Farrugia, D., and D. Woodman (2015), 'Ultimate Concerns in Late Modernity: Archer, Bourdieu and Reflexivity', *British Journal of Sociology*, 66 (4): 626–44.

Fisher, M. (2009), *Capitalist Realism. Is There No Alternative?* Winchester: Zero Books.

Friedman, S. (2014), 'The Price of the Ticket: Rethinking the Experience of Social Mobility', *Sociology*, 48 (2): 352–68.

Friedman, S. (2016), 'Habitus Clivé and the Emotional Imprint of Social Mobility', *Sociological Review*, 64: 129–47.

Guthrie, S., Catherine A. Lichten, Janna van Belle, Sarah Ball, Anna Knack, and Joanna Hofman (2017), *Understanding Mental Health in the Research Environment*, Cambridge: RAND Europe.

Hage, G. (1994), 'Pierre Bourdieu in the Nineties: Between the Church and the Atelier', *Theory and Society*, 23: 419–40.

Hage, G. (2011), 'Social Gravity: Pierre Bourdieu's Phenomenological Social Physics', in G. Hage and E. Kowal (eds), *Force, Movement, Intensity: The Newtonian Imagination in the Humanities and Social Sciences*, 80–93, Melbourne: Melbourne University Press.

Hage, G. (2015), *Alter-Politics*, Melbourne: Melbourne University Press.

Hamilton, C., and R. Denniss (2006), *Affluenza*, Crow's Nest, NSW: Allen & Unwin.

Hil, R. (2012), *Whackademia: An Insider's Account of the Troubled University*, Sydney: New South Wales Books.

Hochschild, A. (1983), *The Managed Heart*, London: University of California Press.

Lahire, B. (2011), *The Plural Actor*, Cambridge: Polity.

Lorimer, H. (2005), 'Cultural Geography: The Busyness of Being "More-Than-Representational"', *Progress in Human Geography*, 29 (1): 83–94.

Mankowski, G. (2013), '"I Can't Seem to Stay a Fixed Ideal": Self-Design and Self-Harm in Subculture', *Punk and Post Punk*, 2 (3): 305–16.

Marx, K. (1978), 'The Eighteenth Brumaire of Louis Bonaparte', in R. C. Tucker (ed.), *The Marx-Engels Reader*, 2nd edn, 594–617, New York & London: W. W. Norton.

McKay, G. (ed.) (1998), *DiY Culture*, London: Verso.

McRobbie, A. (2002), 'A Mixed Bag of Misfortunes? Bourdieu's Weight of the World', *Theory, Culture & Society*, 19 (3): 129–38.

Mead, G. (2016), 'Bourdieu and Conscious Deliberation: An Anti-mechanistic Solution', *European Journal of Social Theory*, 19 (1): 57–73.

Mead, G. (2017), 'Forms of Knowledge and the Love of Necessity in Bourdieu's Clinical Sociology', *Sociological Review*, 65 (4): 628–43.

Milchman, A., and A. Rosenberg 2002, 'Marxism and Governmentality Studies: Toward a Critical Encounter', *Rethinking Marxism*, 14(1): 132–42.

Murphy, M., and C. Costa (2015), *Theory as Method in Research*, London: Routledge.

Noble, G. (2004), 'Accumulated Being', *International Journal of Cultural Studies*, 7 (2): 233–56.

Noble, G., and M. Watkins (2003), 'So, How Did Bourdieu Learn to Play Tennis? Habitus, Consciousness and Habituation', *Cultural Studies*, 17 (3–4): 520–38.

O'Connor, A. (2016), 'Towards a Field Theory of Punk', *Punk and Post Punk*, 5 (1), 67–81.

Probyn, E. (2005), 'Shame in the Habitus', in L. Adkins and B. Skeggs (eds), *Feminism after Bourdieu*, 224–48, Oxford: Blackwell.

Reay, D. (2004), 'Gendering Bourdieu's Concepts of Capitals? Emotional Capital, Women and Social Class', *Theory, Culture & Society*, 20 (6): 57–74.

Reay, D. (2015), 'Habitus and the Psychosocial: Bourdieu with Feelings', *Cambridge Journal of Education*, 45 (1): 9–23.

Robbins, D. (2004), 'The Transcultural Transferability of Bourdieu's Sociology of Education', *British Journal of Sociology of Education*, 25 (4): 415–30.

Robbins, D. (2005), 'The Origins, Early Development and Status of Bourdieu's Concept of "Cultural Capital"', *British Journal of Sociology*, 56 (1): 13–30.

Silva, E. (2016), 'Unity and Fragmentation of the Habitus', *Sociological Review*, 64: 166–83.

Smyth, J. (2017), *The Toxic University*, Basingstoke: Palgrave Macmillan.

Sociology is a Martial Art (2002), [Film] Dir. Pierre Carles, USA: Icarus Films. http://icarusfilms.com/new2002/socio.html

Strand, M., and O. Lizardo (2017), 'The Hysteresis Effect: Theorizing Mismatch in Action', *Journal for the Theory of Social Behaviour*, 47 (2): 164–94.

Sweetman, P. (2003), 'Twenty-first Century Dis-ease? Habitual Reflexivity or the Reflexive Habitus', *Sociological Review*, 51 (4): 528–49.

Thatcher, J., N. Ingram, C. Burke and J. Abrahams (eds) (2015), *Bourdieu: The Next Generation*, London: Routledge.

Threadgold, S. (2017), *Youth, Class and Everyday Struggle*, London: Routledge.

Threadgold, S. (2018), 'Creativity, Precarity and Illusio: DIY Cultures and "Choosing Poverty"', *Cultural Sociology*, 12 (2): 156–73.

Threadgold, S., and P. Nilan (2009), 'Reflexivity of Contemporary Youth, Risk and Cultural Capital', *Current Sociology*, 57 (1): 47–68.

Wacquant, L. (1992), 'Toward a Social Praxeology: The Structure and Logic of Bourdieu's Sociology', in P. Bourdieu and L. Wacquant (eds), *An Invitation to Reflexive Sociology*, 1–60, Cambridge: Polity.

Wark, M. (2017), *General Intellects*, London: Verso.

Wetherell, M. (2013), 'Affect and Discourse – What's the Problem? From Affect as Excess to Affective/Discursive Practice', *Subjectivity*, 6 (4): 349–68.

Willis, P. (1977), *Learning to Labour: How Working-Class Kids Get Working-Class Jobs*, Hampshire: Gower Press.

Woods, P. J. (2017), 'Ethics and Practices in American DIY Spaces', *Punk & Post Punk*, 6 (1): 63–80.

Part Two

Using and Developing Habitus

3

Young People's Educational Expectations, Aspirations and Choices: The Role of Habitus, Gender and Fields

Aina Tarabini and Marta Curran

Introduction

In Spain, most of the sociological research on educational expectations, aspirations and choices is informed by rational choice theories (RAT) (Bernardi and Requena 2010; Elias Andreu and Daza Pérez 2017). Based on the proposals made by Boudon (1983) and Breen and Goldthorpe (1997) these analyses explore the process of young people's decision-making according to the individuals' rational perceptions of costs and benefits associated with different decisions and educational routes.

In this context, the initial aim of our analysis, based on the ABJOVES empirical research project,[1] was to critically engage with previous theories in this field, and frame young people's educational aspirations and choices from a different epistemological angle. RAT and Bourdieu's theory of habitus have often been seen as contradictory, the main difference being that the former put the focus on individual rational decisions and the latter on the structural dimension that shapes these decisions. Despite this, our initial aim was to combine the two approaches in order to better understand the process of educational decision-making of Catalan young people at the end of their compulsory schooling (grade 10) (Tarabini and Curran 2015). In this sense, although we confer key importance on the mechanisms that explain students' educational decisions, we consider that these 'choices' are not exclusively a result of rational calculations. The objective of our analysis was to understand the decision to continue or to stop studying when compulsory schooling was about to end and the reasons for choosing the vocational or the academic upper-secondary track.

With this objective in mind, the ABJOVES project developed a qualitative methodology, based on in-depth case studies in five public secondary schools in Barcelona.[2] Very quickly, however, we discovered that our 'voiced research' analysis (Smyth and Hattam 2001) revealed the limits of RAT theory and made it very difficult to combine it with habitus theory. On the one hand, young people's accounts of their educational decisions and trajectories are not mainly informed by a rationalistic analysis of costs and benefits, but instead by a set of perceptions, dispositions and emotions that make them feel they belong to one place or another. Educational decisions, thus, we found, are not merely instrumental and rational but mostly expressive (in Bernstein's terms) and emotional. In fact, educational choices are not simply driven by potential outcomes but by present feelings, past experiences and subjective perceptions of the future. On the other hand, the possible choices are highly unequally distributed according to students' economic, social and cultural status. In order to properly evaluate the costs and benefits of a given choice, equivalent information and opportunities should be provided. However, crucial differences in information distribution, economic capacity and cultural barriers frame the actual possibilities that young people can choose. Moreover, dropping out of school is not always a question of making a choice but a matter of being excluded, pushed out of the school, in both direct and subtle ways.

In the light of these limitations, our analysis is based on Bourdieu's theory of action (Bourdieu and Passeron 1977) and specifically on his notion of habitus. In the first section, we argue that operationalizing habitus is crucial in order to understand how working-class students imagine and frame their immediate future. In the second section, we incorporate a gender perspective to better comprehend how habitus operates. In the third section, we include the concept of institutional habitus in the analysis. In the last section, we discuss the whole analysis.

Working-class habitus and students' dispositions and subjectivities

According to Bourdieu (1977), disparities in the material conditions of existence of different social classes explain why cognitive and normative predispositions to act vary systematically between individuals from these different classes. Moreover, as Diane Reay (2004b) explains, habitus is not solely composed of mental attitudes and perceptions but it is also embodied in people's ways of standing, speaking, walking, feeling and thinking (Bourdieu 1990: 70). Thus, as a complex interplay (in Reay's terms) between past and present individual histories, habitus reflects the social positions in which individuals are socialized and their subsequent trajectories in the social and educational realms.

The interaction of these elements would explain why working-class students, whatever country is selected and whatever indicator is chosen, always achieve, on the whole, worse educational results than their middle-class peers. It is not because of their economic, cultural or even personal 'incapacity'; neither is it because of their rational decisions and choices. It is, we argue, because their habitus is less aligned with schools' taken-for-granted assumptions, requirements and values, in other words, their institutional habitus. We will develop this argument in the following section. Indeed, when speaking with the students in our sample about their school experiences and their expectations and aspirations for the future, we identified three main types of feelings/reasoning, all of which were different expressions of an internalized social position that conflicted with the schools' expectations and ways of organizing: an internalized sense of incapacity and futility, a resistant disposition and a lack of control over the rules of the game.

Feelings of personal incapacity to cope with academic requirements represent one of the ways in which working-class students in our sample experience the schooling process. Individuals' identities are deeply rooted in social and relational processes and, consequently, self-perceptions and evaluations are mediated by the perceptions and reactions of 'significant others'. As Reay (1997: 226) argues, social class is powerfully internalized and continually plays out in interactions with others across social fields. In this sense, students' reflections on their own capacities and abilities are not independent of their previous educational trajectories or of their daily interactions with teachers and peers. For example, most of the working-class students in our sample have been grouped in low-ability groups within their educational institutions, have repeated some courses and have experienced disrespect, misrecognition and stigmatization from their teachers. As a result, students feel they are not good enough for study and blame themselves for their failed educational trajectory. Some of the interviewed students indicated this feeling as follows: 'I'm not good at studying; this is the main reason I failed' (Maria, 15 years old, grade 9); 'How can I possibly call myself a good student if I've repeated twice?' (Axel, 16 years old, grade 9); 'I was already struggling during compulsory schooling, how can I even think of upper-secondary schooling? No way, I'm not ready. I'm going to fail' (Rut, 15 years old, grade 10). These comments clearly illustrate how a trajectory featuring school troubles and struggles is lived as a personal and private matter. This feeling of being unable to follow the educational trajectory successfully is mainly explained by the students in terms of their perceived individual incapacities to manage the school's instrumental and expressive domains.

One of the consequences of this feeling is the students' sense of futility in the face of present academic requirements and future educational pathways. This is a sense of 'educational worthlessness' in Reay's (2006: 297) terms. As a result of prolonged educational struggles, consisting of referrals, expulsions, repeating subjects and conflicts with teachers, students express a profound lack of trust in the educational system. No matter how much effort they put in to succeed, they feel they are going to fail. Laura and Yanina indicated this: 'I've got this teacher constantly telling me "you are not going to succeed", and finally I ended up doing nothing' (Laura, 15 years old, grade 9); 'I don't see the point of making an effort. No matter if I did nothing, they [teachers] always believe it is me. They are always ready to punish me, to expel me' (Yanina, 17 years old, Second Chance School).[3] Teachers, in fact, play a crucial role in contributing to the way these young people experience schooling. It was precisely in the face of a perception that the teachers lacked trust in their abilities to succeed that the students we interviewed stopped making efforts to achieve. It is then in the interaction with the schools and the teachers, in the interaction with the institutional habitus, that the students' habitus is shaped and reshaped (see Ingram 2009 for a broader understanding of how institutional habitus shapes and mediates students' habitus).

The second expression of the working-class habitus in our sample, somewhat related to the feeling of a sense of futility, is the development of school resistance practices, as classically exemplified by Willis's (1977) lads. In fact, the students in our sample with dispositions towards active resistance to school did not explain their school troubles as a result of their individual abilities or actions, but precisely as a result of features of the school system. These students were the ones making explicit the lack of neutrality of the school organization and the social and cultural parameters defining the curriculum, pedagogy and assessment practices within the school. They rejected school because of this lack of neutrality. This was indicated by the following students: 'I do not study because it is useless. What is the point of studying just for studying? If it has no sense, if I see that it is completely a waste of time I do not study at all' (Evelyn, 15 years old, grade 9); 'I would like to know what it is for but nobody tells me, just general culture the teacher says. General culture is not enough in real life. That's why I disconnect' (Juan, 15 years old, grade 9); 'sometimes I do believe we are wasting our time. We remain here just because we need the certificate, but that's all, waiting, hanging in there until the day we can leave' (Jonatan, 15 years old, grade 9).

In these quotations the main reason the students provide explain why they might drop out is their perception of the lack of utility of schooling. They are not frustrated, unmotivated or feeling incapable. On the contrary, for these young people, the experience of schooling involves boring curricula, constant practices of behavioural control and management, and teachers' biased expectations and practices that remove all sense in continuing studying. One student indicated: 'I do exclude the school. As they exclude me, fuck them!' (Mohamed, 16 years old, Second Chance School).[4] School failure, thus, is externalized because it is not related to individual capacities, abilities or actions, but to the contextual elements and specifically to the school mechanisms enabling – or in this case hindering – the possibilities of school success.

The last expression of working-class habitus in the students' educational experiences, expectations and aspirations is a deep feeling of uncertainty and unpredictability that is explained by a lack of control over the rules of the educational frame. As Gale and Parker (2015) highlight, aspirations are always conceived within the limits of a social imaginary; they are framed by individuals' social circumstances and their imagined place in the world. In this sense, students' assessments of their own possibilities are deeply impregnated by their perception of what is suitable and what is not 'for people like them' (Bourdieu 1990; Burke, this volume; Stahl, this volume). Moreover, based on Appadurai's conceptual tools, Gale and Parker (2015) demonstrate that aspirations are capacity dependent; specifically, they depend on the capacity to navigate the educational system, to understand the implicit rules of the game, and to gain access to families' and peers' previous educational experiences and specific knowledge (or archives of experience in Gale and Parker's terms) to make their aspirations, their future, successful.

Some examples of this lack of navigational capacity are expressed in the following quotations: 'I would love to do something related to sports but I have no idea what you have to study to do that or what kind of jobs you can do' (Juan, 15 years old, grade 9); 'I imagine myself being rich and winning the lottery. If not then I don't know' (Raúl, 16 years old, grade 10). As can be observed in Juan's and Raúl's discourses, the capacity to imagine oneself and to transform this imaginary into a real opportunity is crucially mediated, both in material and symbolic terms, by their social locations, positions and identities.

In sum, Bourdieu's theory of habitus allows us to draw attention to how students experience and feel their educational institutions, accounting for the emotional processes framing young people's educational decisions and not merely the rational-instrumental ones, as highlighted by RAT approaches.

Gendering habitus and students' identities

A large number of feminist scholars have criticized the work of Bourdieu for considering gender as a secondary form of social stratification (Lovell 2004; McLeod 2005; Reay 2004a; Skeggs 1997; Bower-Brown, this volume). Nevertheless, these authors, far from denying the validity of Bourdieu's theoretical approach, adopt his concepts and tools to analyse gender relations. For Skeggs (1997) gender acts as one of the main distributing mechanisms within the social group and provides the relations in which capitals come to be organized and valued. Lovell (2004), for her part, exposes the fact that the processes of representation and recognition that individuals use in the interaction and use of capitals in the social fields differ according to their gender. In this respect, Skeggs (1997) suggests that is it through symbolic capital that different types of capitals are perceived and recognized as legitimated, and states that gender carries different amounts of symbolic capital in different contexts.

McLeod (2005: 19) exposes the fact that gender is an 'inherited' and embodied way of being that is shaped in interaction with social fields, constituting a repertoire of orientations and dispositions. Consistent with this, Reay offers this definition of gender habitus:

> It includes a set of complex, diverse predispositions. It involves understandings of identity premised on familial legacy and early childhood socialization. As such it is primarily a dynamic concept, a rich interfacing of past and present, interiorized and permeating both body and psyche. (1998: 141, quoted in Colley 2006: 26)

This gendered habitus appears to be a very relevant variable to understand how students in the ABJOVES project shape their identities as learners and imagine their academic future. Based on the analysis of the students in our sample, we can identify two examples of the role of this gender habitus: low levels of self-esteem and feelings of 'not fitting in' at school. Even if both mechanisms intersect with social class dispositions, these themes highlight the distinctive features arising from gender ones.

First, as we indicated in the previous section, there is a group of working-class students that express their habitus conflict with the educational institution by showing low levels of self-esteem and high levels of insecurity about their academic abilities. In this group of students, girls are the majority. Julia and Rut say: 'I have totally lost confidence in myself, I see that the class has a very high level and that I do not reach it ... there are some days I leave school crying with a sense of powerlessness' (Julia, 15 years old, grade 9); 'I don't think I'm prepared to go to high school, I find myself unable to do it. I think it will be very difficult and I don't see myself with that' (Rut, 15 years old, grade 9).

In this regard, various studies have demonstrated that girls have less confidence in their abilities than boys, especially in subjects such as mathematics and science, even in those cases where both have the same level of academic performance (Archer and Dewitt 2015). An article recently published in the journal *Science* (Bian, Leslie and Cimpian 2017) shows that, at six years old, girls already define themselves as less brilliant than their male peers, and this has effects on how students shape their educational aspirations and expectations and on the post-school choice-making process. This would explain why there are fewer women, especially from low socio-economic backgrounds, who choose STEM careers, since they perceive them to be beyond their capacities. Along the same lines, Archer (2005) observes that girls perceive these degrees as more difficult and for 'more intelligent' people, which shapes their expectations (see also Archer et al. 2016).

A second example of gendered habitus is the feeling observed in some of the students interviewed of 'not fitting in' with the values and norms of the institution, especially the taken-for-granted gender assumptions and norms. These students perceive that their behaviour is not 'appropriate' according to what the school expects from them and they feel different from the rest of their peers.

> The thing is that they [female classmates] are more posh, more ... . I don't know how to explain it ... . I've always been ruder. In my family, we are all ruder and in class I try to be quiet, to avoid getting myself noticed but sometimes it's difficult. (Rebeca, 15 years old, grade 10)

This feeling of 'not fitting in' is framed by, and contrasts with, the construction of an ideal pupil that relies on the dispositions of the middle class and of passive and obedient femininity. The legitimate way of behaving, dressing, talking, relating with peers and doing schoolwork locates working-class girls in a subordinate and pathologized position within the educational institution.

Moreover, students like Rebeca believe they must modify their attitude and behaviour in order to be more accepted by teachers and peers, because they believe that it would be beneficial for their educational trajectory. These results are consistent with the findings of previous studies (Archer 2005; Ingram 2011; Reay 2002; Stahl 2014) that students who do not meet the profile of the dominant and legitimate culture of the middle-school institution in terms of gender and class may experience social and cultural distancing from the school institution. In this regard, for some working-class girls in the ABJOVES project the only way to be successful in school is to gradually 'leave behind' (Reay 2001) their class and gender identity.

Along the same lines as the previous example, we have also observed a group of students, mainly working-class boys with a migrant background, who present a series of physical characteristics, types of behaviour and ways of relating that move away from the hegemonic patterns of masculinity defined by Connell and Messerschmidt (2005).

> The first year of high school all the rest of the boys were teasing me and bullying me all the time because I was very small and it was terrible. Then I started doing exercise every day and as soon as they saw that I had more strength they stopped bothering me and now I feel more comfortable at school. (Abdul, 15 years old, grade 9)

These students embody the type of masculinity that Connell and Messerschmidt (2005) define as marginalized, who, despite feeling very masculine, present a negative symbolic capital as a consequence of their subordinate position in terms of social class and/or ethnicity. This lack of power and recognition among peers affects their social relations and has negative consequences on their school engagement (Curran 2017).

Overall, as Reay (2015) points out, the configuration of class and gender identities involves affective-emotional elements such as feelings of inferiority, superiority, pride, shame, humiliation and, on occasions, ambivalence, which all contribute to shaping who we are, how we feel and how we act.

Institutional habitus or the crucial importance of educational fields

To this point we have attempted to analyse the effect of social class and gender dispositions on students' educational trajectories and choices. In this section, we will reflect on the utility of the concept of institutional habitus (Reay, David and Ball 2001) in order to understand young people's educational experiences, expectations and aspirations. Following the work of Reay, David and Ball

(2001), we define institutional habitus as the set of predispositions, taken-for-granted expectations and schemes of perception on the basis of which schools are organized. In alignment with Bourdieu's original notion of habitus, then, the institutional habitus allows us to explore how objective structural conditions produce in the habitus particular schemes of perception, appreciation and action, now embedded within an institutional field.

As noted elsewhere (Tarabini, Curran and Fontdevila 2016), the term 'institutional habitus' is of great utility in exploring the role of schools in generating different students' learning identities, dispositions, decisions and ultimately their opportunities for school success. In fact, we have identified two main types of institutional habitus – as Weberian ideal types – the institutional habitus based on inclusion and action and the institutional habitus based on expulsion and reaction. Both types are the result of the interplay between the three components of any institutional habitus, namely, the educational status (social composition, prestige, etc.), the organizational practices (curricular, pedagogical and assessment standards, among others) and the expressive order (mainly teachers' beliefs and expectations)[5] but each type is entrenched by the last factor. In this sense, the two ideal types illustrate crucial differences in schools' logics of action and in teachers' perceptions, beliefs and practices. It is important to analyse the effects of institutional habitus on students' dispositions as well as their educational aspirations and opportunities.

The inclusive institutional habitus, on the one hand, is characterized by a high collective commitment to the educational success of *all* students and, as such, it begins by recognizing students' diversity (in terms of class, gender, ethnicity, etc.). Drawing on empirical data, we see inclusive institutional habitus illustrated in the following quotation:

> All students are different because there is nobody starting from scratch. We are all born in a particular historical period, in a certain country, in a specific family and I mean ... there is no justice. When you are born your path is pretty much defined. It's very difficult to get out of it. They [the students] are the least able to change this situation. (Coordinator, grade 7, school with an inclusive educational habitus)

An exclusive institutional habitus, on the contrary, is mainly characterized by externalizing the responsibility for students' educational failure and, consequently, by a restrictive conception of teachers' role, mostly focused on knowledge transmission and on a very meritocratic and individualistic conception of students' educational trajectories, dispositions and results.

Nowadays, people are afraid to say that with no effort, there is no success. I know this is not a very politically correct statement, but I think we are very paternalistic with our students. Their obligation is to study, no excuses are valid here. And if you want, if you really want it, you can make it! I have seen many students in very difficult family situations with excellent marks. (Tutor, grade 7, school with an exclusive institutional habitus)

Of course, there are intermediate positions between these two extremes, and no doubt more research is needed in this regard. Simultaneously, there are political, social, corporate and other factors explaining the emergence of one or another type of institutional habitus. What our research demonstrates, however, is the crucial role of this analytical tool not just in order to understand the different logics of action displayed by schools but also to properly comprehend the emergence of different students' dispositions, educational aspirations and opportunities. Those schools with an inclusive institutional habitus have a more active role in compensating for social inequalities and, collectively, they increase the possibilities for students' educational engagement. On the contrary, those schools with an exclusive institutional habitus tend to reproduce social inequalities to a greater extent, thus reinforcing working-class students' distance from and misrecognition in the educational field.

The following quotations illustrate the impact of the educational institution, and specifically of the institutional habitus, on the students' educational dispositions and feelings:

Teachers in this school have always helped me. If I don't understand something they explain it twice, they want me to understand. So, this has helped me a lot, it raised my self-esteem a bit and my desire to study. Nowadays I never skip a lesson. I'm more attentive. (Ahmed, 15 years old, grade 9, school with an inclusive educational habitus)

In this school, the teachers are much more attentive to those who study than those who don't. They ignore those who don't study. And remember that what a kid wants is to receive attention. (Ángel, 15 years old, grade 9, school with an exclusive educational habitus)

Conclusions

The analysis developed in this chapter has shown the utility of applying Bourdieu's concept of habitus in order to understand young people's educational experiences and processes of decision-making. Educational dispositions, aspirations and choices are socially and relationally constructed and, as such, are not independent of the students' social identities and their respective educational institutions. Specifically, our analysis of student aspirations in the ABJOVES project has drawn out five main types of educational subjectivities arising from an exploration of the students' social class and gender identities: internalized incapacity and sense of futility, resistant dispositions, lack of control over the rules of the game, low levels of self-esteem and the feeling of 'not fitting in' to the school. These subjectivities allow us to demonstrate the following elements.

First, habitus does not operate in a direct or one-dimensional way but it generates different kinds of dispositions among students. The findings clearly demonstrate that habitus, far from being deterministic, expresses how social structures are internalized by individuals in heterogeneous ways. Moreover, the empirical results suggest the importance of those elements that go beyond purely rational or instrumental thinking – as highlighted by RAT theories – to explain the logic behind people's actions, as well as ways of being and feeling. Habitus is thus a crucial analytical tool to comprehend the impact of social inequalities in the configuration of educational experiences and aspirations.

Second, although the dispositions we found among working-class students in diverse educational settings are diverse, they all express internalized social positions that conflict with the taken-for-granted assumptions of the educational institution. The expressive and instrumental institutionalized rituals in education, in Bernstein's et al. (1966) terms, are built upon the social values and norms of the middle classes, thus explaining the production of symbolic violence, masking power relations, through schooling. Indeed the very presentation of schools as merely meritocratic institutions hinders the class values and relations upon which they are framed, thus turning school failure in a merely personal or individual failure of those students who do not put in 'enough effort'; who 'do not merit' success. Once again, however, our analysis demonstrates that this symbolic violence does not operate in a simplistic or linear way, highlighting the crucial role of specific schools and teachers in generating different opportunities for school success. In this sense, the concept of institutional habitus is of paramount importance in understanding the complex articulations between different types of habitus and different capitals and fields.

Third, our research demonstrates that habitus is also gendered and highlights the importance of taking into account gender dispositions when exploring the configuration of students' learning identities and their educational aspirations. Gender and class dispositions mediate students' self-perceptions about their abilities and capabilities. Hegemonic patterns of femininity and masculinity, being intrinsically connected to social class, have affective and emotional impacts on students' identities, experiences, aspirations and choices.

Notes

1 The project 'Early School Leaving in Spain: An Analysis of Educational Motivations, Decisions and Experiences of Young People' (ABJOVES) is an R&D project funded by the Spanish Ministry of Economy and Competitiveness (Ref. CSO2012-31575) for a period of three years (2013–16) and coordinated by the research group GEPS-UAB (PI Aina Tarabini).

2 The case studies included forty-seven interviews with teaching staff, five focus groups with teachers, fifty-four interviews with students (forty-one of whom were working-class students and the focus of the current analysis), and six focus groups with both middle- and working-class students (thirty-six students included in the groups). Simultaneously, observations of teaching staff meetings, classroom dynamics and informal spaces at the schools were conducted as well as documentary and data analysis for each of them.

3 This quotation is from a young student who had already left the school and was enrolled in a professional course at a Second Chance School. More details are given in Tarabini, Jacovkis and Montes (forthcoming).

4 Ibid.

5 See Tarabini, Curran and Fontdevila (2016) for a systematization of the three dimensions composing the institutional habitus.

Recommended further reading

Tarabini, A., M. Curran and C. Fontdevila (2016), 'Institutional Habitus in Context: Implementation, Development and Impacts in Two Compulsory Secondary Schools in Barcelona', *British Journal of Sociology of Education*, online before print 22 November. doi:10.1080/01425692.2016.1251306

Tarabini, A., M. Curran, A. Montes and L. Parcerisa (2016), 'The Politics of Educational Success: A Realist Evaluation of Early School Leaving Policies in Catalonia (Spain)', *Critical Studies in Education*, online before print 22 June. doi:10.1080/17508487.201 6.1197842

Tarabini, A., M. Curran, A. Montes and L. Parcerisa (2018), 'Can Educational Engagement Prevent Early School Leaving? Unpacking the School's Effect on Educational Success', *Educational Studies*. doi: 10.1080/03055698.2018.1446327

References

Archer, L. (2005), 'The Impossibility of Girls' Educational "Success": Entanglements of Gender, "Race", Class and Sexuality in the Production and Problematisation of Educational Femininities', paper presented at the Economic and Social Research Council Seminar Series 'Girls and Education', Cardiff, 24 November.

Archer, L., and J. Dewitt (2015), *Understanding Student Participation and Choice in Science and Technology Education*, Netherlands: Springer.

Archer, L., J. Moote, B. Francis, J. DeWitt and L. Yeomans (2016), 'The "Exceptional" Physics Girl: A Sociological Analysis of Multimethod Data From Young Women Aged 10–16 to Explore Gendered Patterns of Post-16 Participation', *American Educational Research Journal*, 54 (1): 88–126. doi:10.3102/0002831216678379

Bernardi, F., and M. Requena (2010), 'Desigualdad y Puntos de Inflexión Educativos: el Caso de la Educación Post-obligatoria en España', *Revista de Educacion*, 2010: 93–118.

Bernstein, B., Elvin, H.L. and Peters, R.S. (1966). Ritual in Education. Philosophical transactions of the Royal Society of London. A Discussion on Ritualization of Behaviour in Animals and Man, 251 (772), 429–36

Bian, L., S.-J. Leslie and A. Cimpian (2017), 'Gender Stereotypes about Intellectual Ability Emerge Early and Influence Children's Interests', *Science*, 355 (January): 389–91. doi:10.1126/science.aah6524

Boudon, R. (1983), *La desigualdad de oportunidades*, Barcelona: Laia.

Bourdieu, P. (1977), *Outline of a Theory of Practice*, Cambridge: Cambridge University Press.

Bourdieu, P. (1990), *In Other Words: Essays Towards a Reflexive Sociology*, Stanford, CA: Stanford University Press.

Bourdieu, P., and J.-C. Passeron (1977), *La Reproducción: Elementos para una teoría del sistema de enseñanza*, Madrid: Editorial.

Breen, R., and J. H. Goldthorpe (1997), 'Explaining Educational Differentials: Towards a Formal Rational Action Theory', *Rationality and Society*, 9 (3): 275–305.

Colley, H. (2006), 'Learning to Labour with Feeling: Class, Gender and Emotion in Childcare Education and Training', *Contemporary Issues in Early Childhood*, 7 (1): 15–29. doi:10.2304/ciec.2006.7.1.15

Connell, R. W., and J. W. Messerschmidt (2005), 'Hegemonic Masculinity: Rethinking the Concept', *Gender & Society*, 19 (6): 829–59. doi:10.1177/0891243205278639

Curran, M. (2017), *¿Qué lleva a los jóvenes a dejar los estudios? Explorando los procesos de (des)vinculación escolar desde una perspectiva de clase y género*, Barcelona: Universitat Autònoma de Barcelona.

Elias Andreu, M., and L. Daza Pérez (2017), '¿Cómo deciden los jóvenes la transición a la educación postobligatoria? Diferencias entre centros públicos y privados-concertados', *Revista de la Asociación de Sociología de la Educación*, 10 (1): 5–22.

Gale, T., and S. Parker (2015), 'To Aspire: A Systematic Reflection on Understanding Aspirations in Higher Education', *Australian Educational Researcher*, 42 (2): 139–53. doi:10.1007/s13384-014-0165-9

Ingram, N. (2009), 'Working Class Boys, Educational Success and the Misrecognition of Working Class Culture', *British Journal of Sociology of Education*, 30 (4): 421–34.

Ingram, N. (2011), 'Within School and Beyond the Gate: The Complexities of Being Educationally Successful and Working Class', *Sociology*, 45 (2): 287–302. doi:10.1177/0038038510394017

Lovell, T. (2004), 'Bourdieu, Class and Gender: "The Return of the Living Dead"?', in L. Adkins and B. Skeggs (eds), *Feminism after Bourdieu*, 37–56, Oxford: Blackwell.

McLeod, J. (2005), 'Feminists Re-reading Bourdieu: Old Debates and New Questions About Gender Habitus and Gender Change', *Theory & Research in Education*, 3 (1): 11–30. doi:10.1177/147787850504

Reay, D. (1997), 'Feminist Theory, Habitus, and Social Class: Disrupting Notions of Classlessness', *Women's Studies International Forum*, 20 (2): 225–33.

Reay, D. (2001), 'Finding or Losing Yourself? Working-Class Relationships to Education', *Journal of Education Policy*, 16 (4): 333–46.

Reay, D. (2002), 'Shaun's Story: Troubling Discourses of White Working-Class Masculinities', *Gender and Education*, 14 (3): 221–34. doi:10.1080/0954025022000010695

Reay, D. (2004a), 'Gendering Bourdieu's Concepts of Capitals? Emotional Capital, Women and Social Class', *Theory Culture Society*, 20 (6): 57–74.

Reay, D. (2004b), '"It's All Becoming a Habitus": Beyond the Habitual Use of Habitus in Educational Research', *British Journal of Sociology of Education*, 25 (4): 431–44. doi:10.1080/0142569042000236934

Reay, D. (2006), 'The Zombie Stalking English Schools: Social Class and Educational Inequality', *British Journal of Educational Studies*, 54 (3): 288–307.

Reay, D. (2015), 'Habitus and the psychosocial: Bourdieu with feelings', *Cambridge Journal of Education*, 45 (1): 9–23. https://doi.org/10.1080/0305764X.2014.990420 (accessed 12 October 2017).

Reay, D., M. David and S. Ball (2001), 'Making a Difference? Institutional Habituses and Higher Education Choice', *Sociological Research*, 5 (4). Available online: http://www. socresonline.org.uk/5/4/reay.html (accessed 12 October 2017).

Skeggs, B. (1997), *Formations of Class and Gender: Becoming Respectable*, London: Sage.

Smyth, J., and R. Hattam (2001), '"Voiced" Research as a Sociology for Understanding "Dropping Out" of School', *British Journal of Sociology of Education*, 22 (3): 401–15. doi:10.1080/0142569012006800

Stahl, G. (2014), 'White Working-Class Male Narratives of "Loyalty to Self" in Discourses of Aspiration', *British Journal of Sociology of Education*, 37 (5): 663–83. doi:10.1080/01425692.2014.982859

Tarabini, A., and M. Curran (2015), 'El efecto de la clase social en las decisiones educativas: un análisis de las oportunidades, creencias y deseos de los jóvenes', *Revista de Investigación en Educación*, 13 (1): 7–26.

Tarabini, A., M. Curran and C. Fontdevila (2016), 'Institutional Habitus in Context: Implementation, Development and Impacts in Two Compulsory Secondary Schools in Barcelona', *British Journal of Sociology of Education*, online before print 22 November. doi:10.1080/01425692.2016.1251306

Tarabini, A., J. Jacovkis and A. Montes (forthcoming), 'Factors in Educational Exclusion: Including the Voice of the Youth', *Journal of Youth Studies*.

Willis, P. (1977), *Learning to Labour: How Working Class Kids Get Working Class Jobs*, New York: Columbia University.

4

Putting Habitus to Work: Habitus Clivé, Negotiated Aspirations and a Counter-Habitus?

Garth Stahl

Introduction

Bourdieu's adaptable 'thinking tools' allow researchers to interpret the specific and cultural practices that may produce certain ways of being which can untangle explanations of class, hierarchies, aspiration, status and power in pedagogic contexts. As the habitus has to be apprehended interpretively and 'cannot be directly observed in empirical research' (Reay, David and Ball 2005: 25), I have always been drawn to empirical research where 'habitus is viewed more fluidly as both method and theory' (Reay 2004: 439). While Bourdieu intended his tools to be used relationally, there has also been considerable focus on how habitus is operationalized in social research (Costa and Murphy 2015) and how it can be used to understand experiences of schooling (Ingram 2011ab) and social mobility (Friedman 2016; Burke 2016). Critiquing neoliberal forms of schooling, my research explores the relationship between classed identities and learner identities. I have used habitus due to its capacity to show how class is internalized and individual aspirations and trajectories are mediated in relation to school cultures (Stahl 2015a, 2017a).

In this chapter I reflect upon how I have operationalized habitus in my scholarship to examine how aspirations are made (and remade) by students navigating forms of schooling where the conception of success, embedded within the institution, is exceedingly neoliberal, and where the ideal form of personhood is tied to social mobility (see Stahl 2015a for detailed analysis). I find habitus allows for an investigation of how aspirations are both *realized* and *contested* as students find ways to release themselves from such pressures and search for spaces to constitute themselves as subjects of value. Habitus – as a tool to think with – enhances my understanding of how agents can speak back to the institutional discourses concerning aspiration in their formal schooling, which may heighten various internal contradictions in their habitus. Therefore, in putting habitus to work, I emphasize its rich explanatory potential for understanding how students come to see themselves as aspirant individuals, which can often contrast sharply with the doxic view of aspiration present in formal schooling and wider society.

The formation of aspiration(s) is an ongoing process, bounded by multiple overlapping logics of cultural, economic and social capital. Researching how one comes to aspire, and the complexities and uncertainties this involves, requires sociologists to utilize tools which incorporate the multiplicity of factors influencing their formation. For researchers interested in how aspirations are formed in educational contexts, Bourdieu's theory of practice offers an approach to exploring how relations of privilege and domination are produced through the interaction of habitus, as a matrix of dispositions that shape how the individual operates in the social world. Theorizing with habitus compels me to think critically about the entwined relationship between aspiration, context and agency. After all, Bourdieu's tools are intended to theorize human action in an ongoing dialectical relationship between objective structures and subjective agency (Bourdieu 2004; Bourdieu and Wacquant 1992).

Bourdieu has been widely criticized for proposing concepts that are abstract and not carefully defined (Sullivan 2002; Thorpe 2010). These critiques have resulted in scholars redrawing the boundary lines and reaffirming what in the Bourdieusian canon there is consensus upon and where there may be fragmentation (Reay 2004; Wacquant 2011). We know Bourdieu's conception of habitus became clearer over the course of his scholarship, and scholars who label themselves Bourdieusians may operationalize habitus in a variety of different ways, emphasizing certain facets more than others. As Bourdieu's tools can be applied in different ways, there exist important nuanced differences in how the tool of habitus has been operationalized, where some have adopted the wording of personal and collective 'narratives' in the habitus while others have emphasized 'components', 'elements' and 'performances' (see Stahl, Perkins and Burnard 2017 for a summary). Ingram (2011a) has used the wording of 'tugged' or 'pulled' to explore the competing dispositions of white working-class boys in different school sites accounting for the powerful influence of field and institutions. Specifically, she draws our attention to how institutions can influence the habitus, and how fields can activate features of identity at certain moments. Given its abstract nature, there are certainly different interpretations and different ways of putting habitus to work. For some this arguably depreciates the value of the tool (see Wallace, this volume); for others the differences in interpretation are consistent with Bourdieu's original intent that his tools be considered dynamic and adaptable in social research. With this in mind, in this chapter, I consider the theoretical potential of habitus when researching aspirations before exploring the possibility of a counter-habitus and – if such a thing is possible – how it could be compatible with Bourdieu's logic of practice and useful when researching aspiration.

Habitus, dispositions and aspiration

Habitus is intended to extend our understandings of internalized behaviours, perceptions and beliefs that individuals carry with them and which, in part, are translated into practices. These practices, as products of dispositions, modulate as agents transfer to and from the fields in which they interact. As a tool habitus captures 'the intentionality without intention, the knowledge without cognitive intent, the pre-reflective, infra-conscious mastery that agents acquire in the social world' (Bourdieu and Wacquant 1992: 19). The habitus functions as a locus where agents come to invest their energies, constantly adjusting 'virtualities, potentialities, eventualities' within their social space (Bourdieu and Passeron 1977: 135). Bourdieu's theory of habitus emphasizes that dispositions are generated and shaped through the internalization of structures, the institutions within society, such as family, school and media. Dispositions can be shaped in reaction to new experiences *of* and *within* the world. Therefore, the habitus, in constant negotiation, generates ways of viewing the world, or, according to Bourdieu and Wacquant, the habitus contributes to 'constituting the field as a meaningful world, a world endowed with sense and value, in which it is worth investing one's energy' (1992: 127).

While the concept of habitus originated with Aristotle, and was developed by other sociologists including Durkheim, Weber and Foucault, Bourdieu's approach theorized habitus as a constant interaction between structure and agency where both reside within the habitus, forming and reforming in constant internal negotiation (Reay 2004; Ingram 2011a). After all, to understand habitus, in a Bourdieusian sense, is to approach it as a

> mediating construct that helps us revoke the common-sense duality between
> the individual and the social by capturing 'the internalization of externality and

the externalization of internality', that is, the ways in which the sociosymbolic structures of society become deposited inside persons in the form of lasting dispositions, or trained capacities and patterned propensities to think, feel and act in determinate ways, which in turn guide them in their creative responses to the constraints and solicitations of their extant milieu. (Wacquant 2016: 65)

In considering how habitus can be operationalized to investigate how aspirations are formed, it is important to think of habitus operating within constraints, and as a collection of individual trajectories/histories. The habitus mediates what is possible *but only* from a limited range of possibilities. For Bourdieu, in considering how habitus informs aspiration, the level of aspiration of individuals is 'essentially determined by the probability (judged intuitively by means of previous successes or failures) of achieving the desired goal' (Bourdieu and Passeron 1977: 111). As the habitus is always 'permeable and responsive' (Reay 2004: 434) agents are engaged in complex identity work and this has been particularly notable in research documenting how agents may reconcile competing and contrasting conceptions if they are born in one class status and then engage with the expectation to become upwardly mobile (Reay 2013; Stahl 2015a; Friedman 2016).

Here it is important to note that habitus is both a tool *and* what is being studied (Reay 2004). Therefore, for a social researcher, habitus works as the 'anchor' or a 'compass' keeping one on track (Wacquant 2011: 81). However, while habitus may indeed provide a valuable compass, it remains a tool that must be skilfully operationalized – specifically in regard to its relationship to capital and field – or else we risk losing the 'logic of practice' (Bourdieu 1990). Operationalizing Bourdieu's tools, specifically habitus, is certainly not straightforward and there is both an art and a skill to their application (Murphy and Costa 2016). Habitus demands that the social researcher keep many different overlapping elements in play through both fieldwork and analysis, and it is through this challenging balancing act that habitus becomes an essential point of theoretical orientation (and reorientation). Habitus, working in relation to capital and field, provides an explanatory advantage to explain more cohesively and comprehensively identities within a social context. In considering the skilfulness involved in its operationalization, habitus is not simply a tool to be overlayed, but instead a tool to be put to work in order to understand the interworkings of complex social life (Reay 2004; Adkins, Brosnan and Threadgold 2016; Ingram, 2011a). One of the constitutive elements of habitus is the orientation towards the accrual of capital that gives it weight and sets the trajectory; emphasizing the agentic capacity of the habitus opens up spaces to explore practices of subversion and resistance as the habitus seeks the accrual of both value and symbolic power. Habitus, after all, is the 'internal archive of personal experience', heavily influencing how agents 'strive for different forms of capital that give them a position of place in the social structure' (Murphy and Costa 2016: 7). With this in mind, habitus allows social researchers to move beyond narrow conceptions of aspiration (e.g. motivation, expectations, goal orientation and choice) towards aspirations as *socially realized* and *negotiated* in daily life.

A habitus clivé

Bourdieu talks of his childhood experience as the *transfuge fils de transfuge* (2004: 109) and describes how he considered himself disloyal – a defector – to his class origins during his social ascent. In *A Sketch for a Self-Analysis*, Bourdieu himself describes how social mobility led him to a prolonged feeling of unsettlement and fragmentation in his own habitus. Born the son of a postal worker in a rural town in southern France, Bourdieu became an esteemed chair of Sociology at the Collège de France; thus his life comprised a dramatic rise in social status, an exception that proves the rule. Thus, of particular fascination to Bourdieusian sociologists, especially those interested in the study of the nexus of class and aspiration, has been the dialectical confrontation between one's habitus and new fields that one enters. Bourdieu articulates:

> The relationship between the habitus and the field is, above all, a conditioning relationship: the field structures the habitus, which results from the incorporation of the immanent necessity of this field or of a set of more or less concordant fields; the disagreements may cause a divided, even severed habitus. (Bourdieu and Wacquant 1992: 102–3)

This interplay between the internalization of new experiences, schemes of perception and dispositions of origin can lead to the internalization of conflicting dispositions, commonly theorized as what Bourdieu (1993a: 383) calls a 'cleft habitus' – or habitus clivé. This is where a habitus lacks a certain unity, with either itself or the field, and in this lack of cohesiveness admits some of the messages within the new field while simultaneously adhering to key dispositions structured primarily by the habitus acquired in the field of origin. While the habitus encounters a new field, it is still clearly constrained by the conditioning forces of the field of origin to varying degrees. However, it is important to remain cautious concerning how the habitus may come to see the *legitimacy of the field* as well as the *degree of modification*. For Bourdieu the primary habitus of all agents 'tends to ensure its own constancy and its defense against change' (1990: 60); it has a capacity to counter. The habitus will never fully accept the new field as to do so would negate the power of the dispositions acquired in the field of origin and the desire in the habitus for unity and cohesiveness. Instead, the habitus adapts only *to a certain extent* because the habitus is, after all, generative, with the capacity, albeit fragmented, to resist the logic of the new field. Therefore, a habitus clivé compels social researchers to think critically about the role of agency in the habitus.

Furthermore, social research has shown that this clivé, where the habitus is in disarray, can be incredibly uncomfortable and debilitating (Reay 2013; Friedman 2016; Ingram, 2011ab), which can generate quite serious 'psychic costs' (Reay 2002, 2013). Ingram's research (2011a) illustrates a habitus tug (when pulled by forces of different fields simultaneously), a destabilized habitus (when 'no one knows who you actually are'), and a disjunctive habitus (when the divided habitus causes division). Bourdieu (2004: 127), reflecting on his own experiences, noted that the hysteresis experienced by extreme upward mobility often has profound psychic implications as agents experience prolonged pain and, at times, an 'Icarus effect' (cf. Atkinson 2012; Burke 2016; Friedman 2016). As a habitus clivé is intertwined with emotions of shame and guilt, most people 'tend to remain within compatible fields most of the time'; thus there is habitually a comfortable fit between field and habitus where the habitus knows the logic, its capitals and how to operationalize them accordingly in order to maintain one's social position (Chambers 2005: 340). Therefore, the habitus typically endures an experience of reinforcement – or reaffirmation – in response to the challenges of destabilization in a new field (Stahl 2016).

Theorizing a counter-habitus?

A significant advantage of using habitus as a conceptual tool is how deeply it is rooted in individuals having agency within their social contexts, rather than just being thought of as passive recipients of social structures. In considering the different interpretations and applications of habitus, my emphasis is on the generative capacity of the habitus and its orientation to always seek to accrue value in relation to the capitals one possesses. In Bourdieu's *The State Nobility* (1998: 106–7), he explores the experience of working-class students aspiring beyond their class origins and adapting to the upper echelons of the French education system. Drawing on his conceptual toolkit, specifically habitus, he shows how these 'transfuges' were caught in a sustained and difficult position, feeling the weight of their aspirations which, while unsettling, did not keep them from adopting the cultural dispositions of the elites, though they never quite mastered the game. As Lahire explains:

> Socialised successively but in part also simultaneously in worlds in which habits of taste are different and even socially opposed, these 'class transfuges' oscillate constantly – and sometimes in a mentally exhausting manner – between two habits and two points of view. (2011: 38)

In my own research, the boys I worked with found ways to resist and counter this 'transfuge' process. So while the habitus is 'enduring but *not static or eternal* [where] dispositions are socially mounted and can be eroded, countered or even dismantled by exposure to novel external forces, as demonstrated by situations of migration and specialized training' (Wacquant 2016: 66, original emphasis), we need to question the ways in which habitus may counter such erosions or dismantling, adhering to the security and safety of the primary habitus.

We know historically students from disadvantaged backgrounds have operated within a field of schooling which depreciated their value through continual pathologization of their class background (Jackson and Marsden 1962; Bourdieu and Passeron 1977). In contemporary times, we have seen how certain neoliberal pressures in schooling continue to undervalue working-class culture, privileging certain learner identities and aspirations as doxic (Stahl 2015a, 2017a; Kulz 2017). Oftentimes working-class students are labelled by their school as having 'low aspirations' when this is clearly problematic. My research has shown that working-class boys in these environments often want to learn and do well academically but do not necessarily invest in certain middle-class career-based aspirations which require a university education. I found that, as these young men complete their formal studies, their aspirations are actually more focused on attainable secure employment and maintaining close connections to family and peers. Similar to other studies examining working-class students' experience with education (e.g. Reay 2003; Skeggs 2002), my research found that the boys' habitus was infused with historic working-class dispositions constituted in their habitus of origin, specifically solidarist, communal values (see Stahl 2015a for a detailed analysis). However, as their habitus was exposed to the field of formal schooling which positions one form of aspiration as the only acceptable form, it created various 'identity traps' as they negotiated the precarious production of a valuable learner identity (Youdell 2010). In my research I observed teachers often telling young people they needed to pass their exams in order to be 'the best of the best', or more frequently students were told if they did not pass their exams they would be a 'scrounger', 'on the dole' or a 'benefit thief' (see Stahl 2017b). Clearly, this 'learning equals earning' agenda (Brown 2013), embedded in the institutional discourses of the school, pathologizes aspirations tied closely to working-class culture. As their aspirations become devalued, the habitus of many of the working-class young men I researched found ways to subvert the institutional doxic conceptions of 'success' and 'failure' and, to a certain extent, resist a habitus clivé. To do this they drew on what I call an *egalitarian habitus* (Stahl 2015b) which reaffirmed the habitus inculcated in their field of origin. I argue that this functions as a counter-habitus, directly informing their sense of aspiration (Holt, Bowlby and Lea 2013).

An egalitarian habitus, I argue, is closely aligned with the primary habitus, founded upon a disposition towards not being seen as 'snobby', as wanting to 'fit in' and be 'loyal to oneself', where the boys articulated a belief that 'no one is better than anyone else' or 'above their station' (Stahl 2015a). An egalitarian habitus, which counters a robust and powerful institutional culture, allows the boys to constitute themselves as having value in schools where their aspirations are pathologized; specifically, it is a negotiation where they reconcile certain dispositions within a discourse of aspiration focused solely on increasing status and earning potential (Stahl 2014). To embrace the aspirational discourses of the schooling structure would have required sustained engagement with a habitus clivé, with prolonged fragmentation, which, I argue, they actively resist as the habitus desires cohesiveness (Stahl 2015b).

Discussion

I have discussed how Bourdieu's tool of habitus can be operationalized to understand how working-class young men reconcile their current social and economic realities with the aspirational culture engrained in the fabric of the school. As a habitus is formed through previous experiences as well as new experiences, a counter-habitus is formed when the new experiences present a logic and value structure completely at odds with the habitus of origin. In the eyes of the school the boys are not winners in the game of accumulating capital (economic, cultural and social) yet they are clearly expected to become winners. These experiences of inferiority and abjection should not be under-emphasized;

they considerably influence aspirations and the rationales surrounding how the boys come to be aspirational subjects. Habitus, therefore, is integral to a process of sense-making and the ongoing negotiation concerning aspirations. The boys find ways to counteract the embedded neoliberal expectations of the school, where discourses of credentialism and social mobility are pervasive, through reaffirming the primary habitus based upon traditional working-class values inculcated in family and community life.

In putting habitus to work in the study of aspirations, the habitus served as a guide as I looked for spaces where the participants not only demonstrated both their acceptance of the game of education (e.g. 'learning equals earning': Brown 2013) but also where the participants were agentic, looking for where they could constitute themselves as subjects of value. While the habitus is oriented towards value accrual, the theorizing regarding the counter-habitus discussed above demonstrates an ongoing process through which agents are able to disassociate themselves from the prerogatives of neoliberalism. Bourdieu argues that the habitus does not only 'engender *aspirations* and practices objectively compatible with the objective requirements' (Bourdieu and Passeron 1977: 77), it also '*generates strategies* which can be objectively consistent with the objective interests of their authors without having been expressly designed to that end' (Bourdieu 1993b: 76, emphasis added). The formation of a counter-habitus guards, arguably, against a potential cleft habitus and works to maintain one's sense of value in a field where agents feel they are devalued (Stahl 2015b).

In work on symbolic violence, Bourdieu and Passeron (1977) contend that working-class students do not aspire highly because, through their habitus, they have internalized and reconciled themselves to the 'limited opportunities that exist for those without much cultural capital' (Swartz 1997: 197). This draws our attention to the so-called legitimacy of their exclusion; after all, this is indeed one of the functions of the school – 'for the excluded to persuade themselves of the legitimacy of the exclusion' (Bourdieu and Passeron 1977: 209). Building on this work, Reay, David and Ball write in their analysis of widening participation in the UK that

> working class acquiescence, a propensity to accept exclusion or exclude oneself rather than attempt to achieve what is already denied, arises because the dispositions which make up habitus are the products of opportunities and constraints framing the individual's earlier life experiences. (2005: 24)

As agents come in contact with a doxic version of success, largely beyond their desire, they are on guard against those emotions associated with shame and arguably the habitus finds ways to constitute itself as having value. Therefore, the existence of a counter-habitus can be interpreted as not only a part of the process of symbolic violence, but also, more importantly, as highlighting the capacity of habitus to ameliorate feelings of inferiority and to promote improvisation; after all the habitus is 'creative, inventive, but within the limits of its structures' (Bourdieu and Wacquant 1992: 19). While certainly individuals do internalize painful experiences and, as a result, do exclude themselves, the notion of a counter-habitus, while provocative and a break from Bourdieu in the conventional sense, opens up space to think about how agents negotiate certain expectations concerning aspiration.

Conclusion

Having the capacity to unearth some of the underlying tensions between identity and the dominant culture around aspiration, Bourdieu's theoretical tool of habitus enables interpretation of cultural practices that may produce certain 'ways of being'. It is certainly worth considering whether feelings of dislocation are more frequent in late modernity with increased expectations concerning both social and geographical mobility. While the habitus is continually adaptive and predisposed towards certain ways of behaving and interacting, there exists a complex negotiation when the habitus encounters a new field, as individuals engage in an internalization of possibilities which becomes simultaneously a process of resistance and acceptance.

However, in intentionally complicating habitus through considering the formation of a counter-habitus, in theorizing how it may manifest and what function it could play, we also must recognize its possible critiques. Clearly, if the habitus represents how the social world is in the body (a common way of theorizing with habitus), how can one have a habitus that is counter to the world one inhabits? After all, the habitus never exists in isolation (Wacquant 2016: 69), which is foundational to understanding how it operates. In my thinking on a counter-habitus, I believe it capitalizes and reaffirms certain dispositions structured in the habitus of origin. Clearly the boys spend considerable amounts of time in the school which does not recognize or value their cultural background; while the logic of the field may feel all-encompassing, we need to question *to what extent* it depreciates the capitals the boys enter with. I argue that the counter-habitus is an exciting conceptual space for those studying aspirations as the focus is on reaffirmation of the primary habitus, in this case an egalitarian habitus tied to working-class values. For the boys I researched, I argue they have made sense of 'the game' and may even have a 'feel for the game' but that does not necessarily mean they are compelled to play the game. To be more precise, their habitus enables an active resistance to playing a game where they have not been dealt the necessary cards in order to be a skilled competitor and they find solace in dispositions aligned with their primary habitus.

Recommended further reading

Bourdieu, P. (2004), *Esquisse pour une auto-analyse [Sketch for a Self-Analysis]*, Paris: Raisons d'Agir.

Friedman, S. (2013), 'The Price of the Ticket: Rethinking the Experience of Social Mobility', *Sociology*, 48 (2): 352–68.

Stahl, G. (2015), 'Egalitarian Habitus: Narratives of Reconstruction in Discourses of Aspiration and Change', in C. Costa and M. Murphy (eds), *Bourdieu, Habitus and Social Research: The Art of Application*, 21–55, London: Palgrave Macmillan.

References

Adkins, L., C. Brosnan and S. Threadgold (2016), *Bourdieusian Prospects*, Oxon: Routledge.

Atkinson, W. (2012). 'Reproduction Revisited: Comprehending Complex Educational Trajectories', *Sociological Review*, 60 (4): 734–52.

Bourdieu, P. (1990), *In Other Words: Essays Towards a Reflexive Sociology*, Cambridge: Polity Press.

Bourdieu, P. (1993a), 'A Life Lost', in P. Bourdieu et al. (eds), *The Weight of the World: Social Suffering in Contemporary Society*, 381–91, Stanford, CA: Stanford University Press.

Bourdieu, P. (1993b), 'The Order of Things', in P. Bourdieu et al. (eds), *The Weight of the World: Social Suffering in Contemporary Society*, 60–76, Stanford, CA: Stanford University Press.

Bourdieu, P. (1998), *The State Nobility: Elite Schools in the Field of Power*, Stanford, CA: Stanford University Press.

Bourdieu, P. (2004), *Esquisse pour une auto-analyse [Sketch for a Self-Analysis]*, Paris: Raisons d'Agir.

Bourdieu, P., and J. C. Passeron (1977), *Reproduction in Education, Society, and Culture*, London: Sage.

Bourdieu, P., and L. Wacquant (1992), *An Invitation to Reflexive Sociology*, Cambridge: Polity Press.

Brown, P. (2013), 'Education, Opportunity and the Prospects for Social Mobility', *British Journal of Sociology of Education*, 34 (5–6): 678–700.

Burke, C. (2016), 'Bourdieu's Theory of Practice: Maintaining the Role of Capital', in J. Thatcher, N. Ingram, C. Burke and J. Abrahams (eds), *Bourdieu: The Next Generation*, 107–22, Oxon: Routledge.

Chambers, C. (2005), 'Masculine Domination, Radical Feminism and Change', *Feminist Theory*, 6: 325–46.

Costa, C., and M. Murphy (eds) (2015), *Bourdieu, Habitus and Social Research: The Art of Application*, London: Palgrave MacMillan.

Friedman, S. (2016), 'Habitus Clivé and the Emotional Imprint of Social Mobility', *Sociological Review*, 64: 129–47.

Holt, L., S. Bowlby and J. Lea (2013), 'Emotions and the Habitus: Young People with Socio-emotional Differences (Re)producing Social, Emotional, and Cultural Capital in Family and Leisure Space-Times', *Emotion, Space and Society*, 9: 33–41.

Ingram, N. (2011a), 'Within School and Beyond the Gate: The Complexities of Being Educationally Successful and Working Class', *Sociology*, 45 (2): 287–302.

Ingram, N. (2011b), 'Reconciling Working-Class Identity and Educational Success: A Study of Successful Teenage Boys, Locality and Schooling', Doctoral Dissertation, Queen's University Belfast.

Jackson, B., and D. Marsden (1962), *Education and the Working-Class*, London: ARK Paperbacks.

Kulz, C. (2017), *Factories for Learning: Making Race, Class and Inequality in the Neoliberal Academy*, Manchester: Manchester University Press.

Lahire, B. (2011), *The Plural Actor*, Cambridge: Polity Press.

Murphy, M., and C. Costa (2016), *Theory as Method in Research: On Bourdieu, Social Theory and Education*, Oxon: Routledge.

Reay, D. (2002), 'Shaun's Story: Troubling Discourses on White Working-Class Masculinities', *Gender and Education*, 14 (3): 221–34.

Reay, D. (2003), 'A Risky Business? Mature Working-Class Women Students and Access to Higher Education', *Gender and Education*, 15, (3): 301–17.

Reay, D. (2004), '"It's All Becoming Habitus": Beyond the Habitual Use of Habitus in Educational Research', *British Journal of Sociology of Education*, 25 (4): 431–44.

Reay, D. (2013), 'Social Mobility, a Panacea for Austere Times: Tales of Emperors, Frogs, and Tadpoles', *British Journal of Sociology of Education*, 34 (5–6): 660–77.

Reay, D., M. E. David and S. Ball (2005), *Degrees of Choice: Social Class, Race and Gender in Higher Education*, London: Institute of Education.

Skeggs, B. (2002), *Formations of Class and Gender*, Nottingham: Sage.

Stahl, G. (2014), 'White Working-Class Male Narratives of "Loyalty to Self" in Discourses of Aspiration', *British Journal of Sociology of Education*, 37 (5): 663–83.

Stahl, G. (2015a), *Aspiration, Identity and Neoliberalism: Educating White Working-Class Boys*, London: Routledge.

Stahl, G. (2015b), 'Egalitarian Habitus: Narratives of Reconstruction in Discourses of Aspiration and Change', in C. Costa and M. Murphy (eds), *Bourdieu, Habitus and Social Research: The Art of Application*, 21–55, London: Palgrave Macmillan.

Stahl, G. (2016), 'The Practice of "Othering" in Reaffirming White Working-Class Boys' Conceptions of Normative Identities', *Journal of Youth Studies*, 20 (3): 283–300.

Stahl, G. (2017a), *Ethnography of a Neoliberal School: Building Cultures of Success*, New York: Routledge.

Stahl, G. (2017b), 'Pathologizing the White "Unteachable": South London's Working-Class Boys' Experiences with Schooling and Discipline', in N. S. Okilwa, M. Khalifa and F. Briscoe (eds), *The School to Prison Pipeline: The Role of Culture and Discipline in School*, 91–112, Bingley, UK: Emerald Publishing Limited.

Stahl, G., R. Perkins and P. Burnard (2017), 'Critical Reflections on the Use of Bourdieu's Tools "In Concert" to Understand the Practices of Learning in Three Musical Sites', *Sociological Research Online*, 22 (3): 57–77.

Sullivan, A. (2002), 'Bourdieu and Education: How Useful is Bourdieu's Theory for Researchers?', *Netherlands Journal of Social Sciences*, 38 (2): 144–66.

Swartz, D. (1997), *Culture and Power: The Sociology of Pierre Bourdieu*, Chicago: University of Chicago Press.

Thorpe, H. (2010), 'Bourdieu, Gender Reflexivity, and Physical Culture: A Case of Masculinities in the Snowboarding Field', *Journal of Sport & Social Issues*, 34 (2): 176–214.

Wacquant, L. (2011), 'Habitus as Topic and Toll: Reflections on Becoming a Prizefighter', *Qualitative Research in Psychology*, 8: 81–92.

Wacquant, L. (2016), 'A Concise Genealogy and Anatomy of Habitus', *Sociological Review*, 64 (1): 64–72.

Youdell, D. (2010), 'Identity Traps or How Black Students Fail: The Interactions Between Biographical, Sub-cultural, and Learner Identities', *British Journal of Sociology of Education*, 24 (1): 3–20.

Part Three

Using and Developing Theoretical Approaches to Capital

5

Operationalizing Bourdieu for the Study of Student Aspirations: Conceptual and Methodological Challenges

Jim Albright, Jennifer Gore, Maxwell Smith and Kathryn Holmes

Introduction

The study 'Educational and Career Aspirations in the Middle Years of Schooling: Understanding Complexity for Increased Equity', funded by the Australian Research Council and the NSW Department of Education,[1] sought to identify the relative impact of, and complex interplay among, student- and school-related factors influencing the career and educational aspirations of students. Both the scale of the study and its mixed-method longitudinal design were innovative in the field of aspirations research, where cross-sectional analyses and small samples are common (e.g. Guo et al. 2015). Our goal of providing *comprehensive* quantitative and qualitative longitudinal analyses of factors influencing students' aspirations (see Figure 5.1) drew us to a composite capitals construct. Becker and Tomes' (1986) idea of human capital, or rational decision-making, based on potential gains in productivity as compared with direct/indirect costs, helped us gain insights into academic preparation for tertiary education (e.g. academic achievement, curriculum advice and pathways, test results, and planning and saving for educational expenses). Bourdieu's theory of capital interaction assisted us to conceptualize components contributing to both the differential distribution and the reproduction of aspiration, attainment and achievement. We employed Bourdieu's notions of economic capital (resources generated through labour: income, property, wealth, etc.); social capital (resources available from membership in durable, powerful networks, material and non-material support, etc.); and cultural capital (resources linked to value-based systems: education,

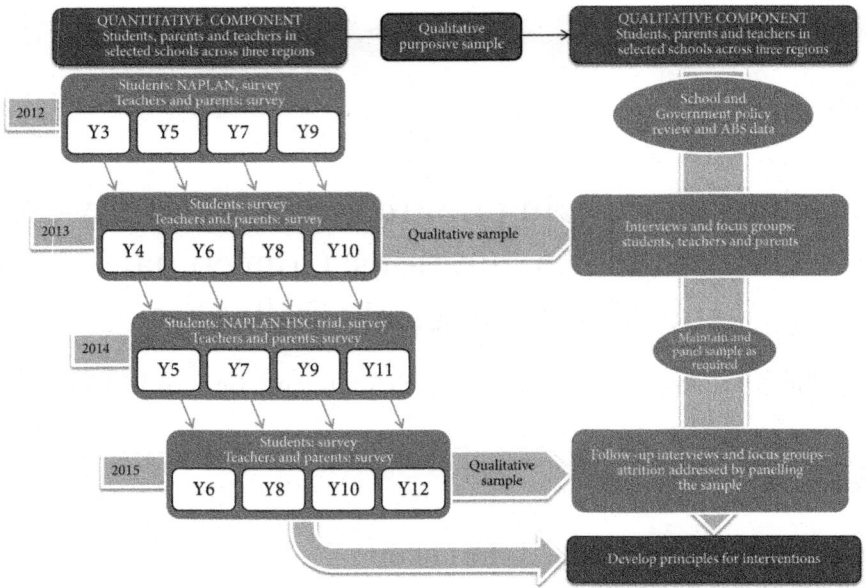

Figure 5.1 Study design and timeline

reputation, language skills, etc.), to identify family, school and community factors that influence students' aspirations, particularly for those from low SES backgrounds.

Sampling 6,492 students, the aspirations study mapped the intersection of the educational and career aspirations of students in Years 3 to 12 (aged 8–18 years) with socio-economic status and other demographic variables. Our aim was to contribute to the evidence base for academic, educational and political work on access to higher education, and the policies, practices and outcomes that might ensue.

We employed a sequential mixed-method approach, with quantitative data collected over a four-year period, including annual online surveys of students (appropriately framed for varying age groups); annual online surveys of parents (with options for paper copy and structured interviews where situational, technological and/or language/literacy situations dictated); annual online surveys of teachers; linkage to education department demographic and student achievement data; school documents and plans; and other publicly available data. Qualitative data were collected through focus groups with students and parents and interviews with teachers in the second, third and fourth years of the study.

In researching educational and career aspirations, we recognized the need for multiple theoretical perspectives to be taken into account using a 'composite capitals framework, similar to that employed by Engberg and Wolniak (2010; cf. Perna and Titus 2005). This framework enabled a comparison of Beckerian rationalist decision-making with Bourdieusian reflective and sonomic modes of action (Reay 2004). Given the importance educationalists and public policy users place on studies that employ capital theories to analyse education achievement and aspiration, we needed to take care in how we employed these concepts in the study. Setting aside the objection that these two notions of capital are incommensurable, our hope was that the relative explanatory power of each would become apparent as a result of the analysis of the data (Hjellbrekke and Korsenes 2009; Veenstra 2009).

Understanding conceptions of capital

A dominant paradigm embedded within educational policy research is rational choice or action theory (see Walker 2012), often associated with Becker and colleagues' notion of human capital (e.g. Becker and Murphy 2009; Becker and Tomes 1986; Coleman 1988). Human capital theorizing and research responds substantially to the social and economic conditions brought about by globalization (Keating and Klatt 2013; Lingard 2010; Sellar and Gale 2011; Sellar, Gale and Parker 2011) and 'the knowledge economy' (Keeley 2007). Policy directions designed to increase the stock of human capital are the main driver motivating the shift from utilitarian to aspirational incentives for human capital accumulation (Feher 2009; Sellar and Gale 2011).

Human capital theorizing contrasts with critical sociological approaches wherein aspirations are understood as influenced by dispositions that are formed in tension within social power structures and are thereby virtually non-conscious (Sellar and Gale 2011). Bourdieusian critical sociology investigates the influence of acquired dispositional traits, or *habitus*, on educational trajectories (Sellar and Gale 2011; Stahl, this volume) and contends that there is a strong link between cultural and social capital and educational attainment. Indeed, Bourdieusian ways of understanding student aspirations are evident in the formulation of education policy predisposed to normative values about the purpose of the educational endeavour and epistemological considerations and judgements regarding reliable knowledge (see for example Bridges 2010; Bridges, Smeyers and Smith 2008; Bridges and Watts 2008; Clark 2011; Hammersley 2002; Levin 2004). Defining cultural capital according to the often limited variables available is common practice in educational research, which affects researchers' interpretations of how cultural capital functions. This conceptual complexity and ambiguity in cultural capital theorizing and research impels students and scholars to be cautious in how the concept is interpreted and applied (Prieur and Savage 2013; Robson and Sanders 2009; Stich and Cipollone, this volume).

Rational choice theory and Bourdieusian notions of reasoning present two seemingly opposing accounts of choice-making regarding career paths and higher education participation (Swedberg 2011). Yet, understanding both somatic and conscious deliberations is important, especially given Australia's goals for greater university participation by under-represented 'equity groups' (Bradley et al. 2008; Bennett et al. 2015; Naylor, Baik and James 2013). Gains made to date have been more quantitative (numbers of student accessing higher education) than qualitative (numbers of student gaining access to high-status institutions and programmes of study) (Gale and Mills 2013; Sellar, Gale and Parker 2011; Whitty, Hayton and Tang 2015).

Applying conceptions of capital

Our composite capitals approach required us to construct a substantive theoretical frame that we could operationalize. We developed a substantive framework that identified clear concepts linked to proxies that would yield data capable of mapping the intersection of educational and career aspirations of students in Years 3 to 12 with socio-economic status and other demographic variables. This framework is depicted in Table 5.1.

These different theorizations of capitals presented challenges. The operationalization of Bourdieu's theories, particularly in Anglophone educational research, is highly contested. For example, researchers have problematized the nexus between highbrow/lowbrow activities and social class (structural homology) (Lareau and Weininger 2003, 2004; Vryonides 2007), the place of gender (Coulangeon and Lemel 2009), and the impact of family practices and resources upon educational outcomes (Lareau and Weininger 2003, 2004; Vryonides 2007). We had reservations about social capital research's failure to provide empirical or theoretical support for a hypothesized positive link between social capital and factors related to education (Dika and Singh 2002). We operationalized social capital as resources available from membership of enduring social networks (Bourdieu 1986) in order to test the veracity of a link between factors relating to education and proxies representing social capital. As a concept, economic capital, identified in terms of economic assets, has not attracted debate like that surrounding cultural and social capital. Hence, in our study we operationalized economic capital as resources generated through labour: income, property and wealth.

Human capital was included as a foil to the other capitals in order to incorporate an explicit representation of conscious decision-making. Of particular interest was the use of rational and conscious decision-making in the conversion of one capital to another; for example, in the conversion of educational qualifications (cultural capital) into economic capital (Veenstra 2009). This was intended to serve as a counterpoint to Bourdieusian capitals, testing whether aspirations emerge as a result of rational and conscious decision-making or as a result of cultural transmission (Andres 2009). The study operationalized human capital as academic achievement, curriculum advice and pathways, test results, and planning and saving efforts for educational expenses.

The student surveys included banks of items that were mapped to the variables listed in Table 5.1. The major areas addressed by the surveys were details of the student's family and personal interests, including books in the home and screen time; schooling, including self-reported opinions of achievement; extracurricular activities and socializing habits; aspects of work and future educational goals; and peer network and support.

We conducted a review of studies on aspirations using notions of capital, focusing on Australia but including international studies. We sourced potential survey questions from prior and existing studies – including the Longitudinal Study of Australian Youth (LSAY), the Programme for International Student Assessment (PISA) and Household, Income and Labour Dynamics in Australia (HILDA). We then collated them, coded them to the relevant form/s of capital, and assessed them for theoretical integrity and likely usability by school students, teachers and parents. A shortlist of possible questions was produced. We conducted a small-group, systematic review process to rank and comment on question suitability with NSW Department of Education staff (including teachers, school executive and regional support staff), academics with expertise in survey design, and academics with expertise in notions of capital. Once this process was complete, a select panel reviewed the responses and refined the questions. Draft surveys were piloted in four representative schools. The piloted survey responses were collated and analysed. The survey was further refined for use in the study.

Table 5.1 Elaboration of variables in relation to the capitals theoretical framework

	Student-level variables		School-level variables
	Students	**Parents**	**School (teachers/exec)**
Economic capital	SES P/T employment Income knowledge and goals	Occupation Income Affordability of tertiary education	SES quartile distribution Per student net recurrent income School SES value Total capital expenditure
Cultural capital	Career and educational aspirations Access to resources outside of school (cultural, educational, leisure) Access to cultural resources in school Language background	Educational and career aspirations for child Educational attainment Parent involvement in cultural, educational, leisure activities Language background	Cultural and linguistic diversity Types and quality of cultural activities available Teacher expectations and aspirations for students' education and career outcomes Tracking practices and curriculum pathways (academic/vocational)
Social capital	Peer educational and career aspirations Number of friends planning VET/university Access to persons with information about VET and university Parent–child discussion about education/career plans	Number of friends who have attended or are attending VET/university Number of friends who have completed Y10/Y12 Involvement with school Level of trust with school Parent–child discussion about education/career plans	Trust in parents to support child's education/career aspirations Types and strength of school connections to parents Types and strength of school connections to local community Connections with employers for career programmes
Human capital	Standardized test results Attendance Courses taken/curricula pathways Education completion plans Concept of career success Aspirations for VET/university Attitude to school/engagement with learning	Saving for education Concept of career success Knowledge of and/or discussion about courses/curricula pathways Aspirations for child to attend VET/university Attitude to education	Standardized test results/trial matriculation results Attendance rates Expectations of academic success Academic curriculum/culture Types and quality of career development programme and other career and equity interventions

Abbreviations: SES = socio-economic status. P/T = part-time. VET = vocational education and training. Y10/Y12 = Year 10/Year 12.

Developing a proxy measure of cultural capital for use in the aspirations longitudinal study

The methodological challenges of operationalizing Bourdieu's fluid and dynamic capitals theories are exemplified in the aspirations study's attempts to find reliable proxies to operationalize cultural capital. Quantitative methodology needs proxies to be discrete units of measurement, which is especially challenging when operationalizing Bourdieusian notions of capital. In fact, Bourdieu is criticized for the fact that his 'theoretical arguments are simply not articulated in empirical terms' (Aschaffenburg and Maas 1997: 584). Even Bourdieu's own operationalization of cultural capital has come under scrutiny (Sullivan 2002). The example provided below is a 'classical operationalization' of cultural capital (De Graaf, De Graaf and Kraaykamp 2000: 96) based on the regularity of student participation in the beaux arts and highbrow cultural activities.

The aspirations study operationalized cultural capital using student survey responses (n = 9,869) to a series of ten questions asking how often they participate in certain activities. These items were derived from the PISA 2000 student survey (OECD 2000). The items began with a common stem: 'How often do you do the following activities?' Frequency of involvement was self-reported by students on a four-point Likert-type scale (1 = never; 2 = rarely; 3 = sometimes; 4 = frequently). Results were as follows: listened to classical music (M = 1.68, SD = 0.91); went to art galleries or museums (M = 1.68, SD = 0.77); talked about news and current affairs (M = 1.99, SD = 0.91); went to the theatre to see a play, dance or opera performance (M = 1.59, SD = 0.80); went to the cinema to watch a movie (M = 2.63, SD = 0.77); went to a library (M = 2.09, SD = 0.98); talked about books (M = 1.98, SD = 1.00); played a musical instrument or sang (M = 2.40, SD = 1.21); and talked about art (M = 1.76, SD = 0.91).

Scale development

Our approach to scale development used random split-half sampling to identify two equivalent subsamples, undertaking exploratory factor analysis (EFA) in the first of these to establish scale structure and confirmatory factor analysis (CFA) in the holdout subsample to specifically model error terms, identify any influential inter-item correlations and obtain p-values to assess the significance of the factor loadings. A principal components analysis was undertaken in the EFA subsample (n = 4,934) using *IBM SPSS Version 23*.

A single factor solution was identified which accounted for 37.86 per cent of the total variance.

A one-factor congeneric model (Jöreskog 1971) was fitted in the CFA subsample (n = 4,935) using *IBM SPSS Amos Version 23* to confirm the structure of the model developed in the EFA. The final CFA model fitted the data well, assessed in terms of the fit statistics recommended by Jackson and Gillaspy (2009) including $\chi^2(29)$ = 507.84, p < .000; *GFI* = .98; *NFI* = .96; *CFI* = .96; *RMSEA* = .05. The pattern of the CFA factor loadings closely matched those of the EFA, cross-validating the two models (see Table 5.2).

The findings of the EFA and CFA analysis underpinned the decision to retain the ten items and formed a scale to act as a proxy representing an embodied form of cultural capital. The low factor loading related to the frequency of attending the cinema as by far the least influential but was nevertheless found to be significant.

Composite scores were calculated as average unit-weighted factor scores, deemed appropriate for this purpose (Klinger et al. 2006). The average cultural capital scale score was 1.97 (*SD* = 0.57), falling almost exactly on the second data point representing 'rarely' on the original frequency-related scale (see Figure 5.2). While not strictly normal, extensive review of research dating back to the 1930s has demonstrated the robustness of parametric methods such as analysis of variance, regression and correlation to violations of this kind (Norman 2010). The cultural capital scale score was adjudged appropriate for its intended use in the project, in some analyses as a continuous variable and in others as an ordinal variable based on tertile or quartile splits.

Table 5.2 EFA and CFA model parameters

Item	Full sample[a]		Factor loadings	
	M	**SD**	**EFA-half**	**CFA-half***
Listen to classical music	1.68	0.91	0.61	0.55
Go to art galleries or museums	1.68	0.77	0.73	0.72
Talk about news and current affairs	1.99	0.95	0.52	0.45
Go to the theatre	1.59	0.80	0.68	0.61
Go to the cinema	2.63	0.77	0.33	0.25
Go to a library	2.09	0.98	0.68	0.58
Talk about books	1.98	1.00	0.71	0.62
Play a musical instrument or sing	2.40	1.21	0.60	0.51
Participate in dancing, gymnastics or yoga	1.87	1.12	0.50	0.42
Talk about art	1.76	0.91	0.70	0.66

[a]N = 9,869. *denotes significance, p < 0.001. Abbreviations: *M* = mean. *SD* = standard deviation. EFA = exploratory factor analysis. CFA = confirmatory factor analysis.

Stem width: .10; each leaf represents eight cases

Figure 5.2 Cultural capital stem-and-leaf plot

Following the development of the cultural capital scale, we conducted subsequent analyses, primarily using this scale in quartiles alongside other variables. For example, in an analysis of student aspirations for occupations requiring a university qualification, we used logistic regression to determine the relative impact of a range of student and school factors on students' career aspirations (Gore et al. 2017). The ten most popular careers were the arts, teaching, veterinary science, architecture, science, engineering, medicine, social work, law and nursing. Using interest in each of these careers as the dependent variable, we examined the extent to which a range of student- and school-related variables were predictive of that interest. The independent variables included in the regression were gender, indigenous status, student cohort, location, language background, socio-economic status, survey year, parental occupation, cultural capital, school ICSEA,[2] prior achievement, self-perception of relative academic performance and access to tutoring. For five of the careers mentioned above – the arts, architecture, science, medicine and social work – the cultural capital variable was a significant predictor of student interest, in the presence of all of the other independent variables. In general, students in the higher quartiles had greater odds of expressing interest in these careers than those in the lowest quartile.

Our measure of cultural capital was also a significant predictor of student interest in science, technology, engineering, maths (STEM) careers, when considered as a distinct grouping, with students in the two highest quartiles having greater odds of expressing interest (Holmes et al. 2017). Given that the careers involved in these analyses require a university qualification, thereby indicating relatively high occupational prestige, it would appear that our measure of cultural capital is capturing an important influence on students' career aspirations.

Discussion

We encountered several methodological challenges in operationalizing capitals theories and in finding reliable proxies to represent the substantive theory with fidelity. While Bourdieu chose correspondence analysis to plot the relationships between various independent variables, other Bourdieusian studies across divergent fields have employed geometric modelling, PCA cluster analysis, structural equation modelling, random effects model, OLS and/or logistic regression, Cambridge scale, latent class analysis, cluster analysis theory/ multilevel modelling, chi-squared bivariate analysis, and cluster analysis (Robson and Sanders 2009).

We have illustrated our own application of Bourdieu's tools in relation to his notion of cultural capital while recognizing that, although widely used, the definition of cultural capital is not without ambiguity. Bourdieu himself defined it as 'instruments for the appropriation of symbolic wealth socially designated as worthy of being sought and processed' (Bourdieu and Passeron 1977: 488). More specifically, Bourdieu (1986) stated that cultural capital exists in three forms: embodied high-status culture, cultural goods or resources, and institutionalized cultural qualifications. Lamont and Lareau (1988) note that even Bourdieu was not entirely clear about its meaning; thus, researchers have defined cultural capital in a number of different ways, all of which connect to Bourdieu's concept at least on some level. Our capitals construct was most helpful in developing a robust tool that surveyed a wide range of proxies to measure.

Although an important part of Bourdieu's theory of social reproduction, cultural capital is only one component of his theoretical framework. In *Distinction*, Bourdieu (1984) noted that capital, habitus and field all work together to generate practice, or social action. The field, the setting in which practices take place, is 'a network, or a configuration, of objective relations between positions' (Bourdieu and Wacquant 1992: 97). Each field is related to one or more types of capital. Capital does not exist or function except in relation to a field.

Furthermore, research has differed when Bourdieu's theory of cultural capital has been applied to societies other than France (Holt 1998; Lareau and Weininger 2003). While our theorizing of a composite capitals model underpinned a methodology that produced significant data and generated important insights about Australian students' educational and career aspirations, our construct bracketed the intersection of capital with field and class habitus. In future studies researchers may wish to attempt to reintegrate field analysis into their conceptual frameworks.

Conclusion

Theorizing capital(s) either in singular, multiple or composite forms to disentangle the various social influences that come into play in the formation of aspirations is an attractive notion. However, the operationalization of capital in educational research is itself problematic and involves two key dimensions. One is the derivation of a robust substantive theory on which to ground and implement the practicalities of the research. The other is the derivation of reliable proxies that have fidelity with the substantive theory used to gather and analyse the data. Each of these is open to varying degrees of complexity. The complexity in deriving a credible substantive theory is magnified with the use of multiple capitals, especially if more than one theorist is invoked. Furthermore, when examining the robustness of the research design, two aspects of validity must be considered: methodological validity and conceptual validity. The validity of quantitative proxies needs to be scrutinized for reliability according to disciplinary standards. Conceptual reliability has to do with fidelity between the proxies and, on the one hand, the conclusions drawn from their use and, on the other, the substantive theory and theorists from which the concepts were drawn. In other words, can the data gathered and analysed be adequately described by the theoretical framework? The problematization of the substantive theory, and the theories from which the substantive theory was derived, through the composite capitals approach, introduces a reflexive critical element in the research design.

Notes

1 This research was supported by the Australian Research Council and the NSW Department of Education through the Linkage Projects funding scheme (LP120100013). The views expressed herein are those of the authors and are not necessarily those of the funding bodies.

2 The index of community socio-educational advantage (ICSEA) is a standardized scale measuring school advantage that enables meaningful comparisons to be made across Australian schools (see https://www.myschool.edu.au/).

Recommended further reading

Alloway, N., P. Gilbert, R. Gilbert and S. Muspratt (2004), *Factors Impacting on Student Aspirations and Expectations in Regional Australia*, Canberra: Department of Education, Science and Training. Available online: http://www.voced.edu.au/content/ngv%3A37399 (accessed 11 August 2009).

Reay, D. (2004), '"It's All Becoming a Habitus": Beyond the Habitual Use of Habitus in Educational Research', *British Journal of Sociology of Education*, 25 (4): 431–44.

Veenstra, G. (2009), 'Transmutations of Capitals in Canada: A "Social Space" Approach', in K. Robson and C. Sanders (eds), *Quantifying Theory: Pierre Bourdieu*, 61–73, Dordrecht: Springer.

References

Andres, L. (2009), 'The Cumulative Impact of Capital on Dispositions across Time: A 15-Year Perspective of Young Canadians', in K. Robson and C. Sanders (eds), *Quantifying Theory: Pierre Bourdieu*, 75–88, Dordrecht: Springer.

Aschaffenburg, K., and I. Maas (1997), 'Cultural and Educational Careers: The Dynamics of Social Reproduction', *American Sociological Review*, 62 (4): 573–87.

Becker, G. S., and K. M. Murphy (2009), *Social Economics: Market Behavior in a Social Environment*, Cambridge, MA: Harvard University Press.

Becker, G. S. and N. Tomes (1986), 'Human Capital and the Rise and Fall of Families', *Journal of Labour Economics*, 4 (3, Part 2): 1–39.

Bennett, A., R. Naylor, K. Mellor, M. Brett, J. Gore, A. Harvey, B. Munn, R. James, M. Smith and G. Whitty (2015), *The Critical Interventions Framework Part 2. Equity Initiatives in Australian Higher Education: A Review of Evidence of Impact*. Available online: https://www.newcastle.edu.au/__data/assets/pdf_file/0016/261124/REPORT-FINAL.pdf (accessed 21 January 2016).

Bourdieu, P. (1984), *Distinction: A Social Critique of the Judgement of Taste*, Cambridge, MA: Harvard University Press.

Bourdieu, P. (1986), 'The Forms of Capital', in J. Richardson (ed.), *Handbook for Theory and Research for the Sociology of Education*, 241–58, New York: Greenwood Press.

Bourdieu, P., and J. C. Passeron (1977), *Reproduction in Society, Culture, and Education*, Beverly Hills, CA: Sage.

Bourdieu, P., and L. J. D. Wacquant (1992), *An Invitation to Reflexive Sociology*, Chicago: University of Chicago Press.

Bradley, D., P. Noonan, H. Nugent and B. Scales (2008), *Review of Australian Higher Education: Final Report*, Canberra: Department of Education, Employment and Workplace Relations. Available online: https://www.mq.edu.au/__data/assets/pdf_

file/0013/135310/bradley_review_of_australian_higher_education.pdf (accessed 9 February 2009).

Bridges, D. (2010), 'Reasoning from Educational Research to Policy', in P. Smeyers and M. Depaepe (eds), *Educational Research: Proofs, Arguments, and Other Reasonings*, vol. 4, 177–92, Dordrecht: Springer.

Bridges, D., P. Smeyers and R. Smith (2008), 'Educational Research and the Practical Judgement of Policy Makers', *Journal of Philosophy of Education*, 42: 5–14.

Bridges, D., and M. Watts (2008), 'Educational Research and Policy: Epistemological Considerations', *Journal of Philosophy of Education*, 42 (S1): 41–62.

Clark, C. (2011), 'Education(al) Research, Educational Policy-Making and Practice', *Journal of Philosophy of Education*, 45 (1): 37–57.

Coleman, J. S. (1988), 'Social Capital in the Creation of Human Capital', *American Journal of Sociology*, 94 (Supp): 95–120.

Coulangeon, P., and Y. Lemel (2009), 'The Homology Thesis: *Distinction* Revisited', in K. Robson and C. Sanders (eds), *Quantifying Theory: Pierre Bourdieu*, 47–60, Dordrecht: Springer.

De Graaf, N., P. De Graaf and G. Kraaykamp (2000), 'Parental Cultural Capital and Educational Attainment in the Netherlands: A Refinement of the Cultural Capital Perspective', *Sociology of Education*, 73 (2): 92–111.

Dika, S. L., and K. Singh (2002), 'Applications of Social Capital in Educational Literature: A Critical Synthesis', *Review of Educational Research*, 72 (1): 31–60.

Engberg, M. E., and G. Wolniak (2010), 'Examining the Effects of High School Contexts on Postsecondary Enrollment', *Research in Higher Education*, 51 (2): 132–53.

Feher, M. (2009), 'Self-Appreciation; or, the Aspirations of Human Capital', *Public Culture*, 21 (1): 21–41.

Gale, T., and C. Mills (2013), 'Creating Spaces in Higher Education for Marginalised Australians: Principles for Socially Inclusive Pedagogies', *Enhancing Learning in the Social Sciences*, 5 (2): 7–19.

Gore, J., K. Holmes, M. Smith, L. Fray, P. McElduff, N. Weaver and C. Wallington (2017), 'Unpacking the Career Aspirations of Australian School Students: Towards an Evidence Base for University Equity Initiatives in Schools', *Higher Education Research and Development*, 36 (7): 1383–400. doi:10.1080/07294360.2017.1325847

Guo, J., H. W. Marsh, P. D. Parker, A. J. Morin and A. S. Yeung (2015), 'Expectancy-Value in Mathematics, Gender and Socioeconomic Background as Predictors of Achievement and Aspirations: A Multi-Cohort Study', *Learning and Individual Differences*, 37: 161–8.

Hammersley, M. (2002), *Educational Research, Policymaking and Practice*, Thousand Oaks, CA: P. Chapman.

Holmes, K., J. Gore, M. Smith and A. Lloyd (2017), 'An Integrated Analysis of School Students' Aspirations for STEM Careers: Which Student and School Factors Are Most Predictive?' *International Journal of Science and Mathematics Education*, online before print 17 January. doi:10.1007/s10763-016-9793-z

Holt, D. B. (1998), 'Does Cultural Capital Structure American Consumption?' *Journal of Consumer Research*, 25 (1): 1–25.

Hjellbrekke, J., and O. Korsnes (2009), 'Quantifying the Field of Power in Norway', in K. Robson and C. Sanders (eds), *Quantifying Theory: Pierre Bourdieu*, 31–45, Dordrecht: Springer.

Jackson, D., and J. Gillaspy (2009), 'Reporting Practices in Confirmatory Factor Analysis: An Overview and Some Recommendations', *Psychological Methods*, 14 (1): 6–23.

Jöreskog, K. G. (1971), 'Statistical Analysis of Sets of Congeneric Tests', *Psychometrika*, 36 (2): 109–33.

Keating, J., and M. Klatt (2013), 'Australian Concurrent Federalism and Its Implications for the Gonski Review', *Journal of Education Policy*, 28 (4): 411–26.

Keeley, B. (2007), *Human Capital: How What You Know Shapes Your Life*, Paris: OECD.

Klinger, D., W. Rogers, J. Anderson, C. Poth and R. Calman (2006), 'Contextual and School Factors Associated with Achievement on a High-Stakes Examination', *Canadian Journal of Education*, 29 (3): 771–97.

Lamont, M., and A. Lareau (1988), 'Cultural Capital: Allusions, Gaps and Glissandos in Recent Theoretical Developments', *Sociological Theory*, 6 (2): 153–68.

Lareau, A., and E. B. Weininger (2003), 'Cultural Capital in Educational Research: A Critical Assessment', *Theory and Society*, 32 (5): 567–606.

Lareau, A., and E. B. Weininger (2004), 'Cultural Capital in Educational Research: A Critical Assessment', in D. Swartz and V. Zolberg (eds), *After Bourdieu: Influence, Critique, Elaboration*, 105–44, Dordrecht: Kluwer Academic Publishers.

Levin, B. (2004), 'Making Research Matter More', *Education Policy Analysis Archives*, 12: 1–20.

Lingard, B. (2010), 'Policy Borrowing, Policy Learning: Testing Times in Australian Schooling', *Critical Studies in Education*, 51 (2): 129–47.

Naylor, R., C. Baik and R. James (2013), *Developing a Critical Interventions Framework for Advancing Equity in Australian Higher Education*, Melbourne: Centre for Research in Higher Education. Available online: https://www.researchgate. net/profile/Ryan_Naylor/publication/266798034_Developing_a_Critical_ Interventions_Framework_for_advancing_equity_in_Australian_higher_education/ links/543cb4730cf20af5cfbf70e6.pdf (accessed 6 September 2014).

Norman, G. (2010), 'Likert Scales, Levels of Measurement and the "Laws" of Statistics', *Advances in Health Sciences Education*, 15 (5): 625–32. doi:10.1007/s10459-010-9222-y

OECD (2000), *Program for International Student Assessment: Student Questionnaire (US English Version)*. Available online: https://nces.ed.gov/surveys/pisa/pdf/quest_ pisa_2000_student.pdf (accessed 27 August 2009).

Perna, L. W., and M. A. Titus (2005), 'The Relationship between Parental Involvement as Social Capital and College Enrollment: An Examination of Racial/Ethnic Group Differences', *Journal of Higher Education*, 76 (5): 485–518.

Prieur, A., and M. Savage (2013), 'Emerging Forms of Cultural Capital', *European Societies*, 15 (2): 246–67.

Reay, D. (2004), '"It's All Becoming a Habitus": Beyond the Habitual Use of Habitus in Educational Research', *British Journal of Sociology of Education*, 25 (4): 431–44.

Robson, K. and C. Sanders (eds) (2009), *Quantifying Theory: Pierre Bourdieu*, Dordrecht: Springer.

Sellar, S., and T. Gale (2011), 'Mobility, Aspiration, Voice: A New Structure of Feeling for Student Equity in Higher Education', *Critical Studies in Education*, 52 (2): 115–34.

Sellar, S., T. Gale and S. Parker (2011), 'Appreciating Aspirations in Australian Higher Education', *Cambridge Journal of Education*, 41 (1): 37–52.

Sullivan, A. (2002), 'Bourdieu and Education: How Useful is Bourdieu's Theory for Researchers?', *Netherlands Journal of Social Sciences*, 38 (2), 144–66.

Swedberg, R. (2011), 'The Economic Sociologies of Pierre Bourdieu', *Cultural Sociology*, 5 (1): 67–82.

Veenstra, G. (2009), 'Transmutations of Capitals in Canada: A "Social Space" Approach', in K. Robson and C. Sanders (eds), *Quantifying Theory: Pierre Bourdieu*, 61–73, Dordrecht: Springer.

Vryonides, M. (2007), 'Social and Cultural Capital in Educational Research: Issues of Operationalisation and Measurement', *British Educational Research Journal*, 33 (6): 867–85.

Walker, M. (2012), 'A Capital or Capabilities Education Narrative in a World of Staggering Inequalities?', *International Journal of Educational Development*, 32 (3): 384–93.

Whitty, G., A. Hayton and S. Tang (2015), 'Who You Know, What You Know and Knowing the Ropes: A Review of Evidence about Access to Higher Education Institutions in England', *Review of Education*, 3 (1): 27–67.

6

Shadow Capital and the Undermining of College-Going Aspirations

Amy E. Stich and Kristin Cipollone

Introduction

In this chapter, we reflect upon our application of Bourdieu's theoretical/ methodological tools and our development of the notion of 'shadow capital'. As a distinct form of cultural capital, shadow capital resembles dominant cultural capital[1] but fails to yield the same kind of exchange value when put to use. While superficially mimicking dominant capital, 'in composition, it is independent of other dominant states and forms of capital and a dominant class habitus – all of which provide the scaffolding necessary to build dominant cultural capital' (Cipollone and Stich 2017). The word 'shadow' signifies the illusory nature of this form of capital; it appears as the dominant form, but its composition differs greatly. Unlike other forms of valuable cultural capital possessed and enacted by non-dominant groups (see Yosso 2005) or subcultures (see Thornton 1995), shadow capital is neither a form of dominant nor non-dominant cultural capital in terms of the value it proffers to students. Instead, shadow capital is produced via social processes that reproduce efforts to stratify rather than democratize, thwarting or capping, in this case, the enactment of college-going[2] aspirations of non-dominant students.

We draw upon representative data from a three-year longitudinal ethnographic study to discuss and illustrate the ways in which the production of shadow capital undermined the enactment of non-dominant students' college-going aspirations within two non-selective, urban, college-preparatory schools in the United States. As we work to conceptualize shadow capital as a distinct form of cultural capital, we further reflect upon the value of Bourdieu's theoretical/ methodological tools in moving our thinking forward in order to better explain existing inequalities and the many unmet promises of US educational reform. By reflecting upon our research practices and analytic process, we reveal the value, power and reach of Bourdieu's 'thinking tools' (Bourdieu and Wacquant 1992).

We begin with Bourdieu's notion of field and a brief discussion of the US secondary education system as it is situated within broader movements to increase access to and democratize post-secondary education. In particular, we focus attention on efforts to reform college preparation that aim to shape non-dominant students' college-going aspirations and their post-secondary destinations. We follow with a brief discussion of Bourdieu's various states of cultural capital relative to other forms of capital and the individual and collective forms of habitus that support the accumulation of capitals. We then discuss our application of these 'thinking tools' relative to our own research and the production of shadow capital. We close with a comment on the usefulness of Bourdieu's tools in researching aspirations in education research.

Understanding Bourdieu's tools: The states of cultural capital and forms of habitus in the field of US secondary education

Our research is historically and contextually situated within the field of US education, accounting for its stratified and exclusionary past in order to examine the inequities of the present. For Bourdieu, a field is a site of struggle (Bourdieu and Wacquant 1992). Arguably, the field of US secondary education is, first and foremost, a site of struggle for class positioning at the post-secondary level and beyond. Because post-secondary education is now viewed as a necessary and nearly universal aspiration in the United States (Goyette 2008; Rosenbaum 2001), the stakes of college admission are greater than ever before. The field now demands increasingly savvy players as the college admissions game has become significantly more competitive in recent years (Epenshade and Radford 2009; Weis, Cipollone and Jenkins 2014).

Within the field of secondary education, affluent parents with a 'feel for the game' and its rules no longer rely upon schools to provide the best opportunities for their children or to help to prepare them for college (Reay 2004). Instead, parents/guardians function as 'co-educators' (Reay 2004) in advocating and securing opportunities for their children (Brantlinger 2003; Weis and Cipollone 2013). Bourdieu (1990) refers to these moves as 'strategies', which derive from one's habitus and the 'objective potentialities' within any given field, rather than from consciousness or intentionality. This is highly evident in the dossier-building investment practices of privileged parents. Using elite college admission as a template for child rearing (Stevens 2007), parents make choices about where to buy homes (Sutcliffe-Braithwaite 2018), work to place children in gifted and talented and accelerated tracks early on (Brantlinger 2003), spend enormous economic resources and time on developing children's extracurricular passions, and arrange for tutoring and enrichment (Weis, Cipollone and Jenkins 2014). The 'package' one must present in order to be eligible for selective college admission cannot be assembled at the time of application; it is a process put into motion early on, often before a child is born. Thus, those without a feel for the game are at a distinct disadvantage. While translating college-going aspirations into action is never a seamless process (Kaufman 2005), it can be particularly challenging for non-dominant students whose childhoods have not been dominated by 'concerted cultivation' (Lareau 2003). In many instances, schools have stepped in to address the packaging gap, attempting to build the apparatus that facilitates students' enactment of college aspirations (Farmer-Hinton 2011; McClafferty, McDonough and Nunez 2002).

For those who play the game, positioning hinges upon the possession, accumulation and 'activation' of various forms of capital (Lareau and Horvat 1999). In the field of education, cultural capital, in particular, plays a central role in the college preparation game. Historically, a 'college-preparatory education' has served as the dominant form of cultural capital necessary for elite social advancement. 'Prep' schools groomed students for entry into exclusive and elite post-secondary institutions (Cookson and Persell 1985; Gamsu, this volume; Gatzambide-Fernández 2009; Khan 2011). Given their high college acceptance rates, educational reformers turned to college-preparatory education as a model for closing opportunity and achievement gaps. Hoping to prepare more students from diverse backgrounds, low-performing schools serving non-dominant students often seek to mimic the visible elements of historically elite college-preparatory education by offering greater college-level curricular and extracurricular opportunities, providing more intensive college counselling, and promoting college-going aspirations for all students (Farmer-Hinton 2011). By doing so, college-preparatory schools serving non-dominant students aspire to reposition students and low-performing schools within the field of education.

However, this kind of reform assumes that cultural capital exists solely in an objectified/material state to be easily acquired and disseminated by the receiver (individual and institutional), irrespective of their position within the field. Though the appropriation of particular forms of cultural capital (e.g. objectified, material forms) may only require economic capital, further appropriation (e.g. to use that object in its intended way) requires access to embodied cultural capital (Bourdieu 1986). Indeed, Bourdieu conceived of cultural capital as existing in three, interrelated states: embodied (e.g. dispositions and tastes), objectified (e.g. material or cultural goods) and institutionalized (e.g. educational credentials) (Bourdieu 1986) – a nuance often neglected by educational research. As our work demonstrates, it is possible to possess a dominant form of objectified cultural capital without appropriating the same cultural capital in an embodied state, which requires prolonged exposure, inculcation and internalization. This distinction, in large part, facilitates the production of shadow capital.

Importantly, the ability to possess and accumulate various amounts and forms of capital is dependent upon one's habitus and one's positioning relative to opportunity structures. Although Bourdieu places great emphasis upon the relational nature of capital, many scholars have argued that it is often presented in isolation from 'the habitus that generates it ... [and] other forms of capital that, alongside cultural capital, constitute advantage and disadvantage in society' (Reay, David and Ball 2005: 21; see also Savage et al. 2013). Bourdieu (1990) defines habitus as a durable, embodied system of dispositions and ways of thinking that reflect how the social world is inscribed in the body (and the ways in which the body is positioned within the social world). For Bourdieu, one's habitus is formed and internalized early in life through socialization with family and group membership and can be either reinforced or transformed through further socialization within various social institutions, like education (Bourdieu and Wacquant 1992). However, some scholars have stretched Bourdieu's notion of habitus to argue that social institutions also embody 'identifiable habituses' (Reay, David and Ball 2005). The highly contested term[3] 'institutional habitus' or 'organizational habitus' can be defined as 'the impact of a cultural group or social class on an individual's behavior as it is mediated through an organization' (McDonough 1997: 107).

As an attempt to theorize collective forms of habitus, the notion of institutional habitus is valuable as it suggests 'schools and other institutions can directly shape the habitus and practices of individuals through their organizational forms and collective practices' (Burke, Emmerich and Ingram 2013: 167). Not unlike Tarabini, Curran and Fontdevila (2016), we utilize this concept to better understand the ways in which institutional structures and practices mediate individual perceptions (e.g. post-secondary aspirations). Relative to secondary education, institutional habitus encompasses curricular and extracurricular offerings and practices as well as the more intangible elements of school culture (Tarabini and Curran, this volume). Importantly, the expressive order represents embodied cultural capital, capital that is embodied in the 'collectivity of students, buildings, rituals, performances, and in the school staff' (Reay, David and Ball 2005: 37). This component of institutional habitus exposes an institution's expectations, values and, ostensibly, its educational discourse – all of which arguably dictate the type of knowledge to be made legitimate, the types of capital to be most valued, the type of student likely to attend, the careers worthy of aspiring to and the post-secondary destinations attended upon graduation.

Applying Bourdieu's tools: Dominant cultural capital within non-dominant schools

In this section, we discuss our application of field, capital and habitus and how we use these thinking tools to conceptualize shadow capital. Shadow capital has the power to explain the reproduction of inequality through education or, rather, why forms of dominant cultural capital (college-preparatory education) do not always result in the same opportunities and outcomes when transferred to non-elite contexts.

Importantly, this section is informed by data collected between 2010 and 2013 within two urban, non-selective,[4] college-preparatory schools serving non-dominant students in Buffalo, NY, USA. Although this research is part of a larger study examining students' pathways from their respective secondary schools to various post-secondary destinations,[5] we focus upon just two schools, Global Horizons (GH) and STEM Academy (STEM)[6] because of their college-preparatory designation. Both schools are composed of majority non-dominant student populations in terms of race and class (as measured by free and reduced lunch rates). STEM students are predominantly black while GH has significant Latino, Asian and black student populations. GH and STEM not only share a college-preparatory distinction and similar student demographics, but also a history of academic 'failure' wherein both schools were subject to turnaround procedures. Following closure, each was reopened as a College Board[7] school. Given their college-preparatory designation, both schools are expected to provide students with viable pathways to college and to compete with the few high-performing schools in the district.

Due to the history and college-preparatory distinction of STEM and GH within the field of education, we were interested in what a college-preparatory education, as a form of dominant cultural capital acquisition, looks like within non-dominant spaces. Our research revealed that the capital transmitted to students was more shadow and illusion than the promised dominant capital. While the schools were able to appropriate some of the more tangible elements of a college-going culture successfully, they were unable to fundamentally alter the institutional habitus in ways that would support dominant capital acquisition. While, in hindsight, the shadows were visible through the institutional cracks, it was at the point of college admission that students and families came to see that they were sold a metaphorical false bill of goods by the schools.

As we immersed ourselves within the two schools, conducting in-depth interviews with students, their families, teachers and administrators, and observing classrooms, school counselling meetings, assemblies and informal spaces within the schools (e.g. cafeterias), we began to identify a stark contrast between the dominant forms of cultural capital students and their families believed they were acquiring and the dominant forms of cultural capital schools were able to disseminate. This contrast became more defined as we assessed the field of secondary education and compared what we observed within STEM and GH to what others, including one of the authors, found within dominant college-preparatory settings.

For example, studies of elite college-preparatory schools reveal an intensive cultivation process designed to position students not just for college, but for selective college admission (see for example Cookson and Persell 1985; Gatzambide-Fernández 2009; Khan 2011; McDonough 1997; Peshkin 2001). This process is found within affluent public high schools as well (Weis, Cipollone and Jenkins 2014). Within these dominant spaces, the expectation of college attendance is taken for granted. Dominant college-preparatory schools do not necessitate the development of college-going cultures because the college-going culture is embodied by the students, who bring this disposition with them, and it is woven into the very fabric of the schools (Weis, Cipollone and Jenkins 2014). We see this in their meticulously landscaped grounds that mimic elite liberal arts colleges, small class sizes, rigorous course offerings, extensive extracurricular opportunities, and comprehensive, intensive college planning/application processes that include early college advisement and progressively build upon students' college knowledge (Weis, Cipollone and Jenkins 2014). Within dominant college-preparatory schools, the college-going culture 'hits you over the head' in overt and tangible ways (e.g. college paraphernalia) (Weis, Cipollone and Jenkins 2014: 27). In these spaces, students' college aspirations are nurtured, making their enactment all but inevitable. As a well-concealed function of privileged schools, a pre-existing dominant class habitus is rewarded in a number of often subtle ways, serving to confirm and strengthen a privileged habitus and further legitimize the unequal structure of schooling (Bourdieu and Passeron 1990).

In non-dominant schools wherein going to college is not the norm or the expectation, schools are tasked with *creating* this kind of culture. This requires not only nurturing student aspirations but also creating an apparatus that allows students to enact them. However, for non-dominant schools, the intention to create a college-going culture often results in simple attempts to mimic the more tangible, visible elements evident within dominant schools (e.g. advanced curricular offerings). These efforts are proposed by reformers and policy makers who too often fail to appreciate the pre-existing, deeper manifestation of a network of dominant capitals and habitus that allows for the acquisition/appropriation of subsequent types and amounts of dominant capitals and reproduces dominant positions within the field of education. The result, of course, is that non-dominant students' ability to enact their aspirations is circumscribed (Deil-Amen and Tevis 2010) by the very environments that promise access.

Producing shadow capital

With targeted reform efforts and an immediate short-term influx of social and economic capital allowing schools to provide what appeared to be, at least in objectified states, dominant cultural capital, students and families trusted in and believed STEM and GH would produce opportunities and outcomes similar to those of more elite institutions. In fact, when we started our research in 2010, GH and STEM outwardly resembled college-preparatory schools. Both schools worked to discursively reinforce going to college as the only option upon graduation. We saw this in counselling offices and throughout hallways, over the morning announcements and reinforced by teachers, administrators and staff in conversations with students. Discursively speaking, GH and STEM appeared successful in articulating going to college as an expectation and in shaping the aspirations of their students. For example, participating students aspired to prestigious careers and believed they would be competitive at highly selective colleges and universities, including Ivy League, elite liberal arts and prominent state research institutions. As part of the expressive order of the schools' institutional habitus, the expectation for students to attend college and the discourse surrounding this expectation is explicit, in part, because going to college is not yet embodied by schools or students.

Moreover, in our first year in the schools, other objectified forms of dominant cultural capital were visible in terms of curricular offerings. As college-preparatory schools, STEM and GH advertised that 'all students' will take 'at least two Advanced Placement (AP) courses before graduation'. AP courses are meant to provide students with rigorous college-level curricula. Many US colleges and universities will grant college credits or placement into higher-level college courses to students who score high enough on an AP final examination. Because not all schools in the district provide these kinds of advanced offerings and accelerated opportunities, students and their families were enthusiastic, noting this as a primary reason for choosing these schools. In other words, curricular offerings appeared, at least on paper, to constitute dominant capital found within dominant college-preparatory spaces. However, despite the stated commitment to rigorous course offerings, we witnessed a reversal of these efforts as many course offerings were gradually watered down or ceased to be offered (see Weis et al. 2015). We observed that the courses, when they were offered, lacked rigour and failed to include the required content. Such changes undermine the college-preparatory mission of the school and the enactment of students' college aspirations, a point not lost on school personnel.

Further, school counsellors at STEM and GH were largely alone in their efforts to guide students through the college process, unlike dominant spaces wherein a team of school counsellors, which often includes college-specific counsellors, work to develop highly competitive candidates for admission to the college of their choice (Weis, Cipollone and Jenkins 2014). Counsellors at both schools complained of feeling overburdened with administrative duties and student concerns, while struggling to attend to college advising and planning. Though well intended, the college advising school counsellors were able to provide little more than the rudimentary elements of this dominant form of cultural capital, which largely took shape as a reactionary set of disjointed practices rooted in objectified forms of cultural capital. As Bourdieu argues, time is central to the development of habitus and the embodiment of cultural capital. As opposed to the longitudinally driven co-production of dominant capitals that transpires within the homes and schools of dominant children, schools like this (though unknowingly) produce a form of capital that neither carries the value of its original dominant form nor a non-dominant form. Rather, schools produce what we call shadow capital:

> As a distinct form of cultural capital, shadow capital is defined by its illusory features. On the surface, shadow capital visibly reflects traces of dominant cultural capital (e.g. advanced curricular offerings, SAT preparation), but in composition, it is independent of other dominant states and forms of capital (e.g. embodied cultural capital, social capital, economic capital) and a dominant class habitus – all of which provide the scaffolding necessary to build highly valued dominant cultural capital. As a result, consumers of shadow capital do not receive the intended return on their investment, but are instead presented with a false bill of goods. (Cipollone and Stich 2017)

Shadow capital constitutes a distinct entity and becomes detectable relative to the habitus that generates it and its activation within the larger field of education (Lareau and Horvat 1999). Although the production of shadow capital was made visible within the two schools during key moments of activation (e.g. applying to college) and ultimately contributed to undermining the enactment of student aspirations, it was not the schools themselves or the actors within them that created the conditions for inequality, but the structuring of the larger field of education itself, influenced by seemingly well-intentioned educational reform efforts. For example, a review of matriculation data revealed the difficulties students faced as they tried to enact their aspirations by activating their shadow capital. Students reported coming to see themselves as college-bound, and often bound for selective colleges, *because of, rather than in spite of,* their attendance at STEM and GH. They shared aspirations to become lawyers, engineers, doctors, nurses, teachers and architects. Yet, only a third of the focal students were accepted to four-year schools and only five enrolled, only one has completed a two-year degree, and a full third opted not to attend college at all.

Importantly, it was not that students did not have high aspirations; it was that the tools they relied upon – the capital proffered by the schools – undercut their ability to enact their aspirations. Like Deil-Amen and Tevis (2010), we argue that students' agency, and ultimately their aspirations, was 'short changed' – in this case by shadow capital – and 'circumscribed by a high school context that promotes college-going while ironically reinforcing a frame of reference that facilitates misperceptions among students about their academic performance and college readiness' (2010: 168).

Discussion and concluding thoughts

For Bourdieu, the separation of theory and method presents a false dichotomy. In fact, Bourdieu describes his 'thinking tools' as methods. Using habitus as an example, Reay reminds us that

> Bourdieu is using the term 'method' in a very elastic sense but what he is stressing is that first and foremost habitus is a conceptual tool to be used in empirical research rather than an idea to be debated in texts. (2004: 439)

In our research, we too approached theory as method through the application of Bourdieu's tools. Rather than a concept to be simply placed upon research or assumed (Reay 2004), we intentionally put individual and collective notions of habitus to use in order to examine what dominant capital looks like within non-dominant contexts. This approach enabled us to build upon the ways in which others have stretched understandings of cultural capital in practice (Carter 2003; Yosso 2005) in order to conceptualize shadow capital within the field of education.

Bourdieu's notion of field provided a powerful relational framework through which we were able to examine the social location of the two schools within our study relative to college-preparatory schools that were situated in contrasting locations within the field of US secondary education. Importantly, for Bourdieu, 'a capital does not exist and function except in relation to a field' (Bourdieu and Wacquant 1992: 101). By locating the two schools and the various forms of capital most rewarded by the larger field, we were able to identify and better understand the 'strategies' employed within non-dominant schools that functioned to reposition students in their post-secondary destinations. Many of these strategies mimicked those within dominant college-preparatory schools in order to reshape non-dominant students' college-going aspirations and produce opportunities and outcomes similar to those within dominant preparatory schools. However, although aspirations remained high, these strategies did not yield the same or similar opportunities and outcomes for non-dominant students. In explaining our findings, we also found the relational concept habitus incredibly useful relative to the acquisition and appropriation of various forms of capital within the field. As noted, the capital that college preparation proffers is advantageous insofar as it is supported by other forms of dominant capital (e.g. economic, social), which are both generated by and reinforce a dominant habitus. As we applied individual and collective notions of habitus to our data, we started to see possible explanations for why embodied forms of dominant cultural capital never materialized within STEM and GH. However, as the schools continued to promote themselves as college preparatory, foster college-going aspirations, and provide students with objectified forms of dominant cultural capital (though incredibly limited), Bourdieu's notion of cultural capital did not quite capture the form of capital produced within these schools – capital that resembles dominant cultural capital but fails to yield the same kind of exchange value when put to use. In order to explain this unique form, we conceived the notion of shadow capital. We believe shadow capital, as a form of cultural capital, can be applied within other spaces or fields (e.g. US higher education) to help make sense of similar inequities.

The use of Bourdieu's tools shaped and improved the quality of analysis that otherwise may have reinforced the very inequality we seek to upend. As is too often the case with educational research and efforts to evaluate policy/reform, particularly within urban spaces, students, teachers, administrators and school staff are blamed for their perceived individual 'failure' to meet students' college-going aspirations (Stahl 2014). In our research, individual-level college-going aspirations remained high, even as structural limitations seemed to increase over time. Further, students exerted their agency within schools that held similarly high aspirations that were also circumscribed.

As the American system of education grows increasingly stratified amidst the persistence of neoliberal policies, Bourdieu's richly relational body of work provides a way forward for education researchers interested in unveiling and better understanding the more hidden mechanisms of social reproduction that are buried within the structure of the social field. Perhaps most importantly, Bourdieu's tools push us to think relationally, allowing us to make invisible structures visible and call attention to the ways in which inequality is reproduced via education.

Notes

1   For Carter, "'dominant cultural capital" corresponds to Bourdieu's conceptualization of powerful, high status cultural attributes, codes, and signals' while "'non-dominant cultural capital" embodies a set of tastes, or schemes of appreciation

and understandings, accorded to a lower status group that include preferences for linguistic, musical, or interactional styles' (2003: 138).

2   Please note that the terms 'college' and 'university' are used interchangeably within the US context.

3   For a spirited debate over collective notions of habitus, see Atkinson (2011, 2013) and Burke, Emmerich and Ingram (2013).

4   Non-selective schools are schools that are open to all students in the given catchment area with no specific admissions criteria. The Buffalo Public School system has a number of criterion-based schools that rely upon several metrics when making admissions decisions. Criteria may include entrance examination scores, course prerequisites, prior marks, and in the case of arts-based schools auditions and portfolios. Criterion-based schools tend to 'cream' the highest-achieving students (ostensibly, the students with most capital). For the purpose of our study, it was important that we used non-selective schools as we wanted to examine the impacts of democratization – in other words, would reform efforts benefit all students?

5   This research was funded by the National Science Foundation (awards DRL 1008215 to Lois Weis and DRL 1007964 to Margaret Eisenhart). For a full description of the research methodology for the larger research project of which this is part, please see Weis et al. (2015) and Eisenhart et al. (2015).

6   All participant names and schools have been assigned pseudonyms.

7   College Board schools are public schools that are supported by the College Board. These schools adopt a model devised by the College Board which includes small class sizes, exposure to advanced course work, intensive college counselling and small-group ongoing advisory sessions. School personnel partake in College Board–led professional development and work with College Board consultants.

Recommended further reading

Cipollone, K., and A. E. Stich (2017), 'In the Shadows: "Democratizing" College Preparatory Education in Two Urban Schools', *Sociology of Education*, 90 (4): 333–54.

Stich, A. E., and K. Cipollone (2017), 'In and Through the Urban Educational "Reform Churn": The Illustrative Power of Qualitative Longitudinal Research', *Urban Education*, online before print 6 February 2017. doi:10.1177/0042085917690207

Weis, L., M. Eisenhart, K. Cipollone, A. Stich, A. Nikischer, J. Hanson, S. Ohle and R. Dominguez (2015), 'In the Guise of STEM Education Reform: Opportunity Structures and Outcomes in Inclusive STEM-Focused High Schools', *American Educational Research Journal*, 52 (6): 1024–59.

References

Atkinson, W. (2011), 'From Sociological Fictions to Social Fictions: Some Bourdieusian Reflections on the Concepts of "Institutional Habitus" and "Family Habitus"', *British Journal of Sociology of Education*, 32 (3): 331–47.

Atkinson, W. (2013), 'Some Further (Orthodox?) Bourdieusian Reflections on the Notions of "Institutional Habitus" and "Family Habitus": A Reply to Burke, Emmerich, and Ingram', *British Journal of Sociology of Education*, 34 (2): 183–9.

Bourdieu, P. (1986), 'The Forms of Capital', in J. Richardson (ed.), *Handbook of Theory and Research for the Sociology of Education*, 241–58, New York: Greenwood.

Bourdieu, P. (1990), *The Logic of Practice*, Cambridge: Polity Press.

Bourdieu, P., and J. C. Passeron (1990), *Reproduction in Education, Society and Culture*, 2nd edn, Thousand Oaks, CA: Sage.

Bourdieu, P., and L. J. D. Wacquant (1992), *An Invitation to Reflexive Sociology*, Chicago: University of Chicago Press.

Brantlinger, E. (2003), *Dividing Classes Negotiates and Rationalizes School Advantage*, New York: RoutledgeFalmer.

Burke, C. T., N. Emmerich and N. Ingram (2013), 'Well-Founded Social Fictions: A Defence of the Concepts of Institutional and Familial Habitus', *British Journal of Sociology of Education*, 34 (2): 165–82.

Carter, P. L. (2003), '"Black" Cultural Capital, Status Positioning, and Schooling Conflicts for Low-Income African-American Youth', *Social Problems*, 50 (1): 136–55.

Cipollone, K., and A. E. Stich (2017), 'In the Shadows: "Democratizing" College Preparatory Education in Two Urban Schools', *Sociology of Education*, 90 (4): 333–54.

Cookson, P., and C. H. Persell (1985), *Preparing for Power: America's Elite Boarding Schools*, New York: Basic Books.

Deil-Amen, R., and T. L. Tevis (2010), 'Circumscribed Agency: The Relevance of Standardized College Entrance Exams for Low SES High School Students', *Review of Higher Education*, 33 (2): 141–75.

Eisenhart, M., L. Weis, C.D. Allen, K. Cipollone, A.E. Stich and R. Dominguez. (2015), 'High School Opportunities for STEM: A Comparative Case Study of Four Inclusive STEM-focused Schools and Four Comprehensive High Schools in Two U.S. Cities', *Journal of Research in Science Teaching*, 52 (6): 763–89.

Epenshade, T. J., and A. W. Radford (2009), *No Longer Separate, Not Yet Equal: Race and Class in Elite College Admission and Campus Life*, Princeton, NJ: Princeton University Press.

Farmer-Hinton, R. (2011), 'On Being College Prep: Examining the Implementation of a 'College for All' Mission in an Urban Charter School', *Urban Review*, 43: 567–96.

Gatzambide-Fernández, R. (2009), *The Best of the Best: Becoming Elite at an American Boarding School*, Cambridge, MA: Harvard University Press.

Goyette, K. (2008), 'College for Some to College for All: Social Background, Occupational Expectations, and Educational Expectations over Time', *Social Science Research*, 37 (2): 461–84.

Kaufman, P. (2005), 'Middle-Class Social Reproduction: The Activation and Negotiation of Structured Advantages', *Sociological Forum*, 20 (2): 245–70.

Khan, S. R. (2011), *Privilege: The Making of an Adolescent Elite at St. Paul's School*, Princeton, NJ: Princeton University Press.

Lareau, A. (2003), *Unequal Childhoods: Class, Race and Family Life*, Berkeley, CA: University of California Press.

Lareau, A., and E. M. Horvat (1999), 'Moments of Social Inclusion and Exclusion: Race, Class, and Cultural Capital in Family-School Relationships', *Sociology of Education*, 72 (1): 37–53.

McClafferty, K. A., P. M. McDonough and A. M. Nunez. (2002), 'What Is a College Culture? Facilitating College Preparation through Organizational Change', Paper presented at Annual Meeting of the American Educational Research Association, 1–5 April, New Orleans, LA.

McDonough, P. M. (1997), *Choosing Colleges: How Social Class and Schools Structure Opportunity*, Albany, NY: State University of New York Press.

Peshkin, A. (2001), *Permissible Advantage? The Moral Consequences of Elite Schooling*, Mahwah, NJ: Lawrence Erlbaum Associates.

Reay, D. (2004), '"It's All Becoming a Habitus": Beyond the Habitual Use of Pierre Bourdieu's Concept of Habitus in Educational Research', *British Journal of Sociology of Education*, 25 (4): 431–44.

Reay, D., M. E. David and S. Ball (2005), *Degrees of Choice: Social Class, Race and Gender in Higher Education*, Stoke on Trent, UK: Trentham Books.

Rosenbaum, J. E. (2001), *Beyond College for All*, New York: Russell Sage Foundation.

Savage, M., F. Devine, N. Cunningham, M. Taylor, Y. Li, J. Hjellbrekke, B. Le Roux, S. Friedman and A. Miles (2013), 'A New Model of Social Class? Findings from the BBC's Great British Class Survey Experiment', *Sociology*, 47 (2): 219–50.

Stahl, G. (2014), 'White Working-Class Male Narratives of "Loyalty to Self" in Discourses of Aspiration', *British Journal of Sociology of Education*, 37 (5): 663–83.

Stevens, M. L. (2007), *Creating a Class: College Admissions and the Education of Elites*, Cambridge, MA: Harvard University Press.

Sutcliffe-Braithwaite, F. (2018), *Class, Politics, and the Decline of Deference in England, 1968-2000*, Oxford: Oxford University Press.

Tarabini, A., M. Curran and C. Fontdevila (2016), 'Institutional Habitus in Context: Implementation, Development and Impacts in Two Compulsory Secondary Schools in Barcelona', *British Journal of Sociology of Education*, online before print 22 November. doi:10.1080/01425692.2016.1251306

Thornton, S. (1995), *Club Cultures: Music, Media and Subcultural Capital*, Cambridge: Polity Press.

Weis, L., and K. Cipollone (2013), '"Class Work": Producing Privilege and Social Mobility in Elite US Secondary Schools', *British Journal of Sociology of Education*, 34 (5): 701–22.

Weis, L., K. Cipollone and H. Jenkins (2014), *Class Warfare: Class and Race in Affluent and Elite Secondary Schools*, Chicago: University of Chicago Press.

Weis, L., M. Eisenhart, K. Cipollone, A. E. Stich, A. B. Nikischer, J. Hanson and R. Dominguez (2015), 'In the Guise of STEM Education Reform: Opportunity Structures and Outcomes in Inclusive STEM-Focused High Schools', *American Educational Research Journal*, 52: 1024–59. doi:10.3102/0002831215604045

Yosso, T. J. (2005), 'Whose Culture Has Capital? A Critical Race Theory Discussion of Community Cultural Wealth', *Race Ethnicity and Education*, 8 (1): 69–91.

Part Four

Advancing Bourdieu's Concepts in the Field of Education

7

Aspirations and the Histories of Elite State Schools in London: Field Theory, Circuits of Education and the Embodiment of Symbolic Capital

Sol Gamsu

Introduction

Students' aspirations to attend elite universities in the UK are embedded in hierarchies of secondary educational institutions that enable or prescribe certain university destinations (Reay, David and Ball 2001, 2005; Donnelly 2014). Schools and colleges are situated within local institutional hierarchies, and simultaneously nested within national hierarchies where they effectively compete to represent themselves as viable options for students who seek to attend elite universities. The field of post-16 education in the UK is a site of struggle for status.[1] Contemporary local and national hierarchies are formed by long institutional histories of struggles for dominant positions within the field. Therefore, I argue that student aspiration must be understood as significantly influenced by the institutional practices and strategies focused upon the accumulation of symbolic capital. Drawing on Bourdieu's approach to history (Bourdieu 1981, 1996: 189–229; Gorski 2013), this chapter will show how student aspirations are shaped by school histories as institutions seek to foster certain socio-spatial trajectories or 'circuits of education' (Ball, Bowe and Gewirtz 1995) to elite universities.

In this chapter, I combine Bourdieu's concept of field, a multidimensional social space within which actors' positions are determined by their stock of cultural, economic, social and, especially, symbolic capital (Bourdieu and Wacquant 1992), with 'circuits of education', developed in the literature exploring the geographies of contemporary educational inequality in the UK (Ball, Bowe and Gewirtz 1995). Combining these approaches allows us to see how prestige is generated over time for institutions through the socio-spatial movement of individuals. Institutional field here is understood as the hierarchy of schools and colleges at the point of university choice, with institutions partly positioned by the symbolic capital gained through sending their students to elite universities. The concept of circuits of schooling, which I apply here to examine the post-16 to university transition, was initially developed to analyse collective socio-spatial patterns in student trajectories and choices at age 11 (Ball, Bowe and Gewirtz 1995). These movements of students may reflect the more individual aspirations of students, but their aspirations are, I argue, significantly shaped by institutional histories of strategies that have sought to directly and more tacitly encourage aspirations to elite universities. The repetition of circuits over time embeds and shapes the school's position within the field. Furthermore, these processes, which are historically cumulative in shaping student's aspirations, are also institutionally accumulative in providing schools with symbolic capital. To illustrate how aspirations can be understood as formed through the interaction of individual habitus and histories of school position takings within the field, I will draw on interviews with staff and students in two high-performing state schools in London, Halsham School and King Henry's School for Boys.[2] Both schools have engaged in the hierarchical struggle for status, and successfully repositioned themselves as elite institutions over the last three decades, now sending large numbers of students to elite UK universities.

To address the relationship between the formation of student aspirations and the historic struggles of schools to gain dominance within the field of education, it is important to recognize that embedding circuits of education which will lead to elite universities require a set of institutional strategies. These strategies respond both to specific political conditions (e.g. shifts in education policy around school admissions) and/or demographic conditions (neighbourhood population change and ethnic class formation). These strategies enabled both Halsham School and King Henry's School for Boys, as state schools, to reposition themselves within the dominant subfield of London's schools where the historic private schools of the capital have traditionally dominated. Adopting a Bourdieusian lens, the aspirations of students currently attending these schools and seeking highly competitive admission to elite universities can be understood as formed 'between the socialized body and the social fields, two products of the same history that are generally attuned to each other, there develops an infra-conscious, corporeal complicity' (Bourdieu 1993: 46).

In this chapter, I emphasize the importance of history. Specifically, I show how institutions create objectified histories which shape and align themselves with the embodied histories and 'aspirations' of students. Throughout Bourdieu's work there is an attention to how institutional histories of the field combine homologically with the positioning of individuals resulting 'from a historical process of progressive and collective creation that follows neither a plan nor an obscure immanent Reason' (Bourdieu 1996: 227). As he describes elsewhere:

> When the history in things and the history in bodies are perfectly attuned to each other ... then the actor does exactly what he has to, the 'only thing there was to do', as we say, without even needing to know what he is doing. (Bourdieu 1993: 46)

Due to this homology, attending an elite university becomes, for these students, a naturalized process and reinforces the position of the school in the field. For Bourdieu, fields function at this juncture of individual *institutional* history, which is always situated within the broader collective history of the institutional field, and the history of the agent themselves. Individuals embody the structure of the field and the history of the institution within their choices. From the perspective of the school, aspirations to attend elite universities and the circuits of education they form function as a valuable form of symbolic capital within the field.

Hobsbawm (2007) argues that 'the past has a central stake in Bourdieu's work since it constitutes the soil in which the present's roots are plunged' and yet, within the sociology of education, Bourdieu's approach to history has been relatively rarely used, particularly in combination with field theory (Maton 2004; Gamsu 2016). Drawing on empirical data, I will theorize student aspirations in two elite state schools in London as the product of institutional histories of struggles for position within the field, in which aspirations to attend elite universities have gradually become normalized. I begin by describing in greater depth Bourdieu's approach to history and how we can combine this with field theory and circuits of education to explore contemporary aspirations of students choosing elite universities.

Bourdieu's historical analysis, field theory and 'circuits of education'

With notable exceptions (Naidoo 2004; Bathmaker 2015), field has not drawn as much attention as other concepts in Bourdieu's oeuvre within higher education research. Habitus has been used more often to understand the relationship between institutions and student identities. For schools in particular, the concept of 'institutional habitus' (Reay 1998; Reay, David and Ball 2001) has been developed to understand how institutional practices become embedded in and shape individual aspirations. This concept has been the subject of some controversy (Atkinson 2011; Burke, Emmerich and Ingram 2013) and is explored elsewhere in this volume (see Tarabini and Curran; Forbes and Maxwell; Stich and Cipollone). While institutional habitus is a useful tool, Bourdieu's approach to field allows us to see how schools seek to accumulate symbolic capital and advantage within interrelated hierarchies of institutions. Tied closely to field theory, symbolic capital has the capacity to impose legitimacy on a vision of the world, hence defining the rules of the game and the field's structure (Bourdieu 1987). Bourdieu (1996) developed an approach to studying institutions in the educational field most clearly in his analysis of the field of *grandes écoles* as part of the broader French field of power. A particularly valuable section explored the 'structural history' of elite French higher education and how these institutions gained dominant positions in the field through historical struggles for symbolic markers of success. This historical analysis of interrelated institutional change allowed an understanding of how the rules, norms and standards of what it meant to be an elite university were shaped; these phenomena in turn shaped the experiences and expectations of students. The way contemporary students' aspirations are used by institutions as markers of success has a long history within UK education and this research considers how contemporary aspirations also *respond to* and *reflect* this institutional history of, as well as current struggles for, position takings within the field.

In his approach to field theory, Bourdieu emphasized the importance of the long processes of accumulation of prestige and power by institutions. His approach underlines the value of understanding how aspirations are formed through institutional histories. Students' aspirations to attend elite universities stem from a set of dispositions that may be shaped by personal habitus depending on gender, class or ethnicity, but are also inculcated by the schools' contemporary and historical–institutional practices (Reay, David and Ball 2005; Ingram 2011; Forbes and Maxwell, this volume). The interaction between individual habitus and school histories of status accrual within the field of education embeds students' aspirations in historical processes of the accumulation of symbolic capital by schools.

Every historical action brings together two states of history: objectified history, i.e. the history which has accumulated over the passage of time in things, machines, buildings, monuments, books, theories, customs, law, etc.; and embodied history, in the form of habitus ... the institution – becomes historical action, i.e. enacted, active history, only if it is taken in charge by agents whose own history predisposes them to do so, who, by virtue of their previous investments, are inclined to take an interest in its functioning, and endowed with the appropriate attributes to make it function. (Bourdieu 1981: 305–6)

Bourdieu insists on understanding how choices and perceptions of the subject engrained in personal habitus combine with, and thus enact, the longer history of the institution in the field. The 'objectified' historical struggles of institutions to accrue symbolic capital within the field of education underpin the aspirations of students in these two schools. Capital, in this case the symbolic capital of students winning places at elite universities, is a form of 'accumulated labour' (Bourdieu 1986), and it is enacted through the combining of institutional history and embodied individual aspirations.

The context and the accrual of symbolic capital within the field

In the UK, the number of students gaining entry to elite universities has long been a marker of institutional secondary school status. The rules of the game and the struggle over the 'principle[s] of domination' (Bourdieu 1996: 265) of the post-16 educational field/s have a specific geography and in the UK the dominant schools remain concentrated in London and the south-east of England. Steedman (1987), focusing on the attempts of selective, state-funded grammar schools to replicate 'public' school norms in the early twentieth century, noted that winning places at Oxbridge was already a key indicator of institutional prestige. Increasing or maintaining the number of students winning places at elite universities remains a key institutional strategy for the accumulation of symbolic capital. 'Winning places' serves a symbolic function, marking the school out from its local peers as a conduit to national institutions associated with middle-class and elite social reproduction (Bourdieu 1996: 197–201). For prospective parents and students, these university successes are a clear sign that the school is working as a node in trajectories of social and academic success.

The way these circuits of education between school and university work as a form of symbolic capital is not static – it is not simply embedded as an architectural form, maintained economically as an endowment or fee income, or physically embodied by the long-term presence of certain staff. Rather, symbolic capital forms dynamically through the flow of students 'upward' to certain universities or courses. This understanding of symbolic capital and institutional position within the field sees institutions not as 'formed wholes' but rather as 'forming and formative processes' (Williams 1977: 128). Drawing upon circuits of education, we see a dynamic of socio-spatial trajectories where young people move through geographical space, transitioning from one educational institution to another. These circuits, and the aspirations of the students who operate within them, are historically formed. Their movements become valuable capital for the institution they are part of. As I will explore below, schools have historically invested time and energy in developing 'traditions' of sending students to elite universities. Schools come to serve as conduits on paths of aspiration for multiple generations of students. Aspiration becomes bound into institutional projects and histories of managing and creating prestige, processes which are sedimented over decades, if not, in the case of some schools, centuries.

Methodology

To situate this analysis of aspiration within a Bourdieusian historical analysis of field and circuits of education, I draw on interviews with two senior teachers from two elite state schools in London and focus groups with students at one of the schools. Halsham School is a state-funded faith school serving a religious community which became increasingly middle class over the twentieth century. King Henry's School for Boys is now once again a selective grammar school, having been a non-selective 'comprehensive' secondary school between 1975 and 1994. This status was deliberately transformed in an institutional project of restoration described below. At King Henry's School for Boys, four focus groups with twenty-one students in their final year were undertaken in March 2014. Just under half were from clearly professional/managerial middle-class families, with other parents from a mixture of other white-collar and more clearly working-class backgrounds. In keeping with the school's increasing ethnic minority intake drawn from London's suburbs, over half of the sample were from families of Indian or Sri Lankan heritage. Both teachers taught at the schools from the 1980s through to the early 2010s. Halsham and King Henry's form part of a cluster of elite, 'super-state' schools in London which now compete with the capital's historic elite fee-paying schools to win places at elite universities (Gamsu 2017).

The institutional trajectories of both schools discussed here have included a conscious decision to reintroduce forms of tacit or explicit selection with the aim of competing with the independent sector. At both schools, students' aspirations to attend elite universities became part of 'cumulative' processes of institutional advantage, with the circuits of education linking these schools to elite universities created and maintained by thirty- to forty-year strategies designed to reinforce academic selection. In these highly selective institutional contexts, 'aspiration' to attend elite universities must be seen as the result of long-term institutional strategies that sought to reposition these state schools closer to the dominant subfield of London's elite private schools. As will be made clear below, students' aspirations clearly sit within and are in part framed by these institutional histories; their 'choices' simultaneously respond to and act to shape an institution's position within the local and national field of post-16 education. Choice and aspiration occur at the juncture of 'corporeal complicity' between the individual, the institution's history and the rules of the field in which that institution sits.

Institutional histories: Framing the development of elite aspirations

Halsham school: The 'cumulative' processes of student aspiration and institutional success

Halsham School felt the need to reposition itself during the 1980s to reflect the changing socio-economic and geographical position of the faith group the school serves. Over the twentieth century the school relocated twice.[3] This process of relocation reflected the growing affluence of fractions of the community who were moving away from the inner-city towards the wealthier suburbs. By the 1980s a substantial number of families were opting into the fee-paying independent sector, depriving the school of potentially higher-attaining students. At Halsham School, I interviewed Susan, the school's former assistant head. She described how, with the arrival of a new head in 1985, the school deliberately set out to attract students who were otherwise attending local private schools.

> Susan: And then Lucy [the new head] took over and she made it her mission
> to increase the able children coming into the school and … she did, she was
> immensely successful. … All the children were interviewed, not with a view
> to 'You can come and you can't come'. But with a view to finding out about

them … . And she would actually say to parents at the interview, 'If you
send your child here, if you come here, I'll guarantee you a place.' And she
would say that to a number of the able children to try and switch, swing this
balance. And she was very successful and we had things called accelerated
classes which … generated enough momentum to increase the able intake.

Sol: Where were the more able students going if not [to Halsham School]?

Susan: It was independent schools that were the main competitors for the able
children. So we would then have a situation where we started to get a better
intake and as those students go through you get better results and better
university whatever.

What we see in Susan's response is how Halsham School adopted institutional
strategies that sought to adapt to the rising affluence among the faith community
served by the school. It did this by *gradually* creating selective environments
and slowly building up an academic reputation. Adopting internal streaming
and tacit selection reflected the policies of Conservative governments of the
1980s that sought to encourage 'differentiation within schools' (Lowe 1989).
These urban demographic and political changes affected Halsham's position in
the field, stimulating strategies which sought to reposition the school within the
dominant subfield of elite London schools.

In considering the composition of Halsham School and the importance
of getting the right 'balance' of students, Susan was also keenly aware of the
importance of fostering links to elite universities to meet families' aspirations:

when I was head of sixth form and Lucy Bergman was head of school, we really
worked hard, we worked our socks off to keep these high-ability children and we
had liaisons, I spent a huge amount of time liaising with Oxbridge, with Russell
Group, I went out to umpteen meetings … I mean [now] it's something like, 70
something per cent go to Russell Group, but that's, that's the staff. And then each
year the kids go, 'My friend went to Nottingham. Can I go to Nottingham?' It
becomes a cumulative thing really.

Susan described the great efforts taken to first attract and then maintain able
students from families wealthy enough to afford independent education. Halsham
School clearly made great efforts to create similar ties to elite universities as the
independent fee-paying schools had. The gradual increase in the proportion of
students choosing to attend the twenty-four self-selecting research-intensive
'Russell Group' universities was a 'cumulative', self-reinforcing process, with
students knowing older friends and peers at these institutions and thus wanting
to attend them themselves. We see with Halsham how student aspirations to

attend elite institutions are not merely the result of a family habitus of higher education choice (Reay 1998). They exist within institutional histories of accumulation of advantage, prestige and reputation and the repeated patterns of circuits of education. Thus, students' aspirations are partly the result of what Bourdieu (1986) would call the 'accumulated history' of schools' efforts to distinguish themselves as elite within the field.

King Henry's school: Naturalizing elite university choices within a project of institutional restoration

King Henry's School for Boys had converted from a selective grammar to a comprehensive school in the mid-1970s. Under a new head, who took over in the mid-1980s, there was a move first to restore the school's 'traditional values' of 'manners and learning' with a system of stricter discipline (Interview with deputy head, 2014). According to the deputy head who had joined the school in 1986, once this shift in the 'pastoral' culture of the school had been achieved, increasing student numbers meant they could think about reintroducing tacit and later explicit forms of selection. To avoid interference from the local education authority, which was opposed to selection, in 1989 the school became a 'grant-maintained' school, opting out of local government control. Using this institutional autonomy allowed selection, initially by interview where parents and students were 'rated according to whether they were in tune with the aspirations of the school' (Interview with deputy head, 2014). From 1994 selection was more formally reintroduced through the return of an entrance exam. These aspirations were strongly oriented towards returning to the selective past of the school and an elite school identity. Already in 1991, national newspapers described the school as 'more like a public school', with high exam results and a strong emphasis on rugby union.

In keeping with this return to selection and repositioning of the school within the subfield of elite schools, students at King Henry's were focused on a subset of elite universities. Ten students in my focus groups had at least one parent who had been to university, of whom four attended a 'Russell Group' university. However, except for two students whose parents had attended King's College London (KCL), students were not from families who had direct experience of the 'golden triangle' of Oxford, Cambridge, and the elite universities of London (KCL, UCL, LSE, and Imperial). These universities, and to a lesser extent the universities of Bristol, Durham, Exeter and Warwick, dominate access to elite positions across a range of professions (Wakeling and Savage 2015). It was precisely this group of universities that students, encouraged by the school, were aiming to apply for:

> Sol: And in terms of universities, what places do people tend to go on to?
> Yajnash: Oxbridge
> Sol: Yeah, Oxbridge and Russell Group, everyone goes there ... are other universities like even on the menu, or?
> Vidu: Yeah there are, like UCL's got quite a lot of people going there.
> Chitesh: The main ones the school tends to focus on for the science ones are UCL, King's and Imperial. I think for history and things like that, Warwick and maybe Durham, um ...
> Sanjeev: There's like kind of ten unis that they look at. Oxbridge, UCL, LSE, Bristol, Warwick, Durham and that's kind of ...
> Chitesh: So generally high-achieving ones. (Focus Group 3, King Henry's Boys)

In keeping with Wakeling and Savage's (2015) findings on the hierarchies *within* the field of elite higher education, the school focuses not simply on the 'Russell Group', but on a smaller subset of elite institutions within that grouping. In producing these aspirations and academic results, which place King Henry's on par with the most academically successful of the UK's private schools, family habitus strongly combined with the school's recent history of restoring its status as an elite school. Familial desire for educational success, discussed elsewhere in the interviews, in keeping with the literature describing the focus among British Asian families on educational success (Modood 2004, 2012), combined tightly with a very distinct institutional orientation towards a small group of institutions:

> Hiren: We've always kind of been put in that direction so we've had like talks and stuff, like Cambridge talks and Oxbridge talks and stuff. Um, yeah, so it's just been a way of life really.
> Girish: I think you're just like expected to go to one of the top places.
> Hiren: You don't think twice about it, it's just ...
> Girish: Yeah, you're just like expected to go to one of the top unis.
> Hiren: That's the way it is.
> Girish: Yeah. (Focus Group 4, King Henry's Boys)

Naturalization and acceptance of the school's focus on elite universities is very clear here. What was at work was the combining of a strong 'education-oriented' (Nitin, Focus Group 1) familial focus on what students will study at university and where with the school's orientation towards elite universities. What was at work was not simply student and familial aspirations; the school's deliberate focus on a small subset of universities plays into the longer history of accumulation of symbolic capital and prestige through which the school's position in the field of education has been recreated. Elite university aspirations are being formed through the combination of familial aspiration and accumulated institutional history, 'the seemingly inextricable dialectic that obtains between the mental structures and the objective structures of the institution' (Bourdieu 1996: 29).

Discussion: A historical–institutional approach to aspiration

This chapter has sought to examine how we can understand the formation of aspirations in the context of institutional strategies that aim to reposition schools within an elite subfield of London schools that dominate access to elite UK universities. Student aspirations are understood here as 'the interaction of two histories and his [*sic*] present is the meeting of two pasts' (Bourdieu 1981: 315), that of the institution and that of the individual themselves. Using Bourdieu, we are reminded as sociologists of the need to embed history, the intersection of biography with the history of social structures within and throughout our analysis. Bourdieu's approach to structural history emphasized the importance of understanding how institutions struggle within the field to accumulate symbolic capital. This allows us to see how changing conditions and rules of the field for a broader hierarchy of schools affect individual institutions. Both King Henry's and Halsham responded to shifting demographic and political conditions by employing long-term strategies which deliberately sought to shape individual choices and aspirations.

The last section examined how students' subjective perceptions regarding where they aspire to go at the end of their school careers are tied into these longer histories of institutional strategizing. Conscious decisions about where to study may not entail a reflection on the long historical processes which have normalized attending certain universities within the culture of particular schools. However, from the perspective of senior teachers with long careers at these schools, it becomes clear that these choices are cumulative processes. From this perspective, aspirations are not simply the result of familial influences but form part of institutional strategies of selection, embedded over years of repeated circuits of education carefully encouraged and maintained by these schools to allow the accumulation of symbolic capital. Students' aspirations and movements to elite universities furnish schools with prestige – through their lives they enact and embody the joining of objective institutional history with their own subjective trajectories. These trajectories are spatial, representing movements between schools and universities across geographical space (see Forbes and Maxwell, this volume). Here I have used the concept of circuits of education from the work of Ball, Bowe and Gewirtz (1995) to suggest how the sedimented patterns of aspiration fostered by institutions involve particular geographies of university destinations. Geographies of education were generally implicit rather than explicit in Bourdieu's analysis of education and as a result his theory is best used in combination with other theory.

Conclusion: History and educational hierarchy as processes of accumulation

By combining field, circuits and institutional history we can see how aspirations are formed by and help create patterns of accumulation within institutions. Circuits allow us to see how students' aspirations create socio-spatial trajectories which are fostered and managed by institutions in slow processes which result in the gradual accumulation of symbolic capital. Accumulation of capital through human labour was central to Bourdieu's sociology (Savage 2017), and this chapter has shown how aspirations are tied into the accrual of capital for schools attempting to reposition themselves within the field. I have explored aspiration in three ways that build on Bourdieu's approach to history: in the coming together of institution and individual, the structural history which shapes the rules of the field, and the processes of accumulation which all dominant institutions must master. This historical element to Bourdieu's work is sometimes overlooked within the sociology of education in the English-speaking world (Gorski 2013). It is worth remembering that Bourdieu saw the 'creation of a unified social science, where history would be a historical sociology of the past and sociology a social history of the present' (Bourdieu and Raphael 1995: 111) as a central aim of the journal he edited, *Actes de la Recherche en Sciences Sociales*. History remains a potent tool to critically understand the sociology of aspirations in the present, and Bourdieu's historical analysis provides rich terrain for further work in the sociology of education.

Acknowledgements

This chapter draws on my PhD thesis which was funded by the Economic and Social Research Council (Reference: 10.13039/501100000269).

Notes

1 The post-16 educational phase in UK education refers to the final two to three years of compulsory education for students aged 16–18/19. Post-16 includes schools with a 'sixth form' (state or private), further education (FE) colleges and sixth-form colleges.

2 All institutional and individual names are pseudonyms.

3 On the history of outward relocation of elite schools from central London to the suburbs, see my paper in *Urban Studies* (Gamsu 2016).

Recommended further reading

Bourdieu, P. (1981), 'Men and Machines', in K. Knorr-Cetina and A. V. Cicourel (eds), *Advances in Social Theory and Methodology: Toward an Integration of Micro- and Macro-sociologies*, 304–17, London: Routledge and Kegan Paul.

Gorski, P. S. (ed.) (2013), *Bourdieu and Historical Analysis*, Durham, NC: Duke University Press.

Hobsbawm, E. (2007), 'Critical Sociology and Social History', *Sociological Research Online*, 12(4). Available online: http://www.socresonline.org.uk/12/6/2.html

References

Atkinson, W. (2011), 'From Sociological Fictions to Social Fictions: Some Bourdieusian Reflections on the Concepts of "Institutional Habitus" and "Family Habitus"', *British Journal of Sociology of Education*, 32: 331–47.

Ball, S. J., R. Bowe and S. Gewirtz (1995), 'Circuits of Schooling: A Sociological Exploration of Parental Choice of School in Social Class Contexts', *Sociological Review*, 43: 52–78.

Bathmaker, A.-M. (2015), 'Thinking with Bourdieu: Thinking After Bourdieu. Using "Field" to Consider In/equalities in the Changing Field of English Higher Education', *Cambridge Journal of Education*, 45: 61–80.

Bourdieu, P. (1981), 'Men and Machines', in K. Knorr-Cetina and A. V. Cicourel (eds), *Advances in Social Theory and Methodology: Toward an Integration of Micro- and Macro-sociologies*, 304–17, London: Routledge and Kegan Paul.

Bourdieu, P. (1986), 'The Forms of Capital', in J. E. Richardson (ed.), *Handbook of Theory of Research for the Sociology of Education*, 241–58, New York: Greenwood Press.

Bourdieu, P. (1987), 'What Makes a Social Class? On the Theoretical and Practical Existence of Groups', *Berkeley Journal of Sociology*, 32: 1–17.

Bourdieu, P. (1993), *Sociology in Question*, London: Sage.

Bourdieu, P. (1996), *The State Nobility: Elite Schools in the Field of Power*, Cambridge: Polity Press.

Bourdieu, P., and L. Raphael (1995), 'Sur les rapports entre la sociologie et l'histoire en Allemagne et en France', *Actes de la Recherche en Sciences Sociales*, 106 (1): 108–22.

Bourdieu, P., and L. J. Wacquant (1992), *An Invitation to Reflexive Sociology*, Chicago: University of Chicago Press.

Burke, C. T., N. Emmerich and N. Ingram (2013), 'Well-Founded Social Fictions: A Defence of the Concepts of Institutional and Familial Habitus', *British Journal of Sociology of Education*, 34: 165–82.

Donnelly, M. (2014), 'The Road to Oxbridge: Schools and Elite University Choices', *British Journal of Educational Studies*, 62: 57–72.

Gamsu, S. (2016), 'Moving Up and Moving Out: The Re-location of Elite and Middle-Class Schools from Central London to the Suburbs', *Urban Studies*, 53(14): 2921–38.

Gamsu, S. (2017), 'A Historical Geography of Educational Power: Comparing Circuits and Fields of Education in Sheffield and London', PhD thesis, King's College London, London.

Gorski, P. S. (ed.) (2013), *Bourdieu and Historical Analysis*, Durham, NC: Duke University Press.

Hobsbawm, E. (2007), 'Critical Sociology and Social History', *Sociological Research Online*, 12 (4). Available online: http://www.socresonline.org.uk/12/6/2.html

Ingram, N. (2011), 'Within School and Beyond the Gate: The Complexities of Being Educationally Successful and Working Class', *Sociology*, 45 (2): 287–302.

Lowe, R. (1989), 'Secondary Education since the Second World War', in R. Lowe (ed.), *The Changing Secondary School*, 4–19, London: Falmer Press.

Maton, K. (2004), 'The Field of Higher Education: A Sociology of Reproduction, Transformation, Change and the Conditions of Emergence for Cultural Studies', PhD thesis, University of Cambridge, Cambridge.

Modood, T. (2004), 'Capitals, Ethnic Identity and Educational Qualifications', *Cultural Trends*, 13: 87–105.

Modood, T. (2012), 'Capitals, Ethnicity and Higher Education', in T. Basit and S. Tomlinson (eds), *Social Inclusion and Higher Education*, 17–40, Bristol: Policy Press.

Naidoo, R. (2004), 'Fields and Institutional Strategy: Bourdieu on the Relationship between Higher Education, Inequality and Society', *British Journal of Sociology of Education*, 25: 457–71.

Reay, D. (1998), '"Always Knowing" and "Never Being Sure": Familial and Institutional Habituses and Higher Education Choice', *Journal of Education Policy*, 13: 519–29.

Reay, D., M. David and S. Ball (2001), 'Making a Difference? Institutional Habituses and Higher Education Choice', *Sociological Research Online*, 5 (4). Available online: http://www.socresonline.org.uk/5/4/reay

Reay, D., M. E. David and S. J. Ball (2005), *Degrees of Choice: Social Class, Race, Gender and Higher Education*, Stoke-on-Trent, UK: Trentham Books.

Savage, M. (2017), 'The Elite Habitus in Cities of Accumulation', in S. Hall and R. Burdett (eds), *The Sage Handbook of the 21st Century City*, 71–86, London: Sage.

Steedman, H. (1987), 'Defining Institutions: The Endowed Grammar Schools and the Systematisation of English Secondary Schooling', in D. Müller, F. Ringer and B. Simon (eds), *The Rise of the Modern Educational System: Structural Change and Social Reproduction, 1870–1920*, 111–34, Cambridge: Cambridge University Press.

Wakeling, P., and M. Savage (2015), 'Entry to Elite Positions and the Stratification of Higher Education in Britain', *Sociological Review*, 63: 290–320.

Williams, R. (1977), *Marxism and Literature*, Oxford: Oxford University Press.

8

Thinking with Bourdieu about Teachers' Pedagogies and Their Dispositions for Social Justice: Unthinkingness in Aspiration Formation

Russell Cross, Carmen Mills and Trevor Gale

Introduction

Despite the best efforts of policy makers and teachers to address educational inequality, the educational attainment gap between students from high and low socio-economic backgrounds continues to grow (Dorling 2011; Gonski et al. 2011; Piketty 2014). Like many nations in the Organisation for Economic Cooperation and Development (OECD) (ETUC and ETUI 2012; Le Donné 2014; NESSE 2012; OECD 2010; UNICEF 2010), the most disadvantaged students in Australia have diminished opportunities to gain from education (Connors and McMorrow 2015; Wilkinson and Pickett 2009). There is an urgent need for new ways to understand how these inequalities are being enacted in and through educational practices, and what possibilities for alternative interventions might exist.

This chapter reflects on the application of Bourdieu's concept of the habitus in a large-scale qualitative study of social justice dispositions, and what these revealed in the practices of teachers working in advantaged and disadvantaged schools located in two major Australian cities. Bourdieu's work resonates with many scholars who seek to understand relations between students from disadvantaged backgrounds and their low academic achievement. Indeed, Bourdieu's own research in 1960s France suggests that, when secondary schooling became more universally available, working-class students falsely imagined they would also gain access to the rewards of the upper classes; their aspirations for a better life were 'inscribed at the deepest level of their dispositions as a sort of blighted hope or frustrated promise' (Bourdieu 1984: 150).

We draw on our research to illustrate how 'dispositions' (collectively, the habitus) offer a useful conceptual tool when working with data to help better identify – and in turn explain – why socially just practices and outcomes are so hard to achieve in schools, even when there is an express desire by teachers and principals to 'do good'. This sits within the broader aim of our research to make visible how more socially just outcomes might be achieved, by interrogating the otherwise taken-for-granted recurring and enduring patterns of teachers' work that unfold in the 'un-thoughtness' of everyday schooling. Of particular interest in the context of this book is how such tools provide a lens into the 'unthinking-ness' of teachers' practice, and its impact on the formation of student aspiration.

Understanding Bourdieu's tools

Bourdieu's conceptual tools for researching social structures have had a significant impact on understanding and critiquing the role of schools in maintaining social inequality, with the *habitus* central to this understanding. As Bourdieu explains, the habitus is 'a system of durable, transposable dispositions which functions as the generative basis of structured, objectively unified practices' (1979: vii). It thus explains recurring patterns of one's social class outlook, inculcated by everyday experiences within families, peer groups and schools over time. Conceived as 'unthinking-ness in action', the habitus operates below the level of strict rational calculation to instead provide guidance and conditions for practice 'without consciously obeying rules explicitly posed as such' (1990b: 76).

As constituents of the habitus, we similarly understand *dispositions* as tendencies, inclinations and leanings shaped and reshaped through the primary and secondary pedagogic work of families and communities (Bourdieu and Passeron 1990). Described as a 'feel for the game' (Bourdieu 1990a: 66), the habitus, and thus dispositions, orient actors to do certain things in certain circumstances, without strictly determining them, enabling actors to 'cope with unforeseen and ever-changing situations' (1977: 72). In the same way, we understand *social justice* dispositions (SJDs) as the particular tendencies, inclinations and leanings that provide un-thought or pre-thought guidance for socially just practice. Conceived in this way, we argue that SJDs offer a new analytical category to advance understandings of how educational advantage and disadvantage are enacted through teachers' pedagogies. Focusing on SJDs enables us to look beyond the (conscious) beliefs that teachers 'claim' as important, to instead focus on the 'un-thought' inclinations that play out as teachers engage with students in practice.

The importance of this way of thinking about and with dispositions has been underestimated and under-theorized in much previous social justice research, particularly in education contexts. While to date such research has focused on outcomes through practices (e.g. policies and programmes) and belief systems (of both policy makers and teachers) (see for example Gale, Mills and Cross 2017), our argument is that social justice research in education should also and perhaps more centrally include a focus on the dispositions that operate between belief and practice, helping to better distinguish between what is said and done. In this chapter we are particularly interested in what this regard for dispositions means for shaping students' aspirations.[1]

Understanding dispositions as the 'un-thoughtness' of practice also has implications for research methods. In contrast to conventional data collection techniques such as interviews (focusing on what is *said*) or observations (focusing on what is *done*), dispositions reside at the level of the unconscious and thus are not easily spoken or observed. Yet Bourdieu's insight that dispositions are *revealed in actions* (Bourdieu and Wacquant 1992) is where theory meets method, on at least two levels: (1) by generating new ways to *read* data, interpreting the unspoken inclinations that operate between beliefs and practice as subtle but enduring *repetitions* and *emphases* unfolding in the rhythm of continuous actions over time; and (2) by evoking new ways to *generate* data, using interview and observation in juxtaposition to scaffold participants' 'reflexive critique' (Gardiner 2000) and, by so doing, provoking them to speak their dispositions (Gale and Molla 2017).

In what follows we illustrate how theory and method come together in the context of our research by focusing on the first of these methodological affordances, made possible through Bourdieu's understanding of the habitus and dispositions. We return to consider the second methodological point in the subsequent discussion. For the purposes of this volume, we particularly draw on data that illustrate the influence of these dispositions in students' aspiration formation.

The research was conducted in three stages. Working with ten case study schools, the first stage utilized extended semi-structured interviews with principals (head teachers) to understand what was significant in terms of the social justice aims in each school context. The second stage data – from which we draw our example for this chapter – used 'stimulated recall' procedures (Gass and Mackey 2000) with one to two teachers from each case school, based on video recordings of a three-lesson sequence with the same class group over one week. These records of what was done (observations), *related to* and *juxtaposed with* what was said (interviews), provide the empirical focus for how we bring theory to method to work with data, and to illustrate the first methodological point above. It provides an example of the analysis that this research process generated, particularly highlighting how one teacher's dispositions were at work to generate particular aspiration-forming practices with her students.

Applying Bourdieu's tools

Our example centres on Caitlyn,[2] an experienced Health and Physical Education teacher at Guildford Girls' College, an all-girls government secondary school in a major Australian city. At the time of our study, Caitlyn was in her forties and lived with her husband and her daughters in an upper-middle-class suburb thirty minutes' drive from the school. Her daughters also attended the same school. For the purposes of our study, the school was deemed 'advantaged' based on standardized test scores published on the Australian government's *MySchool* website (ACARA 2010). We used academic achievement as a proxy measure for sampling dis/advantage in schools given the correlation that has been established between students' levels of achievement and their socio-economic backgrounds (Teese 2011).

As an all-girls school, Guildford is distinct from the vast majority of government schools in Australia, which are typically co-educational. Instead it mirrors the single-sex model of elite schools in Australia's independent sector, which enrol students on the basis of academic performance rather than mandated enrolments based on local zoning. Guildford is an inner-city suburb which neighbours other high-performing government and independent schools, including some that have among the highest tuition fees in the nation. While not officially select entry, demand for student places at Guildford is so high that it has instituted a selection process of interviews and essays to allocate places not already filled by those living in the local zone.

During the early stages of the first interview, Caitlyn was asked directly about how she saw Guilford Girls' College 'being a socially just place' and how the school sees its 'commitment to social justice':

I suppose one of the things I love about the school is the diversity of kids. There's kids that will travel overseas for ten weeks in Year 9 and there's kids that can't afford to leave the city, and they're all together in the classroom and they don't have much of an – they sort of know, but they don't have much of an idea, everyone's still in a school uniform. So there's that sense, and then I like the idea that these kids can [are] all together. And it's not just kids paying thirty-thousand dollars a year at high school so it's good for all the kids to have that.

A recognition of diversity and a collective sense of belonging and inclusion feature strongly in Caitlyn's stated account of what socially just work should look like within the school. She elaborated on this later, speaking about her role within the school as Assistant Year 9 Dean, which has a strong pastoral element, and includes ensuring all students are able to participate in school excursions and camps:

We're conscious of kids and how comfortable things are for them, either [whether they] have payment plans, or help pay or don't pay – so we want the kids to come, particularly because it's a curriculum thing and they have a great time, so we're conscious about making sure all the kids come and if they can't afford it then we just cover that.

Caitlyn was suggested for participation in our study by the school principal because she exemplified the school's social justice goals. Caitlyn herself also volunteered to be part of our study because of her interest in how schools and their teachers approach social justice. She was clearly aware of her own school's diverse student demographics and wanted to ensure that everyone within that school 'felt they belonged'.

Given these explicit interests and commitments, it is instructive to consider the emphases and repetitions revealed in Caitlyn's practice – her disposition guiding action – and how these subtlest of influences follow through to shape her pedagogic work, and in turn the social interactions and arrangements in place and their influence on shaping students' aspirations. The instance we examine below focuses on the first of three Year 8 Health lessons about nutritional substances and the human body. Working from a series of PowerPoints to engage students in a broad discussion about carbohydrates, proteins, fats and vitamins, Caitlyn finished the lesson with a task that had students reflect on foods in their own diet.

When we analysed the emphases and repetitions that emerged in the rhythm of this lesson, the strongest pattern to emerge was the frequency with which Caitlyn referred to herself and her own family to explain the content being studied. During the fifty-minute lesson, she made at least fifteen direct references to herself or her family that were related to the lesson content, for example:

> One of my children – and it's not Natalie! – didn't like brown bread, so she had the Wonder White bread. But I had to find all the different breads and check out their fibre content, and Wonder White actually has quite a lot of fibre, and significantly more fibre than some wholemeal breads.
>
> I don't like cereals, I must say, as I don't like it going soggy.
>
> I have a vegetarian husband. [Some students groan] Yeah, I know – it's a pain sometimes!
>
> When we were away in Tasmania, I kid you not … there's a piece of steak on the menu that was 700 grams. I was just going, I could feed four people with this. 700 grams of steak, huge!
>
> If you're lacking vitamin D it can then increase your risk of osteoporosis, when you're my age.
>
> I think Subway's actually our option if we're on the run, so if we're moving between sports or something like that.
>
> I got so fat in America, it wasn't funny … I just ate [pizza and other American foods] because we were really poor travelling as students [laugh]. We just ate everything.

By using herself as the primary (and essentially only) point of reference, Caitlyn presented a subtle but strong normative model to the girls for making sense of, being able to identify with and relate to the content to be learned. This way of presenting herself speaks directly to the development of her students' aspiration capabilities, and how they are enabled to imagine their own futures (Gale and Parker 2015, 2018; Sellar and Gale 2011; Sen 2009). We are not suggesting that Caitlyn sees herself as the 'perfect' model. For example, when she explained that she likes to add significant amounts of Milo (a brand name for a chocolate and malt powder) to her milk, she also warned 'you shouldn't have too much Milo but don't ask me because whenever I have it … that's what I like to do'. However, she was providing a clear, narrowly defined message about how to make judgements about what is normal, despite these examples being imbued with (and restricted to) her own socio-economic/cultural background, and despite the potential for significant wider socio-economic/cultural diversity within the room. The following extracts from one lesson exemplify how this played out during interactions with her students:

> Caitlyn: Gemma, what's in your lunchbox?
> Gemma: Today?

Caitlyn: Yeah.

Gemma: Um …

Caitlyn: Oh, it's a bit tricky today because you finished so early, but what have you got today?

Gemma: I have carrots and hummus.

Caitlyn: Excellent! And so … carrots, hummus, sandwiches, protein, fruit and vegetables, all really, really good. And as Michelle said, you're getting more independence. Do you have a little bit … a little bit more money in your wallets?

Class: Yes.

Caitlyn: Yes, okay. Do you pass by, pass by milk bars, McDonald's on the way home from school?

Class: Yes.

Caitlyn: Alright, so … what you need to do with the greater independence is to start to think about how to make healthy choices. And you might sort of go, 'oh, that soft serve's looking pretty good there, only 30c' … see how they keep them really cheap? Soft serves, and even chips now at McDonald's, they have $1 things. Really cheap.

And later,

Caitlyn: We actually have pizza once a week, homemade. We get pita bread and we blend up the tomatoes and put mushrooms and salmon and stuff on it.

Student: My mum, she makes the base from scratch.

Caitlyn: Perfect! Because then you have really wholesome ingredients going into it.

In each instance of practice we saw unfolding between Caitlyn and her students – whether one-on-one, or before the class as a whole – her inclination was to continuously come back to her own family as the normative point of reference for engaging with the girls, resulting in a lack of recognition on at least two levels:

1. Whether all students within that group might have access to the types of food choices presented as 'normal'.
2. Whether foods/diets from other socio-economic or cultural backgrounds might also offer nutritionally sound examples (cf. socially 'acceptable' choices).

While on the surface these subtleties might seem innocuous, they came to a head during the main student-centred task for the lesson: having to keep a diary of their family's diet and judge whether the foods they eat are 'good', 'bad' or 'ugly'. Although Caitlyn claimed to recognize diversity and stated a commitment to ensuring all girls feel they belong, she failed to recognize the impact of representing her middle-class examples as normative and how it might feel to do this task if you were a student whose family regularly eats pre-packaged pizza (rather than making them at home, with toppings such as salmon), takeout from McDonald's (rather than Subway), or lunch that is a packet of crisps (rather than carrots and hummus).

> Caitlyn: You're going to evaluate your family's diet [Students groan ...] I want you to think about your family's diet, and you can draw it up ... I thought it might be fun to draw it up like this: 'The good', 'The bad' and 'The ugly' [Writing this up on the whiteboard]. [Class chatters] Shhhh ... right, so let's have a think ... Ingrid?
>
> Ingrid: If your parents have split up, can you just pick one house to do?
>
> Caitlyn: Ah ... good question. You could just put it together; do you know why? That's a good question, if your parents are separated and you are running between two houses, you can put it together because that still influences what you eat. Mary?
>
> Mary: {Inaudible}
>
> Caitlyn: If you are week in week out, you might have to do both. If you are mostly at one parent's house than the other, just do the one you're at the most.
>
> Student: {Inaudible}
>
> Caitlyn: Okay, so do the one you're at the most.

This interaction also provides further insight into Caitlyn's disposition. As with the earlier examples that relied on herself and her family as the central point of reference for making sense of food choices/diet, it was not until questioned by students that Caitlyn considered the possibility of alternative family arrangements. Although beyond the scope of what can be covered in depth here, we saw the same emphases repeated in the subsequent two lessons, with recurring references to 'when you're my age', presenting to the girls an imagined future trajectory that they were all assumed to share.

Discussion

Reflecting on the above example in terms of our own 'thinking with Bourdieu' about teachers' SJDs, and how we have engaged with these empirically as objects of research 'in the field', we return to our earlier points on how we see theory meeting method – in *reading* and *generating* data – as well as the potential of this work to advance research on aspiration.

As noted earlier, dispositions, conceived in the way Bourdieu suggests, afford new ways to approach data by *reading* what operates between what is said and done through attention to the subtle yet constant emphases and repetitions we see revealed through participants' actions unfolding over time. In related work on this project, we have been exploring how we might 'name' such dispositions by overlaying Bourdieu's concepts of 'taste' and 'distinction' to ultimately 'characterize' what participants sense as morally right, just and fair (Bourdieu 1984). In Caitlyn's case, we see her SJD as something akin to 'sororal': her commitment to inclusion resonates most strongly for those within her familiar (family-like) boundaries, and those who are different are welcome but are clearly not an 'insider' (family) member of her group.[3]

For research on aspiration, SJDs offer a powerful new lens to investigate the multifaceted nature of pedagogic work – both primary and secondary (Bourdieu and Passeron 1990) – in terms of the significant but un-thought influence that families, communities and, in this case, teachers have on forming aspiration. If, after Sen (2009), aspiration is understood to be the capability to imagine one's own future, the girls in Caitlyn's class are presented with one very particular, highly curated model of what their future might be. Caitlyn's position as the girls' teacher, in a school modelling itself after elite private schools in the same locale and with a number of students there by a process of select entry, contributes to a very narrow range of aspirations. Absent are other 'socially acceptable' alternatives with which the girls might engage or to which they might relate. Those outside Caitlyn's (metaphoric) family, who struggle to connect with the normative aspirational trajectory being offered to them, are subtly othered in their participation in the school, but also in their futures.

However, to simply 'read' the data in this way suggests a certain inevitability about the influence of teachers' dispositions on the formation of students' aspirations. This is where our second point on theory meeting method is most relevant, specifically the use of data-generation techniques that draw teachers' attention to the enactment of their own dispositions. We see these methods as having potential within teacher education as pedagogic tactics to develop a greater critical consciousness of professional practice. In our study, teachers were 'stimulated' (Gass and Mackey 2000) or provoked by replaying the instances of their teaching recorded to video (like that illustrated above), and asked to 'talk through' each episode as it was played back. In Stage 3 of the study, this strategy was extended to viewing video segments of *other* teacher participants' practice. We deliberately selected video clips of practices that we thought might provoke a response, but this time by juxtaposing other teachers' actions with what we knew of the teacher's own practice and context. Our aim was not just to scaffold self-reflection but to engage our participants in evaluations; initially of others and – through this – eventually of themselves. Through a process of 'stimulated critique' (Gale and Molla 2017), the goal was to scaffold teachers' provocations in a way that would draw on 'both criticism and reasoned reflection' (Dant 2003: 7).

By provoking and scaffolding teachers to see and then speak their dispositions, we sought to elicit 'the logic of practical knowledge' (Bourdieu 1990a) rather than normative accounts. The video clips provided participants with a way to revisit their thinking behind what they were doing at a particular time and in a particular place, rather than to fall into rehearsed accounts of practice. Indeed, at times the conversations were purposefully unsettling (Gale and Molla 2017) and at odds with what might have been the teachers' stated commitments or beliefs. However, through this technique, many of the participant teachers were able to engage in further shared conversations about what this might mean for more deliberative, informed teaching moving forward and critical reflection on plans for subsequent lessons. For example, in Caitlyn's case, this included discussion of how her dispositions influence her students' capabilities to imagine their own futures in the context of her lessons. More generally, it helps enable self-awareness of what alternative approaches might be possible, having brought the un-thought into consciousness.

Conclusion

Through outlining one use of Bourdieu's tools in this chapter we aim to advance new ways of researching social justice, focused on how teachers' dispositions influence practices that either assist or hinder the realization of socially just outcomes – including the impact of pedagogic work on the formation of student aspiration. By using the construct of SJDs as an analytic focus, our goal is to develop tools that help better attend to the subtle but recurring and enduring patterns of teachers' work that unfold in the 'un-thoughtness' of everyday schooling, and the lasting impact they may have on learners' formative stages of schooling.

As highlighted in the introduction, such research is timely given the increasing attainment gap in education between students from advantaged and disadvantaged backgrounds, despite many policy makers, school leaders and classroom practitioners being committed to a fairer, more equitable and socially just system of schooling. The challenges in achieving this are numerous and complex. There is a pressing need for new knowledge that goes beyond the current dichotomy in the literature that tends to focus on how greater fairness might be achieved in terms of beliefs (i.e. what teachers, school leaders and policy makers should claim as being most important or valued) and/ or practices (i.e. strategies and programmes that teachers, schools and school systems should do to improve social outcomes). The belief/practice literature fails to address a persistent problem in educational research: the dissonance that often exists between what is said and done, particularly in relation to social justice.

The creation of new knowledge to move our understandings on, depends on new ways of working with data and innovations in research method. This includes both new ways of approaching how data can be *read*, to attend to the unspoken guidance operating between what is said or done, and new techniques to *generate* accounts of dispositions by practitioners themselves. While the former is especially helpful for understanding more deeply how teachers influence aspiration formation, the latter helps move beyond critique to pedagogical solutions for working with practitioners, and scaffolding their ability to speak, and reflect on, the impact of those otherwise un-thought and unspoken dispositions for themselves.

Notes

1   Informed by the work of Amartya Sen (2009), we understand aspiration as a capability to imagine futures (Sellar and Gale 2011; Gale and Parker 2015, 2018).
2   Pseudonyms have been used for all names presented in the data.
3   Another example has been the use of metaphor as a tool to help name and label SJDs as revealed through practice (Mills et al. 2017).

Recommended further reading

Gale, T., and S. Parker (2018), 'Student Aspiration and Transition as Capabilities for Navigating Education Systems', in A. Tarabini and N. Ingram (eds), *Educational Choices, Aspirations and Transitions in Europe*, 32–49, London: Routledge.

Gale, T., C. Mills and R. Cross (2017), 'Socially Inclusive Teaching: Belief, Design and Action as Pedagogic Work', *Journal of Teacher Education*, 68 (3): 345–56.

Gale, T., and T. Molla (2017), 'Deliberations on the Deliberative Professional: Thought-Action, Provocations', in J. Lynch, J. Rowlands, T. Gale and A. Skourdoumbis (eds), *Practice Theory and Education: Diffractive Readings in Professional Practice*, 247–62, London: Routledge.

References

Australian Curriculum, Assessment and Reporting Authority (ACARA) (2010), *My School*, Available online: http://www.myschool.edu.au (accessed 20 May 2011).

Bourdieu, P. (1977), *Outline of a Theory of Practice*, New York: Cambridge University Press.

Bourdieu, P. (1979), *Algeria 1960: The Disenchantment of the World*, Cambridge, MA: Cambridge University Press.

Bourdieu, P. (1984), *Distinction: A Social Critique of the Judgement of Taste*, Cambridge, MA: Harvard University Press.

Bourdieu, P. (1990a), *The Logic of Practice*, Stanford, CA: Stanford University Press.

Bourdieu, P. (1990b), *In Other Words: Essays Towards a Reflexive Sociology*, Stanford, CA: Stanford University Press.

Bourdieu, P., and J.-C. Passeron (1990), *Reproduction in Education, Society, and Culture*, 2nd edn, London: Sage.

Bourdieu, P., and L. Wacquant (1992), *An Invitation to Reflexive Sociology*, Chicago: University of Chicago Press.

Connors, L., and J. McMorrow (2015), *Imperatives in Schools Funding: Equity, Sustainability and Achievement*, Melbourne: Australian Centre for Educational Research.

Dant, T. (2003), *Critical Social Theory: Culture, Society and Critique*, London: Sage.

Dorling, D. (2011), *Injustice: Why Social Inequalities Persist*, Bristol: Policy Press.

ETUC and ETUI (2012), *Benchmarking Working Europe 2012*, Brussels: ETUI.

Gale, T., C. Mills and R. Cross (2017), 'Socially Inclusive Teaching: Belief, Design and Action as Pedagogic Work', *Journal of Teacher Education*, 68 (3): 345–56.

Gale, T., and T. Molla (2017), 'Deliberations on the Deliberative Professional: Thought-Action, Provocations', in J. Lynch, J. Rowlands, T. Gale and A. Skourdoumbis (eds), *Practice Theory and Education: Diffractive Readings in Professional Practice*, 247–62, London: Routledge.

Gale, T., and S. Parker (2015), 'Calculating Student Aspiration: Bourdieu, Spatiality and the Politics of Recognition', *Cambridge Journal of Education*, 45 (1): 81–96.

Gale, T., and S. Parker (2018), 'Student Aspiration and Transition as Capabilities for Navigating Education Systems', in A. Tarabini and N. Ingram (eds), *Educational Choices, Aspirations and Transitions in Europe*, 32–49, London: Routledge.

Gardiner, M. E. (2000), *Critiques of Everyday Life*, London: Routledge.

Gass, S., and A. Mackey (2000), *Stimulated Recall Methodology in Second Language Research*, Mahwah, NJ: Lawrence Erlbaum.

Gonski, D., K. Boston, K. Greiner, C. Lawrence, B. Scales and P. Tannock (2011), *Review of Funding for Schooling: Final Report*, Canberra: Commonwealth of Australia.

Le Donné, N. (2014), 'European Variations in Socioeconomic Inequalities in Students' Cognitive Achievement', *European Sociological Review*, 30 (3): 329–43.

Mills, C., T. Molla, T. Gale, R. Cross, S. Parker and C. Smith (2017), 'Metaphor as a Methodological Tool: Identifying Teachers' Social Justice Dispositions Across Diverse Secondary School Settings', *British Journal of Sociology of Education*, 38 (6): 856–71.

NESSE (2012), *Mind the Gap: Education Inequality Across EU Regions*, Brussels: European Commission.

OECD (2010), *PISA 2009 Results – Overcoming Social Background: Equity in Learning Opportunities and Outcomes (Vol. II)*, Paris: OECD.

Piketty, T. (2014), *Capital in the Twenty-First Century*, Cambridge, MA: Belknap Press of Harvard University Press.

Sellar, S., and T. Gale (2011), 'Mobility, Aspiration, Voice: A New Structure of Feeling for Student Equity in Higher Education', *Critical Studies in Education*, 52 (2): 115–34.

Sen, A. (2009), *The Idea of Justice*, Cambridge, MA: Belknap Press of Harvard University Press.

Teese, R. (2011), *From Opportunity to Outcomes*, Melbourne: Centre for Research on Education Systems.

UNICEF (2010), *The Children Left Behind*, Innocenti Report Card 9, Florence, Italy: UNICEF.

Wilkinson, R., and K. Pickett (2009), *The Spirit Level: Why More Equal Societies Almost Always Do Better*, London: Allen Lane.

Part Five

Bourdieusian Perspectives on Aspirations and Gender

9

'It Was Noticeable So I Changed':
Supergirls, Aspirations and Bourdieu

Tamsin Bowers-Brown

Introduction

In recent years girls have been positioned as winners in the educational game, often depicted as fulfilling their role as 'good pupils' who, through hard work, are able to achieve success in the schooling system (see Mendick, Allen and Harvey 2015). Educational success is embodied by the 'supergirl' who is 'popular, well adjusted, easy going, stress free, college [university] bound, and beyond oppression' (Pomerantz, Raby and Stefanik 2013: 191). Allen reflects on how this discourse has crystallized the configuration of the 'top girls', who she argues are depicted as 'central figures in propagating the neoliberal dream of upward social mobility' (2016: 807). Upward social mobility also requires the so-called supergirl to have 'high' aspirations in line with a doxic expectation that she will invest in herself through her schoolwork and extracurricular activities to ensure that she remains a competitor in 'the game'. The game is constituted by the social practices required to be successful within certain fields; these practices are not equally accessible to all competitors.

Studies which draw on intersectionality are concerned with identifying, discussing and addressing the ways that systems of inequity, including sexism, racism and class bias, intersect to produce complex relations of power and (dis)advantage (Crenshaw 1991; Cho, Crenshaw and McCall 2013). Race, class and gender do not operate as distinct categories of experience but are lived conjointly (Crenshaw 1991) and should be understood as complex, multiple and dynamic. To understand the formation of girls' aspirations as gendered and classed across social and cultural contexts, I operationalize intersectionality. The supergirl status presents a misconception of girls as 'evidence of meritocracy at work' (Shain 2013), which marginalizes intersectional differences and stratified levels of attainment, so that 'persistent gender (as well as class and race) inequalities' are conveniently ignored (Allen 2016: 807). The problematic nature of the 'successful girls' discourse (see for example Harris and Dobson 2015; McRobbie 2009) compelled me to undertake research that explored how girls 'do' education and how they perceive their aspirations (Bowers-Brown 2015, 2016).

Bourdieu discusses how different fields operate as 'games in themselves', each with their own logic requiring players to operationalize different capitals. Therefore, the practices required to be successful in a particular field are tied to the familiarity of the habitus in that field, in this instance the schooling system. The odds of successfully negotiating the field of formal schooling are stacked heavily in favour of those whose habitus has been structured by an accumulation of capitals within primary socialization (in the home). As Bourdieu asserts: 'The earlier a player enters the game and the less he is aware of the associated learning ... the greater is his ignorance of all that is tacitly granted through his investment in the field' (1990: 67). The misrecognition of what is tacitly granted allows the field of schooling to be seen as a ladder enabling upward social mobility, offering an equal opportunity of success to all those who work hard, when in fact it often does the opposite, 'reproducing the condition of its own perpetuation' (Bourdieu 1990: 67). This reproduction occurs because the inequalities that skew the game in favour of those with a practical sense for the game are not addressed by policy makers as a structural issue of inequality, rather as an individual deficit (Spohrer, Stahl and Bowers-Brown 2017).

In this chapter I explore how the expectations of the supergirl subject position are perpetuated by practices of formal schooling. I draw on data from discussions I had with girls in one state co-educational comprehensive secondary school, Greenlea, in the North of England (see also Bowers-Brown 2016). I did not wish to explore the differences between boys' and girls' aspirations; instead, I aimed to explore how girls 'do' education and how this relates to their aspirations. I drew upon Bourdieu's theories along with an intersectional approach which enabled me to think beyond my immediate interpretation of the girls' talk and to understand their expectations of reaching their aspirations in the context of broader societal issues. In the next section I demonstrate how I came to use Bourdieu despite his relative lack of engagement with issues of gender.

Thinking gender and aspiration through Bourdieu's theory

Although there is little engagement with gender in the corpus of Bourdieu's scholarship he does argue that there is a 'double-edged privilege' awarded to men which endows on them the capability to play social games which largely involve 'some form of domination'. This capability relies on skills which are 'socially instituted and instructed', inculcated early on through the 'rites of institution' (Bourdieu 2002a: 75). Dillabough confirms that 'male domination can be traced to historical ideas that are embodied by social actors in the present' (2004: 494). Although Bourdieu's evaluation of masculine domination still holds resonance in contemporary society, as Lovell recognizes there is also 'female–female domination across the lines of class' (2004: 50) and this is where my interest lies. Analysis drawing on intersectionality avoids reductionist attempts to claim homogeneity merely for categorical expediency. Furthermore, combining intersectionality with Bourdieu's theory of practice enabled me to think about both the individual, conceptions of femininity, and society in tandem and to understand how the system is inherently skewed to perpetuate middle-class advantage (Reay 2017).

Specifically, Bourdieu's theory of practice helped me to understand how girls' choices are situated in a web of opportunities that are influenced by their habitus, field and the capitals to which they have access: [(habitus) (capital)] + (field) = practice (Bourdieu 1984: 101). This formula helped me to identify inequality that is concealed within practices, enabling a mode of interrogation that looks beyond individual deficit. To this end, I drew on both Bourdieu and an intersectional approach to demonstrate how inequalities exist in ways that compound intersectional disadvantage and indeed purposefully ensure the avoidance of 'instantaneous mechanical equilibria between agents' (Bourdieu 1986: 15).

By using Bourdieu's approach to forms of capital I was able, through my analysis, to identify the unequal distribution of valued capitals as well as the intersectional differences in the experiences of my participants. Both theoretical approaches, I believe, enabled me to understand how some girls rejected aspirations which were privileged by the school but that they perceived to be unattainable in favour of the probable: 'to refuse what is anyway denied and to will the inevitable' (Bourdieu 1990: 54), while others understood that there was a game to play and took deliberate action to ensure they remained competitors, continuing to participate in what Bourdieu terms the *illusio* (see Threadgold, this volume).

Like Bourdieu, my area of research is political, situated in a commitment to challenge inequality in educational opportunity and outcomes. For me, as a researcher, Bourdieu's (2002b) contention that 'sociology is a martial art' holds great resonance and has become central to my positionality. The role of sociology in defending those who face the greatest societal inequalities is integral to my beliefs about the need to highlight and make explicit systemic injustices. In working with these principles, my recent research has attempted to both employ and extend Bourdieu's theoretical concepts in order to offer explanations for the inequity that is evident across formal education systems in relation to process and outcomes (see for example Reay 2017; Morrin 2016; Stahl 2015; James 2015; Bathmaker et al. 2016). Considering critical analysis of aspiration and how we conceptualize aspiration, I was particularly drawn to the work of Allen and Hollingsworth, who highlight that there is a 'deficit construction of aspiration which holds young people responsible for their own (lack of) ambition and (im)mobility in education and work' (2013: 501) rather than considering the structural factors that mean that their aspirations become difficult to achieve. Bourdieu's theory of practice and the relationship between habitus, field and the forms of capital ensures that success or failure is not attributed to individual excellence or deficit. Rather, Bourdieu's theories address the power dynamics of institutions and the legitimacy bestowed on different experiences. As McKenzie argues, 'Bourdieu's model of capital exchange can expose the mechanisms of how power works to advantage some groups whilst disadvantaging others' (2016: 31). Bourdieu's approach, therefore, seemed appropriate in ensuring that my analysis did not lead to a hierarchical evaluation that reinforced deficit labels and notions of 'escape' from a working-class background (Francis and Hey 2009). In the next section I reflect on how I operationalized the combination of intersectionality and Bourdieu's concepts.

Operationalizing habitus, field and the forms of capital

Bourdieu uses the concept of habitus to refer to the non-reflective human actions that each person undertakes because of their 'habitual expectations and assumptions' (Crossley 2005: 108). Habitus is not enacted; it is an embodiment of certain behaviours and actions that are then undertaken without thought. Bourdieu writes that the habitus does not lead to considered behaviours, rather 'spontaneity without consciousness or will' (1990: 73). In relation to aspiration, habitus, as a tool, compelled me to question whether certain decisions would be ruled out by my participants before they were even considered either because of a perceived misalignment of the field with their habitus or due to no prior experience or knowledge of that field. Young people's future choices may be limited to what appears probable if the options that are considered are determined by their familiarity. For the young women I spoke to in the sixth form this was not the case, whereas conversations I had with younger pupils indicated that subject choices were made at an early stage that would limit their options later on.

Nevertheless, for Bourdieu the 'habitus becomes active in relation to a field, the same habitus can lead to very different practices and stances depending on the state of the field' (Reay 2004: 432). As 'fields' become more familiar to an individual, their habitus will begin to acclimatize. Therefore, according to a Bourdieusian logic, practices may have to be adapted or indeed 'performed' in certain situations to compensate for the unfamiliarity, and these performances are not part of the habitus at the point of origin but are understood as part of the acclimatizing process or behaving as is seen fit for the particular logic of the field. These performances may go against the habitual actions of an individual in order to meet the expectations of those in the field.

In order to fully operationalize Bourdieu's theory of practice, the researcher needs to adeptly consider habitus and field along with the forms of capital. The difference in possession and volume of capitals, Bourdieu argues, is what distinguishes the 'conditions of existence' of the different social classes. As well as social, economic and cultural capital, Bourdieu also refers to the closely associated 'academic capital' or the 'guaranteed product of the combined effects of cultural transmission by the family and cultural transmission by the school (the efficiency of which depends on the amount of cultural capital directly inherited from the family)' (Bourdieu 1984: 23). Considering academic capital, I found, is important to the study of the supergirl phenomenon because supergirl status assumes high volumes of academic capital. The influences on aspirations for the girls in my study could not then be isolated to their schooling experience and I had to find different ways of asking them about life outside of school.

Methodology and the study

In *The Weight of the World* (1999), Bourdieu discusses how the writing up of method can often be misleading; it offers a précis of the research that was undertaken, formalizing the process which in reality may have been very different to the way it appears in the researcher's presentation. Bourdieu writes of the lack of usefulness of discussing the methodological principles of research, 'often derived from the desire to imitate the external signs of the rigor of the most established scientific disciplines' when in practice, as with my own research, this 'does not do justice to what has been done' (1999: 607).

Drawing on an interpretivist, qualitative approach in gathering my data I used a variety of methods to understand the formation of aspirations (see Bowers-Brown 2015, 2016). The research was undertaken in a comprehensive co-educational state-funded secondary school, which I have given the pseudonym 'Greenlea'. The area where Greenlea Comprehensive School is situated is more affluent than its surrounding geographical areas; the school's position in league tables is also higher than other schools within a five-mile radius. The sixth form, for pupils aged 16–18 who wish to pursue advanced level (A level) qualifications,[1] attracts pupils who have not previously attended the school. The school has high expectations of its pupils and a strong adherence to policies that support the school inspectorate's expectations of outstanding academic achievement. The girls I observed and spoke with were aged 12–18, largely of white British ethnicity but of mixed socio-economic backgrounds; the sixth-form participants all self-identified as working class and spoke freely about the influence of their background on their aspirations.

In keeping with an intersectionality framework, my analysis recognizes the multidimensional disadvantage (and privilege) that was articulated according to the sociopolitical context of the time that the research was undertaken; my research findings are therefore partial, dynamic and situated in multiple, complex processes. As a researcher, I consider the perspectives that are drawn from my research participants, both in and outside the education system, as their representation of 'truths' as personally experienced. In interpreting these truths I valued Bourdieu's call for a reflexive approach. I found it imperative to be reflexive in analysing the data on the aspirations of young women in order to avoid preconceptions determining the outcome of the research. My research methodology, therefore, reflected an epistemological view that 'truths' are 'experiential, personal, subjective and socially constructed' (Wellington et al. 2005: 102). Bourdieu calls for researchers to strive 'to make reflexive use of the findings of social science' (1999: 608). I applied a reflexive approach to my research data, which involved my own independent decisions about the interpretation and representation of the data (Hammond and Wellington 2013: 59), but analysis also occurred through the collaborative practices of discussion situated beyond the moment of data collection, with research colleagues and the research participants. Verification and further discussion with participants ensured that interpretation was a collaborative process with reflexivity at its core.

Using theory to interrogate the data

After completing focus groups and interviews with pupils the discussions were transcribed and organized in order to identify patterns which were then labelled as belonging to a particular 'theme'. As themes emerged from my data I found myself 'cycling back and forth between theory and data to identify patterns and regularities' (Barton and Hamilton 1998: 69). This process – although I did not realize it at the time – was Bourdieusian, 'a spiral between theory, empirical work and back to reformulating theory again' (Maher, Harker and Wilkes 1990: 3).

As an introduction to the focus group discussion, pupils were asked to think about anyone or anything that had influenced or influences their decision-making and to situate them on a 'target circle' (see Figure 9.1). Those components

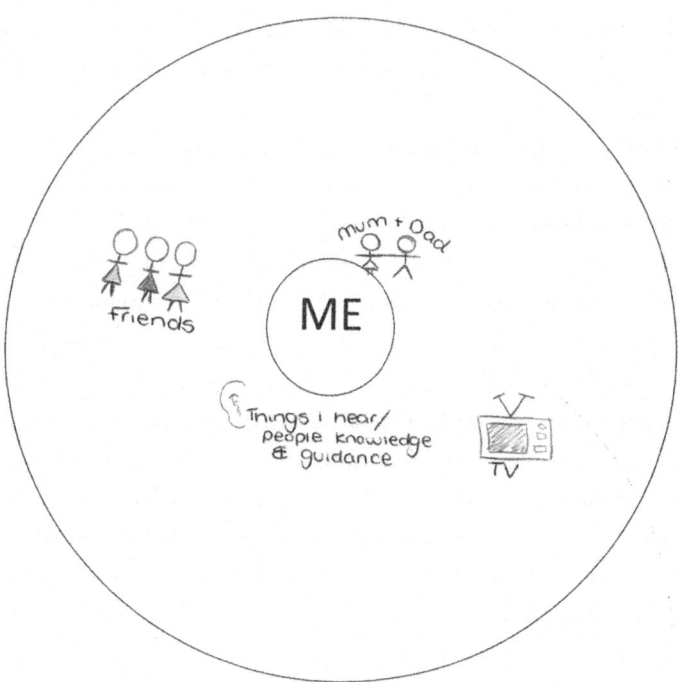

Figure 9.1 Map of important influences (Hannah, Year 12)

who were closest to the centre and the word 'ME' were considered to be most influential (Spencer and Pahl 2006). This activity promoted discussion about how various factors/components influence girls' aspirations. In figure 9.1, we see an example from Hannah, a Year 12 pupil who was in the process of making decisions about her post-16 opportunities.

Throughout my research, the young women discussed influences on their aspirations in relation to their access to different forms of capital: extracurricular activities, people that they knew and the experiences that they had. These discussions assisted in understanding the origins of their aspirations as well as their relationship with the social world. Bourdieu's forms of capital were therefore entirely relevant to understanding how these experiences had shaped their aspirations, with social and cultural capital in particular being evident in the types of influences that girls expressed as important in relation to their hopes for the future. For example, Chloe, who spent most of her time outside of school looking after horses, discussed how this motivated her to study: 'Like, I sort of want to do textiles in technology because I like horses and, like, I'd rather, like, make stuff for horses' (Chloe, Year 9). Her aspirations to work with horses had led her to see the value of her studies only through the lens of how they would assist her in reaching her goal. Although participation in activities influenced some pupils' aspirations, conversely a perceived lack of participation in 'noteworthy activities' was seen to close off certain fields (Bowers-Brown 2016).

Familiarity because of exposure to activities or people was a prominent theme; accepting the familiar, or making choices because of their familiarity, can be linked with Bourdieu's concept of habitus and field, but we also see the influence of familial networks or social capital on decision-making. When considering how aspirations are formed, the habitus – in constant negotiation with field and capitals – reproduces social positions: 'It adjusts itself to a probable future which it anticipates and helps to bring about because it reads it directly in the present of the presumed world' (Bourdieu 1990: 64). This often leads to choices that may incline 'agents to cut their coats according to their cloth, and so to become the accomplices of the processes that tend to make the probable a reality' (1990: 65). For example Casey, a Year 9 pupil, discussed her consideration of a career in administration in the police force: 'I've got parents and friends and people that are either doing the job or have done the job. Well, my mum worked there and then it's just people like her friends.'

Probable realities were evident also in the way that one girl accepted advice from her mother as a fait accompli. She believed that she could not undertake a course of study that she perceived to involved sustained academic work and her mother's confirmation of this meant she closed down the opportunity:

> Me and my mum decided for me not to do Business Studies because I know and my mum knows that I wouldn't do the work and wouldn't get the grades because I'm not like the sort of person who can do a lot of work. (Lucie, Year 10)

However, this was not always the case, and many of the young women I researched also discussed their desire to have different experiences to their parents, most notably in the discussions of first-generation applicants to university. It is important to note here that the discussions about going to university were not about moving away from a community, or 'escaping' a certain lifestyle (Reay 2001) but furthering employment opportunities and making their family proud. Indeed, several respondents discussed either wanting or needing to stay at home in order to continue their studies.

An important finding was how the perceived futures discussed through the focus groups differed significantly from the private disclosure of hopes that were presented in the survey which offered more anonymity. Despite a number of the young women identifying their aspirations to go to university, the survey responses also demonstrated 'private hopes', goals related to family, marriage and happiness which were not discussed in the focus groups. This was perhaps because aspirations to have a family or, as one of the respondents stated, 'be a happily married housewife' did not align with the supergirl subjectivities that were expected of them. Nevertheless, family was clearly an important influence in almost all the target circles. The alignment of the data with theory is discussed further in the following section.

Academic capital, supergirl status and aspiration to higher education

At Greenlea Comprehensive School, situated in an affluent area, I observed institutional attempts to mould the habituses of its pupils to accept that the gold standard in terms of aspiration is to go to university. Similar to Ingram's research, I found that 'pupils are shaped to conform to these dispositions' (2009: 426). Indeed Greenlea propagates the value of individual success, which imbues in its learners an understanding of self-responsibility and self-monitoring through the use and ownership of individual target grades. Value was endowed on those pupils whose subject positions demonstrated a habitus that incorporated academic capital and therefore complied with the rules of the field. However, the 'pressures to succeed are frequently transmuted into pressures not to fail' (Jackson 2006: 49), and this led to anxieties that reinforced their need to ensure target grades were met.

Despite the anxieties that the expectation of high attainment placed upon them, the young women anticipated that the effort would enable them to pursue their intended aspirations for the future and therefore they continued to 'play the game'. Where the girls in my study had aspirations that aligned with those of the school, they were able to use the capitals available to them within the school to follow pathways that they believed would enable their aspirations to evolve. Therefore, operationalizing Bourdieusian concepts alongside intersectionality allowed me to situate the practices of the school and its pupils in a wider frame of reference and to understand how the school implicitly supported the aspirational supergirl status through its hierarchical values and emphasis on progression to higher education.

Bourdieu's theory and intersectionality can be operationalized to demonstrate how aspiration is constructed in a way that rewards and misrecognizes privilege. The young women's lives outside of school, and their accumulation of valued capitals, demonstrated that aspirations were not equally accessible. The data indicates that the girls from working-class backgrounds understood this inequity but also that there was a 'game' to be played and they attempted to participate in the hope that the long-term gains would effectively serve their aspirations. Similarly to Allen's research, the findings reveal how young people are expected to aspire but are subject to 'conditions that place (ever greater) limits on agentic practice' (2016: 817).

Zara's aspirations

Bourdieu argues that when the habitus feels unease in unfamiliar fields it can become 'expressed in behaviours such as avoidance or unconscious adjustments such as the correction of one's accent' (2000: 184). For the purposes of this chapter I draw on one particular participant, Zara. Although not the only one to discuss the difficulties of transition into sixth-form, she articulated very clearly the processes of reflection and adaptation that she underwent in order to achieve her 'supergirl' status and indeed how this enabled her to aspire to study at university.

Yang (2014: 1530) argues that 'change in a field rarely happens suddenly' and therefore the relationship between habitus and field returns to one of 'adjustment' rather than 'revolt', or what Bourdieu calls hysteresis when there is severe disjuncture between habitus and field. In theorizing the relational nature of social class, Sayer highlights how 'accent, language, taste and bearing' (2005: 70) form part of the judgement of a person's social standing. This was evident in Zara's narrative, in which she highlighted class pathologization and discussed the need to change in order to aspire to her goals of a successful career: 'My accent and stuff was just really awful. I don't know, I sounded really common, if that sounds really cocky. I sounded really common and then I came to Greenlea and then like it was noticeable, so I changed.'

Reay discusses this adjustment process as a 'refashioning of the working-class self into a middle-class persona' (2003: 62). Kulz too discusses how the pupils in her research study were expected to '"adjust" themselves to accrue value' (2014: 685) in line with institutional habitus. Zara's stance demonstrates how she actively understood the game and took action to 'refashion' herself in order to fit in with her peer group and meet the institutional expectation of the 'supergirl'. Her comments reflect that there is an expectation or perception that there is a particular way of being that aligns with what it is to be a successful girl in the field of education. Zara needed to adapt if, according to her, she was to achieve success:

> I came from like being really streetwise and being really mouthy, to being really quiet and really like hardworking, not that I wasn't anyway, but you know, and I wanted to like have a future for myself and I didn't like looking at other people in the area and stuff. (Zara, Year 13)

As other research on working-class women confirms (Skeggs 2004), social class pathologization contributes to how aspirations are formed. Zara also highlighted how negative preconceptions about the council estate where she lived culminated in a 'general attitude' or prejudice: 'Oh you come from this estate so you're not really going to get a good job. You're not going to get a good career.'

In order to gain a place at university the doxic representation of the supergirl stretched beyond the acquisition of a scholarly habitus (Watkins and Noble 2013) and the girls understood that they would need to present themselves as accruing capital beyond their educational qualifications in order to pursue higher education. For some young women this was more difficult to access than for others; Skeggs (2004: 91) refers to this as a process whereby self-production and the resources required to achieve it are 'class making'. The girls in my study, including Zara, understood the rules of the game and could also see that their access to capitals was unequal. The expectation by the system of participation in often expensive forms of 'dominant symbolic' culture demonstrates how symbolic violence works to misrecognize middle-class privilege, judging it rather as evidence of motivation or engagement rather than wealth (Skeggs 2004: 88). Zara, like other working-class girls aspiring to university, was arguably placed in a position of negotiating her perceived lack of value as the institutional logic is not concerned with disparity of access to the forms of capital. Nonetheless, Bourdieu claims that investment in the game, or 'the illusio', requires the conviction that the game is worth playing or as Bourdieu states 'is worth the candle' (1998: 76). Zara, after all, still believed that the game was worth playing. Despite recognizing the systemic inequity and how they would have to disassociate themselves from facets of working-class culture, the girls in my study were complicit in accepting the rules of the game because exclusion from the game was seen to be worse than adhering and accepting the symbolic violence of the system.

Discussion

This chapter shows how Bourdieu's theory, used alongside intersectionality, opens up new spaces to explore how aspirations are gendered and shaped in and by schooling practices. In critically thinking about aspiration, the Bourdieusian notion that certain opportunities are 'probable' even though others are 'possible' was helpful, but I also saw how girls maintained their aspirations by adapting themselves through the cultivation of the capitals that the field requires in order to achieve 'supergirl' status. In so far as habitus inclines 'agents to cut their coats according to their cloth' which in due turn makes the 'probable a reality'; the girls in my study demonstrated that some would reject the inevitable (Bourdieu 1990: 64–5). However, for those young women who had succeeded academically, attempting to embody the supergirl subjectivity and rejecting the inevitable came with a requirement for self-adaptation. The data indicates that, particularly for the girls in the sixth form who had entered a field that was unfamiliar, there was a requirement to acclimatize but the academic disposition embodied in their habitus had offered them familiarity in an unfamiliar field (see Reay, Crozier and Clayton 2009). Zara discussed how she had actively pursued supergirl status in order to live a life that would not see her in the poverty she had experienced in her early years. Nonetheless, the process of self-adaptation left me as the researcher with a feeling of unease and anger. The process of avoiding social reproduction relied heavily on habitus transformation – often in line with the status of the field of higher education and its doxic expectations of the supergirl. The research left me with questions about the symbolically violent nature of the higher education application process which requires evidence of adherence the dominant symbolic order. While employing Bourdieu shows how social class is powerful, drawing on an intersectional approach, Omi and Winant argue that 'race, class, and gender are not fixed and discrete categories ... . They overlap, intersect, and infuse with others in countless ways' (1994: 68) especially when they rub up against institutional logics.

Conclusion

The expectation that all girls will embody supergirl aspirations misrecognizes the differences in privilege that create an uneven platform to achieve this subjectivity and for many this may involve self-adaptation. Using Bourdieu's concepts allowed me to understand how young people negotiate the dominant discourses of deficit when aspiring. Combining these with intersectionality enabled me to interrogate the more complex relationships often hidden in discussions of high-achieving girls. Although Bourdieu has been criticized for a lack of engagement with gender, academics interested in intersectionality have engaged with his work (Fowler 2003) and his tools can be easily combined with other frameworks (see Ayling and Adewumi, this volume). In my research discussions of aspiration could not be properly understood without recognizing the structural intersectional inequalities faced by different sectors of society. Therefore, in the study of working-class young women's aspirations, the combination of intersectionality and Bourdieusian theory offers us the opportunity to highlight certain opportunities, how aspirational discourses work, as well as what may get sacrificed along the way.

Note

1   In the UK, at age 16, pupils can choose where they intend to study/pursue further training. Not all schools have their own sixth-form centre.

Recommended further reading

Allen, K. (2016), 'Top Girls Navigating Austere Times: Interrogating Youth Transitions Since the Crisis', *Journal of Youth Studies*, 19 (6): 805–82.

Allen, K., H. Mendick, L. Harvey, and A. Ahmad (2018), *Celebrity, Aspiration and Contemporary Youth: Education and Inequality in an Era of Austerity*, London: Bloomsbury Press.

Spohrer, K. (2016), 'Negotiating and Contesting 'Success': Discourses of Aspiration in a UK Secondary School', *Discourse: Studies in the Cultural Politics of Education*, 37 (3): 411–25.

References

Allen, K. (2016), 'Top Girls Navigating Austere Times: Interrogating Youth Transitions Since the Crisis', *Journal of Youth Studies*, 19 (6): 805–20.

Allen, K., and S. Hollingworth (2013), 'Social Class, Place and Urban Young People's Aspirations for Work in the Knowledge Economy: "Sticky Subjects" or "Cosmopolitan Creatives?"', *Urban Studies*, 50 (3): 499–517.

Barton, D., and M. Hamilton (1998), *Local Literacies: Reading and Writing in One Community*, London: Routledge.

Bathmaker, A.-M., N. Ingram, J. Abrahams, T. Hoare, R. Waller and H. Bradley (2016), *Higher Education, Social Class and Social Mobility: The Degree Generation*, London: Palgrave.

Bourdieu, P. (1984), *Distinction: A Social Critique of the Judgement of Taste*, Cambridge: Cambridge University Press.

Bourdieu, P. (1986), 'The Forms of Capital', in J. Richardson (ed.), *The Handbook of Theory and Research for the Sociology of Education*, 241–58, Westport, CT: Greenwood.

Bourdieu, P. (1990), *The Logic of Practice*, Cambridge: Polity Press.

Bourdieu, P. (1998), *Practical Reason: On the Theory of Action*, Cambridge: Polity Press.

Bourdieu, P. (2000), *Pascalian Meditations*, Cambridge: Polity Press.

Bourdieu, P. (2002a), *Masculine Domination*, Cambridge: Polity Press.

Bourdieu, P. (2002b), 'Sociology is a Martial Art', *YouTube*, posted 13 September 2013. Available online: http://www.youtube.com/watch?v=_9PCp9oKPRw (accessed 8 November 2017).

Bourdieu, P. et al. (1999), *The Weight of the World, Social Suffering in Contemporary Society*. Cambridge: Polity Press.

Bowers-Brown, T. (2015), 'How Girls "Do" Education: Achievement, Choices and Hopes for the Future', PhD thesis, University of Sheffield, Sheffield.

Bowers-Brown, T. (2016), '"It's Like If You Don't Go to Uni, You Fail in Life": Bourdieu, Decision Making and the Forms of Capital', in J. Thatcher, N. Ingram, C. Burke and J. Abrahams (eds), *Bourdieu: The Next Generation*, 55–72, London: Routledge.

Cho, S., K. Crenshaw and L. McCall (2013), 'Toward a Field of Intersectionality Studies: Theory, Applications, and Praxis', *Intersectionality: Theorizing Power, Empowering Theory*, 38 (4): 785–810.

Crenshaw, K. (1991), 'Review: Mapping the Margins: Intersectionality, Identity Politics, and Violence against Women of Color', *Stanford Law Review*, 43 (6): 1241–99.

Crossley, N. (2005), *Key Concepts in Critical Social Theory*, London: Sage.

Dillabough, J. (2004). 'Class, Culture and the "Predicaments of Masculine Domination": Pierre Bourdieu's Encounter with Contemporary Feminist Sociology', *British Journal of Sociology of Education*, 25 (4): 489–506.

Fowler, B. (2003) 'Mapping the Obituary: Notes Towards a Bourdieusian Interpretation' in Adkins, L. and B Skeggs (2005) *Feminism after Bourdieu*, 148–72, Oxford: Blackwells.

Francis, B., and V. Hey (2009) 'Talking Back to Power: Snowballs in Hell and the Imperative of Insisting on Structural Explanations', *Gender and Education*, 21 (2) 225–32.

Hammond, M., and J. Wellington (2013), *Research Methods: The Key Concepts*, Abingdon: Routledge.

Harris, A., and A. Dobson (2015), Theorizing Agency in Post-Girl Power Times, *Journal of Media and Cultural Studies* 29 (2), 145–56.

Ingram, N. (2009), 'Working-Class Boys, Educational Success and the Misrecognition of Working – Class Culture', *British Journal of Sociology of Education*, 30 (4): 421–34.

Jackson, C. (2006) *'Lads' and 'ladettes' in school: Gender and a Fear of Failure*, Maidenhead: Open University Press.

James, D. (2015), 'How Bourdieu Bites Back: Recognising Misrecognition in Education and Educational Research', *Cambridge Journal of Education*, 45 (1): 97–112.

Kulz, C. (2014), '"Structure Liberates?": Mixing for Mobility and the Cultural Transformation of "Urban Children" in a London Academy', *Ethnic and Racial Studies*, 37 (4): 685–701.

Lovell, T. (2004) Bourdieu, Class and Gender. 'The Return of the Living Dead?' in Adkins, L. and B. Skeggs, (2004) *Feminism after Bourdieu*, Oxford: Blackwell Publishing.

Mahar, C., R. Harker and C. Wilkes (1990), 'The basic theoretical position', in R. Harker, C. Maher and C. Wilkes (eds), *An Introduction to the Work of Pierre Bourdieu: The Practice of Theory*, 1–25, London: Macmillan.

McKenzie, L. (2016), 'Narrative, Ethnography and Class Inequality: Taking Bourdieu into a British Council Estate', in J. Thatcher, N. Ingram, C. Burke and J. Abrahams (eds), *Bourdieu: The Next Generation*, 25–36, London: Routledge.

McRobbie, A. 2009, *The Aftermath of Feminism: Gender, Culture, and Social Change*, London: Sage.

Mendick, H., K. Allen and L. Harvey (2015), '"We Can Get Everything We Want If We Try Hard": Young People, Celebrity, Hard Work', *British Journal of Educational Studies*, 63 (2): 161–78.

Morrin, K. (2016), 'Unresolved Reflections: Bourdieu, Haunting and Struggling with Ghosts', in J. Thatcher, N. Ingram, C. Burke and J. Abrahams (eds), *Bourdieu: The Next Generation*, 123–39, London: Routledge.

Omi, M., and Winant, H. (1994), *Racial Formation in the United States*, New York: Routledge.

Pomerantz, S., R. Raby and A. Stefanik (2013), 'Girls Run the World? Caught between Sexism and Postfeminism in School', *Gender & Society*, 27 (2): 185–207.

Reay, D. (2001), 'Finding or Losing Yourself? Working Class Relationships to Education' *Journal of Education Policy*, 16 (4): 333–46.

Reay, D. (2003), 'A Risky Business?: Mature Working Class Women Students and Access to Higher Education' *Gender and Education* 15 (3): 301–18.

Reay, D. (2004), '"It's All Becoming Habitus": Beyond the Habitual Use of Habitus in Educational Research', *British Journal of Sociology of Education*, 25 (4): 431–44.

Reay, D. (2017), *Miseducation*, Cambridge: Polity Press.

Reay, D., G. Crozier and J. Clayton (2009), '"Strangers in Paradise"? Working-Class Students in Elite Universities', *Sociology*, 43 (6): 1103–21.

Sayer, A. (2005), *The Moral Significance of Class*, Cambridge: Cambridge University Press.

Shain, F. (2013), '"The Girl Effect": Exploring Narratives of Gendered Impacts and Opportunities in Neoliberal Development', *Sociological Research Online*, 18 (2): 1–11.

Skeggs, B. (2004) *Exchange, Value and Affect: Bourdieu and The 'Self'* in L. Adkins and B. Skeggs (2005), *Feminism after Bourdieu*, Oxford, Blackwells.

Spencer, L., and R. E. Pahl (2006), *Rethinking Friendship: Hidden Solidarities Today*, Princeton, Princeton University Press.

Spohrer, K., G. Stahl and T. Bowers-Brown (2017), 'Constituting Neoliberal Subjects? "Aspiration" as Technology of Government in UK Policy Discourse', *Journal of Education Policy*, online before print 15 June. doi:10.1080/02680939.2017.1336573

Stahl, G. (2015), *Identity, Neoliberalism and Aspiration: Educating White Working-Class Boys*, London: Routledge.

Watkins, M., and Noble, G. (2013), Disposed to Learn: Schooling, Ethnicity and the Scholarly Habitus, London: Bloomsbury.

Wellington, J. J., Bathmaker, A., Hunt, C., McCulloch, G. and Sikes, P. (2005), *Sage Study Skills: Succeeding with Your Doctorate*, London: SAGE Publications Ltd.

Yang, Y. (2014) Bourdieu, Practice and Change: Beyond the Criticism of Determinism, *Educational Philosophy and Theory* 46 (14), 1522–40.

10

Bourdieu Plus: Understanding the Creation of Agentic, Aspirational Girl Subjects in Elite Schools

Joan Forbes and Claire Maxwell

Introduction

This chapter examines the social and intellectual habitus of Wagril (a pseudonym), an elite 'all-through' (ages 3–18) school for girls, located in Scotland. In what follows we operationalize theory to explore how elite education can facilitate the development and realization of aspirations. Through drawing on Bourdieu's concept of habitus (e.g. Bourdieu 1977, 1996), we examine how the Wagril institutional habitus works spatio-temporally to extend the family habitus and, in doing so, supports the emergence of girls' agentic selves. The girls' belief in their capacity to act, and the examples set by those who successfully achieve within their families and through the school, is critical in fostering their aspirations and a surety about the future in terms of higher education, work and social networks (Maxwell and Aggleton 2013a; Forbes and Lingard 2015).

We argue that Wagril is a carefully constructed school space that combines the academic with more practical experiences. The school's dining room, for instance, combines the 'civilizing' and largely socio-community practices of eating together with hearing from 'old girls' about the future world that awaits today's Wagrilians. Families are regularly invited to join students and teachers in these events. These are carefully constructed to align students' (family) experiences with the institutional culture (i.e. the habitus and field) in order to embed this developing habitus of agentic aspiration and make it a more durable part of the habitus.

This chapter is informed by our previous work on the elite education of girls in Scotland and England. Wagril was one of the three schools involved in an earlier study of elite education in Scotland, the *Scottish Independent Schools Project* (SISP) (see for example Forbes and Weiner 2008). The SISP project used a case study methodology, comprising a number of different data collection tools – document analysis, observations, field notes, semi-structured interviews and a short questionnaire (see Forbes and Weiner 2014). Wagril's students are predominantly day pupils who reside locally, within the limits of the city in which the school is based, as well as the surrounding rural areas. It has accommodation for about fifty boarders from wider afield in Scotland and other countries. The ethnic profile of Wagril is predominantly white Scottish and white British.

We have extended elements of the SISP project, particularly our work at Wagril, through our current *Leading Women* study – where we focus on how female head teachers conceptualize elite education and lead their schools. Some of the interview data analysed here comes from the latter research, where we reinterviewed Wagril's now retired head teacher. We have also drawn on our first interview with the head teacher, the student survey data (of all 13–14-year-olds in the school) and school documentation (from magazines, prospectuses and their websites) from SISP.

Following Bourdieu, we work *with* the concept of habitus – both as a method for analysing our data and as the focal point of what it is we are studying (Reay 2004). Habitus is understood here as the embodiment of particular historical cultural experiences that shape dispositions, which, in turn, may drive certain practices. We conceive of all practices as enactments of agency, and highlight the role of affect in this process (Maxwell and Aggleton 2014a). Affect here, we argue, shapes and characterizes relations between people, as well as people and objects. We see affect as a different concept to emotions, which captures the kinds of feelings that are experienced, or observed on or within the body/a person (Maxwell and Aggleton 2013c). Thus, Clegg (2013) argues that emotions are something people have, but these are socially constituted by the affective structures that shape how these 'emotions' are experienced.

The habitus is initially strongly shaped by family (Reay 1998, 2004; Archer et al. 2012), but is subsequently further embedded or challenged through a subject's interactions with different fields. Where family dispositions align with the institutional habitus of the school (Bourdieu 1996: 44), we argue that this particular type of orientation to the self, others and the future is more likely to 'stick' (Maxwell and Aggleton 2014b). Ahmed emphasizes that affect is 'what sticks' (2010: 29), so we see the affective nature of the spaces created within the school and the relations being fostered there as central to the process.

Another central element in our deployment of Bourdieu's theorizations of habitus is his emphasis on how the past is likely to play a role in informing the future. For Bourdieu, the habitus is the product of history; history produces individuals and collective practices. The 'system of dispositions' constitutes 'a past which survives in the present and tends to perpetuate itself into the future' (1977: 82). Thus, in our research we examine closely how family has shaped the habitus of the girls studying at Wagril, and then trace how the habitus becomes challenged, further embedded and/or moulded through their time at the school. The interactions between family and school habitus, in turn, prepare the ground for the dispositions the girls take with them into their future lives (Bourdieu 1977; Maxwell and Aggleton 2014b). Anterior family and institutional influences are therefore 'restructured but not erased' (Brubaker 1993: 226) as these privileged young women move into higher education and work, and start their own families. In this chapter we argue that, where family and institutional habitus are closely aligned, it is more likely that a fairly clearly articulated set of dispositions and congruent practices will emerge that inform future desires, interactions and destinations.

Extending Bourdieu's conceptual toolkit, we understand the relationship between habitus and aspiration as particular spatio-temporal investments constituting specific ideals and commitments towards the future. Thus, students' aspirations for expected futures are already present, generated in the spatio-temporalities of their habitus. In the words of Bourdieu, the future is already to a certain extent inscribed in the present; today's practices significantly influence what is to come. However, our research has focused on seeking to understand more fully the ways in which the present interacts with the past and therefore embeds and/or remoulds the habitus of young women being educated in elite schools. In this way we can start to understand more fully the processes of social reproduction, but also potentially of social mobility, that are facilitated through different kinds of elite education – as young women/people take another step through the 'institutional wormholes' (Nespor 2014) of elite reproduction.

Despite the intense debates among Bourdieusian scholars about whether the concepts of family habitus and institutional habitus are coherent with his theoretical framing (see for example Reay 1998; Atkinson 2011; Burke, Emmerich and Ingram 2013; Tarabini, Curran and Fontdevila 2016), for our purposes, we find both notions helpful in thinking about the effect the young women's immersion in these two spaces has on their orientations to the future. We seek to understand how family and school offer particular ways of knowing and being, and specifically how the interactions between these two spaces – of family and school – unsettle or reinforce their understandings of the world, their desires, their interactions with others and the trajectories they seek to forge into their futures.

The concepts of both family habitus and institutional habitus are critical for us in making sense of processes of social reproduction (Bourdieu 1977). However, in our so-called 'Bourdieu-plus' approach, we seek to provide further insights into the underpinnings of Wagril's particular articulation of an elite aspirational habitus by drawing on other theoretical inflections, such as those relating to space, the sticky-ness of affect and a reflexive disposition.

Family and aspired-to futures in school: Habitus knittings that stick

> I worked with the architecture ... two listed buildings ... the buildings are just as much part of the learning ... and what we did was ... turn it into a campus ... and people can live and move and different ages can live and move around and feel they're coming to this sort of really [lovely place]. ... We thought ... if we could get an eating [space] that would open it up, feeling you know, here is this building [the community centre] which is for living and open. (Head teacher (HT), Interview (Int.) 1)

Introduced above, the community centre was very specifically designed and built as the hub of Wagril. It represented the centre of the social and intellectual life of the school. The school community centre was central in the social practices of the daily thrum or rhythm of school life (hence our emphasis on spatio-temporalities as a concept: Lefebvre 1991; Massey 1994; Forbes and Weiner 2012). The centre also served to strongly link and merge home and school, with parents often having breakfast there with their daughters before classes, and the head teacher ever present to mingle and chat with all. In this way, the affective atmosphere created in this space sought to ensure that families felt themselves to be a central part of the school, where their expertise and desires could be shared. Parents were therefore asked to invest their time and energies into the educational endeavour of the school. These regular moments of bringing family and school together in the young women's lives meant that the link between family and school was strengthened affectively. Furthermore, because these interactions were occurring within the school space itself, these moments of sociability opened up opportunities for the institutional habitus to influence the families' ways of thinking and being.

Wagril's intensive social-spatial 'knittings' included conscious work with and through the school's elegant architecture to open up redesigned historic buildings, and to create architect-designed physical spaces that aimed to 'effortlessly' facilitate these critical social and intellectual moments. The aesthetic surroundings at Wagril were aimed at promoting ease, well-being and proactive participation, and inculcating dispositions that would, we would argue, 'stick' into the future.

> The [community centre] developments were always intended to provide better facilities for teaching and learning, to improve the school's ethos and social life and to enable sharing with others. We could have the kind of setting that enabled students to feel that they were in almost a university world. … With proper, inviting and appropriate facilities, boys and girls from neighbouring schools joined the students for drama, music, sport, social life, lectures, action, research, projects, trips. (HT, Int. 2)

The centre hosted myriad events during all parts of the day from morning breakfast to late-night opera. The community centre was the intellectual, cultural and social hub of the school's expansive spatio-temporalities, facilitating social interactions between family, school, and representatives of local and national cultural and social elites. Thus, a particular social and intellectual institutional habitus was being facilitated that aimed to extend the families' habitus and be carried over in post-school habitus. Critical in securing the effective inculcation of a particular habitus was the role of the head teacher. Beyond her presence within the formal curriculum and school day, the head teacher and her husband were always visible at the numerous cultural events held by and at the school, to be seen on the touchline at sporting fixtures shouting encouragement, and always talking animatedly and knowledgeably with girls and families.

Furthermore, attempts to knit together family and school can be seen in the discursive representation of the school. For instance, in a student survey conducted at Wagril, responses to the item 'School is like …' received responses such as 'home', 'second home' and 'family'. Meanwhile, boarders at the school, just like the day pupils, were encouraged to view Wagril as their second home. Additionally, all employees of the school were expected to provide a 'pastoral', socially inclusive, caring attitude towards all students.

The head teacher emphasized that relationships across the school should be characterized by, in her words, interpersonal respect; trust and confidence; openness to others and to a range of ideas; involving and getting on with everybody and everybody 'counting'; liveliness; being available and relating to others; collaborating equally and leading collaboratively; being honest, capable, responsible, caring and dedicated; and valuing oneself, belonging and being of independent mind (HT, Int. 2).

Through numerous events, across different spaces within the school, and throughout the years the girls attended Wagril, the habitus of the young women was being moulded in very particular ways that would, in turn, shape their aspirations. The frequent and repetitive nature of these moments, the consistency with which particular values were affectively reiterated (as outlined by the head teacher above), is likely to ensure that a fairly stable habitus is promoted. Wagril therefore aims to promote alignment instead of disjuncture between family and institution, which is more likely to secure the particular habitus of its students.

We argue that by applying Massey's (1994) conceptualization of scalar space-time we gain further analytical purchase and insights into how social and intellectual relations are constituted and in turn shape, among many other things, young women's understandings of 'the future' and their desires to become particular 'future-girl-subjects'. Massey argues that

> the spatial is thought of in the context of space-time and as formed out of social relations at all scales, then one view of a place is of a particular articulation of those relations, a particular moment in those networks of social relations and understandings. (1994: 5)

Therefore, in understanding how aspirations are formed, we view social–intellectual relational space as 'scalar' in analysing spatio-temporalities production at different levels – different times, places and occurring with different rhythms in the school life. The use of a spatio-temporalities frame in analysis emphasizes the scales at which we need to research, analyse and, in doing so, more fully understand the formation of habitus. Spatio-temporalities theorizations have provided us with the necessary analytical purchase to understand the effects of different spatial repetitive rhythms (Lefebvre 2004).

Furthermore, we contend that affective agentic resources are central to the Wagril head teacher's professional habitus and the school institutional habitus, which shape the structures moulding the Wagril girls' habitus (see for example Tarabini, Curran and Fontdevila 2016). We understand affect as driving and underlying agency – 'infusing and circulating around the space, the person and broader discourses' (Maxwell and Aggleton 2013b: 5). Following Bourdieu (1986), we view social–emotional affect norms as the mostly unwritten aspects of family and institutional habitus, inculcating the typical feelings we should have towards our social networks. Thus, affect structures the girls' affinities, engagements, motivations and broader dispositions, which inform each individual's future envisioning and actions.

Habitus and aspiration

The girls' collective schooling habitus intensively inculcated personal and professional future-orientated dispositions. The girls' anterior family habitus was extended, but also modified or diversified in particular ways, through a Wagril schooling which lay down specific dispositions they should draw on when reproducing school-envisaged futures (Bourdieu 1977; Brubaker 1993). We argue that three particular aspects of the institutional habitus emerged that relate directly to the young women's capacity to aspire and to fulfil those aspirations: the promotion of a sense of agency, the use of affective resources and the development of a reflexive approach.

A sense of agency

The school fostered a habitus which was grounded in a strong self-belief and high levels of self-esteem, a confidence and sense of efficacy about the self and the future – a positive agentic self (see also Gaztambide-Fernández, Cairns and Desai 2013). We view agency as accomplished by individuals in particular contexts, but facilitated by drawing on their available resources or, following Bourdieu, their stocks of capitals, here, namely: economic, social and intellectual (Bourdieu 1986, and see for example Forbes and Weiner 2008). Thus, individuals' capacity to act in a particular social context derives from their specific current and prior habitus-inculcated dispositions. The head teacher recalled,

> Overall the students wanted to be themselves and articulate what they really cared about. If it was art, for instance, they would tell you that and they would be in on Saturdays for the art class with a life model. If it was sport, they would come to tell you and you would talk to them about their experience and their team. If it was academic work, they would tell you. You knew that they would be competent in themselves. (HT, Int. 2)

We found these girls to be extraordinarily resourced with individually tailored stocks of capitals, and with the necessary underlying reflexive habits and trust relations with their teachers, so as to feel empowered to positively envision and work towards their futures. Our broader research at Wagril, namely, the student survey and focus groups interview data, found that these girls exuded confidence, which we have termed 'assured optimism', in being well equipped to pursue their desired futures (Forbes and Lingard 2013, 2015). Applying an analytical frame examining for social capital, using key terms including trust and confidence, our data again and again showed these students' high levels of self-confidence. For example, the data revealed that they assuredly and optimistically took for granted high levels of academic attainment, as well as broader co-curricular achievement. They saw public examinations success as a key means to navigate not only their tertiary education futures (seen as Oxbridge and Ivy League university destinations), but also beyond in terms of their individual professional futures and life choices around future marital partnerships and children.

Inflected by affect

Wagril's institutional habitus foregrounds sociability and the formation of generative relations – particularly of 'soft power' relations regarding present and future leadership, and acting knowledgeably, authoritatively, but respectfully in relation to others. In and through Wagril's particular affective commitments and engagements, its girls consciously and reflexively understand and work with affect – their own and others' feelings – and critically seek out and expect 'to belong' in these elite, aspirational, meaningful spaces that the school works so hard to create for them. Through these positive affective experiences of caring for oneself and others and through a sense of rightfully 'belonging', the agentic aspiration self is more likely to emerge successfully and be sustained.

One way in which the school foregrounds the affective structures that promote belonging and aspiration is to tackle the girls' sense of self and self-worth, and encourage them to 'talk'. The head teacher emphatically stated,

> We know that women can easily be put down and are very self-critical. ...
> In practice, we must give young women of every age the chance to become
> themselves, not to feel ashamed of anything about themselves ... some will be
> bitchy to their friends. That has to be approached [dealt with] and it is essential
> to talk to young women ... [about these various issues] in the appropriate
> context of trust. (HT, Int. 2)

Thus, informed by the head teacher and other staff, knowledge of reflexivity and values of trust and regard are promoted – made to stick – at Wagril with a view to equipping its girls with affective capacities for school success and aspired-to futures. The effects of girls' individual practices, their feelings of self-worth, and their extant affective social capital relations with friends and other members of the Wagril community (current and past pupils, family networks using the school and so forth) are understood and quite explicitly worked with here.

A habitus of reflexivity fostering resilience

Wagril's institutional habitus actively emphasized the importance of the intellectual habit of reflexivity, which was seen as a valuable capacity for the girls' futures. While scholars have engaged with ideas of reflexivity and habitus to date – see Sweetman's (2003) account of 'reflexive habitus', Adams (2006) for critical debate on habitus and reflexivity, and Threadgold and Nilan (2009) for further critique – here we draw on Archer's (2003) idea of the internal conversation to integrate reflexivity and affect into our theorization of an agentic and aspirational habitus. The internal conversation, which is prompted by the emotional responses that are elicited following any interaction, leads to a commitment to a course of action both in the present and also connected to future possible imaginings. In our work we have argued that if such a course of action is acted upon it constitutes agency (Maxwell and Aggleton 2014a). Thus, at Wagril, we found that the girls are inculcated into the habit of reflecting on their practices, seeking to understand the factors shaping these, the value of the outcomes of such practices and assessing whether to do things differently in the future. The head teacher explicated,

> I take it for granted that an excellent school must have dedication to the development of the mind. ... [Staff] would be working all hours and taking trips in holiday time. They were people who believed in their subject and their pupils, who would go the extra mile. They did all they could in giving support to pupils with extra abilities in maths, for instance, and equally to pupils with additional support needs. ... Every teacher was concerned about the whole person. (HT, Int. 2)

Here, school structures, including the ongoing and committed support teachers offer (one aspect of the overarching institutional habitus), spatio-temporally underpin the laying down of particular habits of the mind.

Inculcation of mental resilience is underpinned by the constant practice of incarnating reflexive self-awareness. For example, Institutional 'Pastoral' Guidance (Personal and Social Education) efforts focused intensively on habits of reflexive thinking. The Wagril head teacher remarked, for example, the following:

> I think students were generally able to articulate what they felt … on the whole they would find someone to confide in … I was told all the time what people were feeling like. This is the result of having exceptional women staff in charge of the ethos of the school. [The Deputy Head of Guidance] was sensible as well and often made it clear that their problem was part of life. Life is full of contradictions and sometimes it is going to go wrong for you: what is important is to tackle the issues and to find ways to overcome them. (HT, Int. 2)

The Wagril institutional habitus therefore inculcates the capacity to be resilient among its students, through the in-built habit of being reflexive, almost continuously. We observed this during our discussions with the young women, whose narratives were usually constructed in a reflexive manner as they talked about themselves, their relationships with others and their futures. The process of being reflexive was understood within the school to facilitate a form of tenacity in the girls' approach to life. Thus, Wagril girls were expected to be (or at least learn to be) resilient – even 'tough' on themselves; and, somewhat paradoxically, to be 'soft' and convivial in their orientations towards others.

The vast majority of Wagril girls and their parents aspire to a form of schooling tuned in to the needs and (re)production of 'academic high flyers'. But it is the emphasis on agency, positive affective relations with others and being resilient – driven by the intellectual practices of reflexivity – that creates the discursive and affective structures facilitating the development of the particular positive and ambitious aspirations we found at Wagril. We suggest similar types of dispositions, which legitimate the kinds of futures that come to be expected, will be mirrored across a range of elite education spaces, particularly those in all-girls elite schools (Maxwell and Aggleton 2013a; see also Wardman et al. 2010).

Final reflections

This chapter has drawn on the concepts of family and institutional habitus (developed by scholars inspired by Bourdieu) to provide an analysis of how girls' aspirations are fostered and their capacities to pursue these are developed in a very particular school setting. The effects of a privileging institutional habitus configuration, evidencing high levels of social-cultural connectedness and academic excellence, inflected by gender and (upper-middle) social class resources, become a 'forcing ground' for intense cultivation of societally prized dispositions. This secondary – institutionally acquired – habitus underlies Wagril girls' acquisition of socially connected, intellectual, agentic dispositions of 'assured optimism' that carry over to valuably resource their personal and professional futures (Forbes and Lingard 2015).

In Wagril, we found a collective institutional habitus that is very clearly discursively articulated, proactively driven by its head teacher, and practised through its girls' intense and broad – indeed, vast – repertoire of activities and experiences. In this way, the habitus is intensively layered in and through the daily, weekly and annual repetitive intensive rhythms and flows of school: particular tightly timetabled yet naturalized spatio-temporal regimes of learning in formal academic work, and informally through sport, community engagements and social relations. The institutional secondary habitus actively mediates, makes malleable and builds upon the individual family-conditioned primary habitus possessed by each girl. The primary-family and secondary-school spatio-temporal habitus engagements strongly underlie the (re)production of and future possibilities for agency so effectively because they durably align.

While, for many, there is a relatively seamless knitting together of family and institutional habitus, which is, we argue, especially critical in ensuring the social reproduction fostered successfully by elite schooling, we found some cases of seemingly almost unbridgeable non-alignment of (working-class) family habitus and (upper-middle and middle-class) institutional habitus. Similarly, the institutional habitus could not adequately connect to or overlay the individual needs of a bright girl with autism. In such examples of inadequate primary–secondary habitus alignment, anterior dispositions survive, if somewhat altered. Thus, in these few cases the secondary (institutional) habitus has proven insufficiently malleable to take up and integrate the initial family disposition and overlay these with the necessary resources (capitals) to fully secure a set of the right kind of dispositions for Wagril graduates. Moving beyond school may therefore be less predictable and more fraught than for 'normal' Wagrilians. Gaztambide-Fernández, Cairns and Desai (2013) draw on Ahmed's work to explain how such experiences of non-alignment can lead to students feeling like 'affect aliens'; while Maxwell and Aggleton (2014b) show how non-alignment makes the social reproduction of privilege less secure and unpredictable.

We found Bourdieu's theoretical toolbox – particularly the concept of habitus – to be central in this endeavour. Yet, like research colleagues, often within the Anglophone world, tend to, we have found that we need to draw on other theoretical ideas – such as agency, affect and spatio-temporalities – to offer a more in-depth analysis of how elite school social and intellectual (re)production is usually so effective in laying down dispositions that are likely to facilitate the fulfilment of particular articulations of future aspirations. Using a 'Bourdieu plus' conceptual approach, we draw on the foundational ideas in Bourdieusian theory as the framework within which we situate the development of our research and therefore our analysis, but overlay this with other concepts to help make greater sense of our data. Methodologically we have found that this hybrid approach offers analytical flexibility which we see as generative of new and nuanced insights into Wagril's structuring conditions – the spatio-temporalities across which its girls' habitus agentically, affectively and reflexively operates.

Recommended further reading

Kenway, J., and A. Koh (eds) (2017), *New Sociologies of Elite Schooling*, London: Routledge.

Maxwell, C., and P. Aggleton (eds) (2013), *Privilege, Agency and Affect: Understanding the Production and Effects of Action*, Basingstoke: Palgrave MacMillan.

Maxwell, C., and P. Aggleton (eds) (2016), *Elite Education: International Perspectives*, London: Routledge.

References

Adams, M. (2006), 'Hybridizing Habitus and Reflexivity: Towards an Understanding of Contemporary Identity?', *Sociology*, 40 (3): 511–28.

Ahmed, S. (2010), 'Happy Objects', in G. J. Seigworth and M. Gregg (eds), *The Affect Theory Reader*, 29–51, Durham, NC and London: Duke University Press.

Archer, M. S. (2003), *Structure, Agency and the Internal Conversation*, Cambridge: Cambridge University Press.

Archer L., J. DeWitt, J. Osborne, J. Dillon, B. Willis and B. Wong (2012), 'Science Aspirations, Capital, and Family Habitus', *American Educational Research Journal*, 49 (5): 881–908.

Atkinson, W. (2011), 'From Sociological Fictions to Social Fictions: Some Bourdieusian Reflections on the Concepts of "Institutional Habitus" and "Family Habitus"', *British Journal of Sociology of Education*, 32 (3): 331–47.

Bourdieu, P. (1977), *Outline of a Theory of Practice*, Cambridge: Cambridge University Press.

Bourdieu, P. (1986), 'The Forms of Capital', in J. Richardson (ed.), *The Handbook of Theory and Research for the Sociology of Education*, 241–58, Westport, CT: Greenwood.

Bourdieu, P. (1996), *The State Nobility. Elite Schools in the Field of Power*, Cambridge: Polity Press.

Brubaker, R. (1993) 'Social Theory as Habitus', in C. Calhoun, E. LiPuma and M. Postone (eds), *Bourdieu: Critical Perspectives*, 212–34, Cambridge: Polity Press.

Burke, C. T., N. Emmerich and N. Ingram (2013), 'Well-Founded Social Fictions: A Defence of the Concepts of Institutional and Familial Habitus', *British Journal of Sociology of Education*, 34 (2): 165–82.

Clegg S. (2013), 'The Space of Academia: Privilege, Agency and the Erasure of Affect', in C. Maxwell and P. Aggleton (eds), *Privilege, Agency and Affect*, 71–87, Basingstoke: Palgrave Macmillan.

Forbes, J., and B. Lingard (2013), 'Elite School Capitals and Girls' Schooling: Understanding the (Re)production of Privilege through a Habitus of Assuredness', in C. Maxwell and P. Aggleton (eds), *Privilege, Agency and Affect: Understanding the Production and Effects of Action*, 50–68, London: Palgrave MacMillan.

Forbes, J., and B. Lingard (2015), 'Assured Optimism in a Scottish Girls' School: Habitus and the (Re)production of Global Privilege', *British Journal of Sociology of Education*, 36 (1): 116–36.

Forbes, J., and G. Weiner (2008), 'Understated Powerhouses: Scottish Independent Schools, Their Characteristics and Their Capitals', *Discourse: Studies in the Cultural Politics of Education*, 29 (4): 509–25.

Forbes, J., and G. Weiner (2012), 'Spatial Paradox: Educational and Social In/exclusion at St Giles', *Pedagogy, Culture & Society*, 20 (2): 273–93.

Forbes, J., and G. Weiner (2014), 'Gender Power in Elite Schools: Methodological Insights from Researcher Reflexive Accounts', *Research Papers in Education*, 29 (2): 172–92.

Gaztambide-Fernández, R., K. Cairns and C. Desai (2013), 'The Sense of Entitlement', in C. Maxwell and P. Aggleton (eds), *Privilege, Agency and Affect*, 32–49, Basingstoke: Palgrave Macmillan.

Lefebvre, H. (1991), *The Production of Space*, trans. D. Nicholson-Smith, Oxford: Blackwell.

Lefebvre, H. (2004), *Rhythmanalysis: Space, Time and Everyday Life*, trans. S. Eldon and G. Moore, London: Continuum.

Massey, D. (1994), *Space, Place and Gender*, Cambridge: Polity Press.

Maxwell, C., and P. Aggleton (2013a), 'Becoming Accomplished: Concerted Cultivation Among Privately Educated Young Women', *Pedagogy, Culture & Society*, 21 (1): 75–93.

Maxwell, C., and P. Aggleton (2013b), 'Introduction: Privilege, Agency and Affect – Understanding the Production and Effects of Action', in C. Maxwell and P. Aggleton (eds), *Privilege, Agency and Affect: Understanding the Production and Effects of Action*, 1–14, Basingstoke: Palgrave MacMillan.

Maxwell, C., and P. Aggleton (2013c), 'Privilege, Agency and Affect: Moving Further Debate', in C. Maxwell and P. Aggleton (eds), *Privilege, Agency and Affect: Understanding the Production and Effects of Action*, 248–57, Basingstoke: Palgrave Macmillan.

Maxwell, C., and P. Aggleton (2014a), 'Agentic Practice and Privileging Orientations among Privately Educated Young Women', *Sociological Review*, 64 (2): 800–20.

Maxwell, C., and P. Aggleton (2014b), 'The Reproduction of Privilege: Young Women, the Family and Private Education', *International Studies in Sociology of Education*, 24 (2): 189–209.

Nespor J. (2014), 'Schooling for the Long-Term: Elite Education and Temporal Accumulation', *Zeitschrift für Erziehungswissenschaft*, 17 (3 Supp): 27–42.

Reay, D. (1998), '"Always Knowing" and "Never Being Sure": Familial and Institutional Habituses and Higher Education Choice', *Journal of Education Policy*, 13 (4): 519–29.

Reay, D. (2004), '"It's All Becoming Habitus": Beyond the Habitual Use of Habitus in Educational Research', *British Journal of Sociology of Education*, 25 (4): 431–44.

Tarabini, A., M. Curran and C. Fontdevila (2016), 'Institutional Habitus in Context: Implementation, Development and Impacts in Two Compulsory Secondary Schools in Barcelona', *British Journal of Sociology of Education*, online before print 22 November. doi:10.1080/01425692.2016.1251306

Threadgold, S., and P. Nilan (2009), 'Reflexivity of Contemporary Youth, Risk and Cultural Capital', *Current Sociology*, 57 (1): 47–68.

Sweetman, P. (2003), 'Twenty-first Century Dis-ease? Habitual Reflexivity or the Reflexive Habitus', *Sociological Review*, 51 (4): 528–49.

Wardman, N., R. Hutchesson, K. Gottschall, C. Drew and S. Saltmarsh (2010), 'Starry Eyes and Subservient Selves: Portraits of "Well-Rounded" Girlhood in the Prospectuses of All-Girl Elite Private Schools', *Australian Journal of Education*, 54 (3), 249–61.

Part Six

Ethnic Inequalities and Identities: Assessing Bourdieu's Tools

11

Aspirations in Britain's Caribbean Diaspora: Applying Bourdieu's Doxa

Derron Wallace

Introduction

To date, much of the political discourse on aspirations has been centred on young people, especially those from disadvantaged and ethnic minority backgrounds. From parliamentary pronouncements to new school-based schemes, young people across Britain are continually the subjects of plans to 'raise aspirations'. Such policy initiatives frame young people's aspirations as a primarily psychological impediment rather than a discerned disposition based on the opportunity structure (Spohrer 2011; Spohrer, Stahl and Bowers-Brown 2017; Wallace 2017a). More often than not, these initiatives personalize, or perhaps psychologize, aspirations without attending critically to the impact of austerity measures in British society that constrain students' aspirations. According to Reay and Lucey (2010), Britain's national narrative on aspirations has been deployed as an 'ideological whip' to cultivate more productive citizens, rather than address the structural conditions that might make more productive citizenship possible. By drawing on Bourdieu's conception of doxa, this chapter offers a departure from mainstream discourse. I interrogate the role of a deficit doxa – a shared or taken-for-granted logic that is largely negative and prejudicial but deemed legitimate or socially significant. My interest is in how doxa contributes to the formation of high career aspirations among black Caribbean youth who are deemed to 'lack' aspirations according to select government officials policy makers. Through my analysis, I point to the need for more nuanced interpretations of Bourdieu's work that emphasize more generative, asset-based analyses of black and ethnic minority youth and their aspirations.

A rigorous reassessment of Bourdieu's contributions – which includes engaging with the less frequently used tools in his oeuvre – is important for increasing our engagement with his work, especially when studying the formation of aspirations (see Threadgold, this volume). Owing to the fact that Bourdieu ranks among the most celebrated and influential sociologists of the twentieth century, the interpretation, application and extension of his work can function as symbolic capital, signalling the quality of one's intellect and/or academic training. Unfortunately, this can result in random name-dropping, cherry-picking of his key terms and sophomoric appraisals of Bourdieu's concepts, as opposed to putting his theories to work (Reay and Lucey 2010). Instead, I argue, the popularity of Bourdieu's work should inspire new modes of inquiry regarding differences in the manifestation of inequalities, arguably the goal of this collection. However, operationalizing Bourdieu's conceptual toolkit in new ways in order to explore new terrain also involves addressing long-standing critiques of Bourdieu's scholarship. For instance, what are the consequences of a colour-blind class analysis for understanding the lived experiences of ethno-racial minority communities? How can Bourdieu's theoretical approach to doxa be used to further understandings regarding how ethno-racial minorities form their aspirations? The chapter offers answers to the latter question.

The analysis presented in this chapter works from the context that black Caribbean communities in Britain have experienced significant marginalization in various sectors of British society over several decades, including in the field of education (Jones 2011; Treviño, Harris and Wallace 2008). Specifically, the chapter addresses how the social and political marginalization black Caribbean people have endured over the course of several decades have resulted in a pervasive deficit doxa regarding black Caribbean youths' educational and career aspirations. The sections that follow provide (1) an overview of the theoretical utility of Bourdieu's conception of doxa in understanding the lived experiences of minority communities, (2) context on the historical formation of deficit doxa through an examination of the history of Caribbean migration and disadvantage, (3) a synthesis of contemporary perspectives on aspirations among black young people in education, (4) an outline of the study and its design, and (5) empirical data and analysis of counter-narratives of black Caribbean young people and their aspirations.

The utility of doxa: Challenging the deficits

Engagement with Bourdieu's scholarship is at times restricted to the application of his master concepts: habitus, capital and field. However, as this edited volume confirms, there is much more to Bourdieu's theoretical approach. To explore the experiences and aspirations of black Caribbean young people, this chapter illustrates how doxa is informed by history. A historical understanding of doxa formation can add richness and depth to our understandings of contemporary formulations of aspiration. For Bourdieu, doxa is a 'set of fundamental beliefs, which does not even need to be asserted in the form of an explicit, self-conscious dogma' (2000: 15). In other words, doxa is the unspoken but widely accepted logic that informs and structures social life. In her explication of doxa, Deer contends that

> doxa refers to pre-reflexive, intuitive knowledge shaped by experience, to unconscious inherited physical and relational predisposition ... [it is] the misrecognition of forms of social arbitrariness that engenders the unformulated, non-discursive, but internalized and practical recognition of that same social arbitrariness. It contributes to its reproduction in social institutions, structures and relations as well as in the minds and bodies, expectations and behaviours. (2008: 119–20)

Put simply, doxa is an arbitrary, taken-for-granted set of assumptions considered so normative that it remains generally unquestioned. Operating as a largely well accepted orthodoxy, doxa is an infrequently spoken norm rendered objective and perhaps universal. Doxa is but one in a series of mechanisms that shape field relations, contributing significantly to how inequality is maintained and reproduced. As a prevailing logic that may prove illogical, doxa refers to the powerful discourses influencing social relations and the order of social life. Such powerful discourses influence individual and institutional engagement with social actors, which can have negative consequences for disadvantaged and minority groups.

Doxa is structured *by* and *through* history (Deer 2008). Throughout British history, a long-standing doxa has capitalized on racist stereotypes to influence how black Caribbean students are depicted, especially in the field of education. Assumptions about black Caribbean educational underachievement in Britain are so ubiquitous that many in Britain are startled to learn that in the United States black Caribbeans are regularly associated with academic success. The association between Caribbean identity and economic, educational and political success is, for some, an unimaginable prospect in British society. Inherent to the deficit doxa, black Caribbeans (parents and pupils) are assumed to have a poverty of aspirations and those that aspire beyond their present circumstances are considered exceptions to an otherwise failing group. Such suppositions are worth challenging.

Black feminist scholars like Heidi Mirza (2009) call into question claims about black Caribbeans that do not attend to the particularities of gender and social class. For example, black Caribbean schoolgirls fare much better on GCSEs, university admission and employment than their male counterparts, and have done so for several years (Mirza 1992). However, as Mirza (2009) points out, black girls from poor and working-class backgrounds do not succeed at the same rates as those from the upper and middle classes. So, interestingly, the substantive role that gender and social class play in differentiating academic success is obscured by doxic narratives of black Caribbean underachievement. For instance, black Caribbean working-class girls are marginalized, while significant attention and policy focus is geared towards addressing the moral panic around boys' underachievement (Gillborn 1997; Warrington and Younger 2000; Wright, Weekes, McGlaughlin and Webb 1998; Younger and Warrington 1996; Younger, Warrington and McLellan 2005).

For Bourdieu, doxa serves as the foundational pillar of the field, where it orients social relations within it; agents form their aspirations and goals in reference to the doxa. Deer confirms:

> Doxa is understood as comprising field-specific sets of beliefs that inform the shared habitus of those operating within the field. It is the result of a conquest via normative and even performative statements often expressed and represented by and/or around influential elements in the field which sets the field as a world apart with its own fundamental rules and laws (nomos), discursive forms (logos), normative beliefs (illusion), expected actions and behaviours and barriers to entry. (2008: 125)

If we are not to simply understand the influence of doxa, but to challenge deficit doxas, we must focus on the constitutive fields that shape them – in this case schools. The power of schools as sites of reproduction and resistance should not be underestimated (Bourdieu and Passeron 1977). As fields of symbolic power are informed and shaped by the doxa, schools are significant fields in the lives of young people that either erase or emphasize what the doxa holds in high regard, however problematic it may be. Doxic notions of black Caribbean failure or underachievement – as reinforced by teachers' assumptions, educational expectations and pedagogical practices – can shape students' aspirations. But while the doxa influences institutions, relationships and outcomes, it does not determine them. One way that students counter these deficit doxas in schools is formulating and enacting counter-narratives (Stahl, this volume), which, in the case of the African diaspora in the UK, is evident in the fields of families and black supplementary schools (Gerrard 2013; Mirza and Reay 2000). As will be revealed in subsequent sections, these practices of resistance that seek to counteract deficit doxas are significant in understanding how black Caribbean students form their aspirations in British society.

Caribbean migration to Britain: A history of diaspora, disadvantage and disappointment

Through what can be considered three waves of immigration, black Caribbeans sought full inclusion in British society as members of the British Empire (Gilroy 1992). They left the shores of Trinidad and Tobago, Jamaica, Barbados, the Bahamas, and other Commonwealth nations in the Caribbean with high aspirations in pursuit of upward social mobility. However, discrimination and other expressions of structural disadvantage limited the full realization of their aspirations. During each of the three waves, namely the pre-Windrush era (1880s to 1947), the Windrush generation (1948–62) and the post-Windrush period (1962 to present), black Caribbeans struggled as cultural outsiders and political subalterns to have their aspirations and senses of belonging affirmed in a nation they were technically citizens of (through the Commonwealth) but were substantively marginalized in. As British historians such as Fryer (1984) and Sivanadan (1982) among others suggest, following their arrival, black Caribbean immigrants encountered widespread de facto discrimination in the labour market, the housing sector, and the educational and immigration systems. In fact, the recent public disputes regarding the deportation and mistreatment of black Caribbeans from the Windrush era by then home secretary Amber Rudd and her office illustrate the ongoing civic estrangement Black Caribbean people negotiate in twenty-first-century British society. The aspirations of black Caribbeans in the UK must therefore be understood holistically and historically in this context of struggle, self-determination and structural disadvantage. This section shows how the deficit doxa has been structured through history, with particular attention to the educational experiences of this diverse Caribbean immigrant.

Black immigration to the UK is often considered a post-World War phenomenon (Rastogi and Stitt 2008). Waters, for example, suggests that Britain largely became 'a country of postcolonial immigration, only' (2008: 11). Others contend that postcolonial Windrush migration is not the definitive historical portal through which narratives of black life are inaugurated in British history (Jones 2011). Though often disregarded in postcolonial history, cultural criticism on black immigration in Britain suggests that the pre-Windrush era is a vital part of black Caribbean migration history. It is indeed fair to consider black migration in the pre-Windrush years more of a ripple than a wave (Phillips and Phillips 1998); nevertheless, its significance, minor though it be, is worth bearing in mind as part of this historical framework. These years saw the slow introduction and steady settlement of black Caribbeans, mainly along seaports in Liverpool, Cardiff, Bristol, Manchester and East London (Brown 2005; Gerrard 2013). These immigrants gained legal access to England as subjects of the British Empire, and economic elites from their respective 'colonies'. The members of this first wave were mainly colonial seamen, top-ranked soldiers and professional businessmen. Commenting on the class heritage of these first wave pioneers, Jones points out that 'prior to the Second World War, the migration of Blacks to Britain had consisted almost entirely of middle- and upper-class individuals' (1986: 218). The Caribbeans émigrés among these blacks were small in number and limited in their impact on Britain's social and political landscape. Solomos (2003) suggests that the presence of this small cohort of black Caribbeans who came to England to work and fight for the British Army was tolerated but not fully accepted by the local population. However, white fear and racial conflict would intensify when other black Caribbeans arrived in droves after 1947 (Winder 2004). This reveals that a supportive context of reception is perhaps just as important as high aspirations. The latter becomes difficult to maintain without the former.

Immigration historians often contend that calls for workers after the Second World War to aid in the infrastructural and economic redevelopment of Britain led to the largest and most politically significant wave of black Caribbeans to enter Great Britain (Dabydeen, Gilmore and Jones 2008; Fryer 1984; Loury, Modood and Teles 2005; Modood 1992). Under the auspices of the *British Nationality Act* of 1948, which confirmed all colonial subjects as full-fledged citizens of Great Britain, 492 Caribbean professionals sailed to the shores of Tilbury in Kent on the SS *Empire Windrush* on 22 June 1948 seeking greater opportunities and a respite from the economic difficulties emerging in the Caribbean (Peach 1995; Phillips and Phillips 1998). A sizeable contingent of the Windrush arrivals were returnees from the First and Second World Wars, along with their relatives, who could afford the fifteen-pound fare for the journey (Fryer 1984). Arriving to a curious crowd and some fanfare, these black Caribbeans filled gaps in the labour market as farm workers, electricians, railway workers and plumbers, despite being qualified to do more (Phillips and Phillips 1998). Although the number of black Caribbean newcomers would remain relatively small for a number of years, it would swell after 1951. Prior to 1951, the intake of black Caribbeans was limited to 1,000 per year, but subsequent years would see a steady increase (Fryer 1984). The increase is not surprising given the entry restrictions imposed on black Caribbeans interested in coming to the United States through the 1952 *McCarren-Walter Act*. England, the much revered 'Mother Country', seemed the next best option (Phillips and Phillips 1998). The emigration of black Caribbeans to Britain was arguably an expression of high aspirations, but widespread interpersonal and institutional racism limited the conversion of high aspirations into outcomes.

With the sharp rise in the number of black Caribbeans, the arrival of new ethnic minorities and the increased presence of early black settlers, latent racial tensions matured to inform a divisive public political debate. Immigration became – and arguably still is – a source through which 'race' and racism were expressed and enforced. Jones (2011) asserts that Britain's white majority grew increasingly sceptical and fearful of the country's new 'coloured' minority. Members of the British Empire were essentially deemed a threat in the 'Mother Country'. And not only were they a threat, they were deficient, by European standards (Dabydeen, Gilmore and Jones 2008; Phillips and Phillips 1998; Winder 2004). Fryer points out that the white British population deemed 'coloured' immigrants 'ignorant and illiterate, speaking strange languages, and lacking proper education' (1984: 347). This pathologization contributed to the doxa, which would later be legitimated in the educational experiences of ethnic minorities across Britain. The fear harboured by British whites inspired a series of talks on immigration control, which eventually led to the creation of the *Commonwealth Immigrants Act* on 1 November 1961 to be enforced on 31 July 1962. This legislation restricted free access to Great Britain for all members of the Commonwealth. Rushing to win entry before the enforcement of the ban, the number of black Caribbean immigrants and other ethnic minorities increased considerably between 1961 and 1962 (Dabydeen, Gilmore and Jones 2008). Never again would Britain witness a flood of black Caribbeans in such volumes to its shores. It is in this second wave and the next that Britain would experiment with black Caribbeans in its educational system and entrench a deficit doxa that would stymie the aspirations of a number of black Caribbean immigrants and their children for generations.

The *Commonwealth Immigrants Act* proved effective in limiting access to Britain; however, it did not stem the tide of migration completely. A voucher system was built into the Act so that dependants could be reunited with their loved ones and qualified black Caribbeans seeking jobs could be sponsored by friends and family already in England. This 'chain migration' led to continued incorporation, but one with a decreasing flow of black Caribbeans. In the years that followed, black Caribbeans came to Britain more as dependants of immigrant relatives than as job seekers. Dabydeen, Gilmore and Jones (2008) estimates that between 1962 and 1967, 1,550 workers came to England through the voucher system, and 55,310 as dependants seeking reunification with relatives. They settled into previously existing black communities (in London, Liverpool, Manchester, etc.) and turned sections of some cities into new ethnic niches (e.g. Brixton). Although the third wave of immigration has been much smaller than the first and the second, its political significance in education is unmatched by the waves that preceded it. During this time period, 1962 to present, a pattern of resistance in education emerged (Dabydeen, Gilmore and Jones 2008; Gerrard 2013; Reay and Mirza 1997; Gillborn and Mirza 2000; Tomlinson 1981). As Anglophone black Caribbean immigrants settled into England, and sent their children to school, they were forced to confront racial, cultural and political tensions in an educational system that deemed them educationally subnormal, and oppositional learners. The remainder of this chapter puts doxa to work in a multi-part project. First, I capitalize on how doxa is structured through history, emphasizing how there has long been public activism shaping spaces of opportunity to establish the aspirations of black Caribbeans beyond the doxa. I highlight recent research that focuses on young black Caribbeans living in South London to establish the current doxa which portrays them as a largely disadvantaged group. Finally, I draw on Bourdieu to show that doxa, while powerful, is not all-encompassing but waxes and wanes in its salience so that social actors can think and act beyond it.

Deficit doxa: Caribbeans failing?

Historically informed doxic logics continue to shape the educational experiences of black Caribbean young people in contemporary British society. Nearly seventy years after the children of Caribbean immigrants began enrolling in British state schools en masse, popular and academic presses continue to describe black Caribbeans with much anxiety, often framing them as a low-achieving, 'problem' minority (Mirza 2009; Demie 2005; Coard 1971; Gillborn et al. 2011). Much of the concerns can be attributed to the comparatively low educational performance linked to substandard schooling experienced by black Caribbeans from the late 1960s to date, high levels of material deprivation, and high rates of unemployment (Coard 1971; Gillborn and Mirza 2000; Loury, Modood and Teles 2005; Modood 2004; Tomlinson 1991).

However, the continual presence of deficit doxas has informed activism which has sought to change the opportunity structures available to black Caribbeans. For example, in the late 1950s, black Caribbean women educators and community workers in London grew concerned at the number of black Caribbean children being designated as 'educationally subnormal'. Statistics produced by the Inner London Educational Authority through the 1960s were difficult to refute. Black children, mainly black Caribbeans, comprised 15 per cent of students in London's primary and secondary schools, but 28 per cent of students in London's special educational schools. Caribbean mothers and fathers, suspicious of the state, were disconcerted by what they believed was the over-referral of black children to 'educationally subnormal schools' based on the poor assessment of the needs and performance of black children. The activism of these parents was rooted in their understanding of a doxa regarding black Caribbean pupils derived from the misrecognition of their children's language, their intelligence, the perceived unruliness of black children and myths about Caribbean children's home lives. Much of this continues today. Year after year, black Caribbean pupils rank among the lowest performing group on GCSEs, surpassed only by Roma and Travellers (Strand 2014; Strand and James 2008), which contributes to deficit perspectives on the educability of black Caribbean pupils in Britain. Despite this phenomenon, important activist work continues (see Gerrad 2013 for detailed analysis).

But deficit perspectives on black Caribbean people are not only shaped by Caribbean youth's educational performance. National survey data suggest that black Caribbeans do not fare as well as their white British peers on a number of socio-economic indicators (Law and Swann 2011). For example, a 2012 Runnymede Trust report suggests that 30 per cent of black Caribbeans in the UK currently live in low-income households, compared to 20 per cent of white working-class British people. What is more, a disproportionately high percentage of black Caribbeans are considered homeless (Law & Swann 2011). The 2006–08 Labour Force Survey also suggests that unemployment is higher for black Caribbean men (13%) than it is for white British men (4%). Commenting on the ongoing stigmatization of black Caribbeans in the UK, Warikoo argues that 'British Afro-Caribbeans have not attained socioeconomic parity with whites, have lower-than-average educational outcomes, and are stereotyped as dangerous and lazy' (2011: 13). Such findings give credibility to the doxic narrative concerning the aspirations of black Caribbean youth. The doxic narratives these datasets informed do not offer due recognition to the sociopolitical and racialized class conditions that stymie aspirations. As the history of the Caribbean diaspora in Britain is one shaped largely by structural discrimination and disadvantage, aspirations of second- and third-generation black Caribbeans that would be deemed low according to a policy logic should not be surprising. Bourdieu contends that doxa is unquestioned orthodoxy structuring societal and institutional logics, inculcating the habitus. However, there is significant evidence that black Caribbeans hold high aspirations as an expression of resistance (Treviño, Harris and Wallace 2008; Wallace 2017a). I now turn to examples of this.

The study

This chapter draws on a subset of data from a comparative ethnographic study exploring the educational experiences of second-generation black Caribbean working-class and middle-class pupils in London and New York City. The larger study seeks to understand how various social agents (teachers, parents and peers) influence the educational experiences and outcomes of black Caribbean pupils. Given the space constraints of this anthology, I focus exclusively on second-generation black Caribbean pupils in London. In this study, second-generation black Caribbean young people were identified through an initial screening survey. This instrument was administered to all black Caribbean students in Years 10 and 11 in two of the largest secondary schools in London and New York City with the greatest share of black Caribbeans. Students were identified as second generation if one or more of their parents hailed from the Anglophone Caribbean, but the participants were born in the UK. The survey also provided insights into the class standing and class histories of their families. Surveys were followed by semi-structured interviews with second-generation black Caribbean pupils whose parents consented to their participation in the study: thirty in London and thirty in New York. The London case study included pupils between 14 and 17 years of age; sixteen female and fourteen male; seventeen working class and thirteen middle class.

Interviews with London participants took place between 2012 and 2013 in schools, homes and community centres with parental consent and staff support. Semi-structured interviews explored topics such as educational and career aspirations, cultural authenticity, perceptions of teachers' expectations and much more. Interviews generally lasted between fifty-five and eighty-five minutes. To ensure accuracy and precision, interviews were digitally recorded and professionally transcribed. Transcripts were uploaded to and analysed through NVivo. To allow for inductive and deductive analyses, and transitions in between the two, I pursued two rounds of coding after reading through the transcripts thoroughly for contextual meanings. Using NVivo, I then identified broad themes before refining the initial coding scheme with more precise codes, all the while searching for more patterns to deepen the analysis. For more details on the design of the study and the analytic processes that guided it, see Wallace (2017d).

In what follows, I outline the findings of this study in relation to aspirations. All participants expressed high aspirations, in a school and policy context that often assumed they had low educational aspirations, especially the working-class pupils among them. The students strategically held and expressed high aspirations to counter-dominant claims about black Caribbean failure and to advance counter-hegemonic ideas of black Caribbean identities.

The rewards of articulating aspirations

The evidence from this study supports the view that black Caribbean youth hold a wide range of aspirations in spite of their current circumstances and the limits of Britain's political economy in an era of austerity. For the participants, their aspirations are not simply wishful dreams; instead, their aspirations are active, goal-oriented endeavours geared towards participants' educational, career, religious, political, financial and social mobility. To better explicate the diverse nature of the aspirations of black Caribbean young people in South London, I focus on their career aspirations and the importance to the participants of expressing high aspirations in public settings. I do not wish to suggest that the all participants consistently held high aspirations across the life course. As Hart (2012) suggests, aspirations held by young people are often in flux and are at different developmental stages, from the latent to the mature, the realistic and the reaching, to the short term and the long term. In putting Bourdieu's tools to work, I draw on data that show the participants articulating and pursuing career aspirations – noting their expressed aspirations for higher education as both acts of resistance and expressions of resilience.

The working-class and middle-class black Caribbean students in this study simultaneously held multiple career aspirations. Despite the doxa regarding black underachievement, which participants were very much aware of, they wished to become business owners, barristers, teachers, professional footballers, physicians, real estate managers, TV producers, police officers and so much more. These aspirations were often informed by their own desires, access to or one-off encounters with professionals in those posts, the economic rewards of such work, along with the personal fulfilment and talent cultivation such work affords. As their aspirations refute common doxic claims about Caribbean pupils' low aspirations, we see their habitus rebuffing these narratives in distinct ways (see Stahl, this volume).

In terms of his approach to doxa Bourdieu has been criticized for emphasizing the internalization of dominant and oppressive beliefs, which leaves little room for agency. To this end he responds by showing how his approach is central to 'consciousness' and symbolic violence, specifically 'false consciousness', where one cannot 'grasp the main ideological effects, which most of the time are transmitted through the body' (Eagleton and Bourdieu 1992: 115). So while Bourdieu allows for agency, he emphasizes that it is very difficult for many to break from the doxa. According to Atkinson, people can come to

> perceive their trajectories as driven by external forces, which from a Bourdieusian perspective – and sticking with indicators of the influence of class – would comprise recognition of the external forces and conditions issuing from capital possession in shaping the constraints and expectations that have characterised their path. (2010: 2.4)

The participants I interviewed believed that they could challenge the influence of the dominant doxa on their day-to-day life. In fact, not only did they articulate their primary career aspiration, twenty-five of the thirty black Caribbean participants in London also held what I regard as contingent aspirations: secondary and tertiary career aspirations that serve as a viable backup plan if their primary career aspirations fail. What is especially striking is that for all the participants articulating their aspirations in public settings was arguably just as important as having high aspirations. Consider, for instance, the following examples. Akilah, a Year 10 pupil, explained:

People don't think positive things about black Caribbean young people ... they don't think we want to become serious leaders in our community. Well they are wrong. A lot of my Caribbean friends, yeah, have so many big dreams. ... I want to be a barrister, but when most people see that I am Caribbean, they might just think I'm dreaming. ... People in this community have low expectations for black Caribbean young people, and that's kind of why it is so important to tell them what you want to become. That's how we change their perceptions of us.

Devon, a Year 11 student athlete, affirmed Akilah's claims about the importance of not just having high aspirations, but expressing them in public. He maintained:

Whatever you want to be in the future, it's really important to let people know ... wanting to be a doctor or a teacher like I do is one thing, yeah, but because so many people look down on black Caribbean boys, I have to let them know that I know where I am going and who I want to be.

In the case of Anthony, a Year 11 student of working-class background, expressing high aspirations aids in the production of counter-narratives that challenge the dominant doxa regarding black Caribbean pupils across gender boundaries. The consistent, collective expression of high aspiration among black Caribbean pupils can serve as a defence mechanism against doxic claims of Caribbean identity. Anthony reported:

In this country, when you are black and especially when you are Caribbean it can help you if you tell people what you want to become ... they start seeing you as more than just another black Caribbean boy destined to get in trouble. ... Even older black Caribbean people at the supermarket or shop 'round here can start to treat you differently ... they start to see you as someone who will lift up the community. ... When I tell people I want to be a football player, they are like, yeah, another black boy wants to be a football player ... but when I tell them I want to be a PE teacher or a headteacher, they celebrate ... they big me up.

Anthony was not alone in his assessment of the benefits of high aspirations. While he noted the extrinsic benefits (positive recognition, adult support and ethnic pride), some students like Imogen, a Year 10 working-class student, pointed to the intrinsic benefits of expressing high career aspirations in public settings. Imogen maintained:

In a way, telling people about the career I want to have in the future can change how they think about Caribbean young people, but that's not really why I do it. I do it because it motivates me to make sure I do what I say I want to do. I know that a lot of people expect Caribbean young people to fail in school. I can't become another statistic. When I tell people what I want to do in the future, it motivates me … it stops me from believing what they say about Caribbean young people.

These comments from Anthony, Imogen, Akilah and Devon are emblematic of common claims made by the participants regarding the important benefits of expressing high career aspirations: (1) intrinsic motivation, (2) extrinsic praise, (3) resistance to stereotypic identity claims based on ethnicity, gender and age, and (4) the active reimagining of black Caribbean identities in public domains. In their words, we see the rewards black Caribbean pupils associate with expressing high career aspirations in public settings throughout their local communities.

In expressing high career aspirations, four of the thirty black Caribbean pupils (including Imogen) point to expressing high aspiration as a strategy for resisting the internalization of the dominant doxa. Within the study, eighteen participants underscored the value of the public praise they received from adults in their neighbourhood upon expressing their aspirations. Five of the thirty black Caribbean participants believed that the articulation of high career aspirations was not only significant for convincing those outside the black Caribbean community, but that such expressions were also useful for garnering support within it. Eight participants pointed out that the expression of high aspirations became a way of cultivating ethnic pride in local enclaves. Finally, all thirty participants noted that the expression of high career aspirations is a useful formula for engendering counter-hegemonic claims about black Caribbean identities and disrupting the dominant doxa. In this regard, expressing high aspirations becomes a political, if performative, strategy for challenging the deficit doxa, and reimagining more positive representations of Caribbean identity (Wallace 2017a). It also becomes a way of avoiding what Bourdieu would regard as misrecognition (Wallace 2017d).

The participants' investments in positive narratives on black Caribbeans that privilege certain careers are beneficial in the short term, but arguably risky in the long term. Such a shift in identity representation may inadvertently suggest that it is only through middle-class career routes that black Caribbean youth can find value in British society. Or, simply put, that having high aspirations regarding class mobility minimizes or erases ethnic stigmatization (Wallace 2017b). The career options cited by Anthony, Imogen, Akilah and Devon assist them in distinguishing themselves in the community from other black Caribbean young people, but do little – if anything at all – to transform the structural conditions that maintain ethnic stigmatization, or the constraints of the political economy that inform the doxa and limit the transformation of aspirations into reality. Given the orthodoxy of the doxa and the way it informs institutional practices and stereotypes, chances are participants will come to experience barriers to realizing their aspirations (Warikoo 2011). Bourdieu's notion of doxa, as applied throughout his many works, points not only to the importance of cultural change, but structural transformation of the class order.

As this chapter illustrates, doxa is formulated through history and has consequences in the contemporary moment. Those invested in challenging deficit doxa regarding black Caribbean young people in Britain must move beyond career aspirations and social mobility focused on the politics of recognition, to a more critical appraisal of the material reality of black Caribbean people and the need for a politics of redistribution, not just recognition (James 2015).

Recommended further reading

Strand, S., and W. James (2008), 'Educational Aspirations in Inner City Schools', *Educational Studies*, 34 (4): 249–67.

Wallace, D. (2017b), 'Cultural Capital as Whiteness? Examining Logics of Ethno-Racial Representation and Resistance', *British Journal of Sociology of Education*, online before print 2 August.

Winder, R. (2004), *Bloody Foreigners: The Story of Immigration to Britain*, London: Abacus.

References

Bourdieu, P. (2000), *Pascalian Meditations*, Stanford, CA: Stanford University Press.

Bourdieu, P., and J. Passeron (1977), *Reproduction in Education, Society and Culture*, Beverly Hills, CA: Sage.

Bourdieu, P. and Eagleton, T. (1992), Doxa and Common Life, *New Left Review*, 191 (1), 111–21.

Brown, J. N. (2005), *Dropping Anchor, Setting Sail: Geographies of Race in Black Liverpool*, Princeton, NJ: Princeton University Press.

Coard, B. (1971), *How the West Indian Child is Made Educationally Subnormal in the British School System*, London: New Beacon Books.

Dabydeen, D., J. Gilmore and C. Jones (eds) (2008), *The Oxford Companion to Black British History*, Oxford: Oxford University Press.

Deer, C. (2008), 'Doxa', in M. Grenfell (ed.), *Pierre Bourdieu: Key Concepts*, 119–130, Durham: Acumen.

Demie, F. (2005), 'Achievement of Black Caribbean Pupils: Good Practice in Lambeth Schools', *British Educational Research Journal*, 31 (4): 481–508.

Fryer, P. (1984), *Staying Power: The History of Black People in Britain*, New York: Pluto Press.

Gerrard, J. (2013), 'Self-Help and Protest: The Emergence of Black Supplementary Schooling in England', *Race, Ethnicity and Education*, 16 (1): 32–58.

Gillborn, D. (1997), 'Ethnicity and Educational Performance in the United Kingdom: Racism, Ethnicity, and Variability in Achievement', *Anthropology & Education*, 28 (3): 375–93.

Gillborn, D., and H. Mirza (2000), *Educational Inequality: Mapping Race, Class and Gender. A Synthesis of Research Evidence*, London: Office for Standards in Education.

Gillborn, D., N. Rollock, S. Ball and C. Vincent (2011), 'Race, Class and Disability: The Wrong Kind of "Special"?' Paper presented at the British Education Research Association Annual Conference, London, 6–8 September.

Gilroy, P. (1992), *There Ain't No Black in the Union Jack*, 2nd edn, London: Routledge.

Hart, C. S. (2012), *Aspirations, Education and Social Justice: Applying Sen and Bourdieu*, A&C Black.

James, D. (2015), 'How Bourdieu Bites Back: Recognising Misrecognition in Education and Educational Research', *Cambridge Journal of Education*, 45 (1): 97–112.

Jones, C. (2011), 'The Importance of Hubs and Context for West Indian Immigrants: A Review Essay on New Scholarship on West Indians', *Black Diaspora Review*, 2 (2): 52–4.

Jones, V. (1986), *We Are Our Own Educators! Josina Machel: From Supplementary to Black Complementary School*, London: Karia Press/Josina Machel Supplementary School.

Loury, G. C., T. Modood and S. M. Teles (eds) (2005), *Ethnicity, Social Mobility and Public Policy: Comparing US and UK*, Cambridge: Cambridge University Press.

Mirza, H. S. (1992), *Young, Female, and Black*, New York: Routledge.

Mirza, H. S. (2009), *Race, Gender and Educational Desire: Why Black Women Succeed and Fail*, New York: Routledge.

Mirza, H., and D. Reay (2000), 'Spaces and Places of Black Educational Desire: Rethinking Black Supplementary Schools as a New Social Movement', *Sociology*, 34 (3): 521–44.

Modood, T. (1992), *Not Easy Being British: Colour, Culture Citizenship*, Stoke-on-Trent: Runnymede Trust and Trentham Books.

Modood, T. (2004), 'Capitals, Ethnic Identity and Educational Qualifications', *Cultural Trends*, 13 (50): 87–105.

Peach, C. (1995), 'Profile of the Black Caribbean Population in Great Britain', in C. Peach (ed.), *Profile of the Ethnic Minority Populations in Great Britain*, London: Office of the Population Censuses and Surveys.

Phillips, M., and T. Phillips (1998), *Windrush: The Irresistible Rise of Multi-Racial Britain*, London: Harper Collins.

Rastogi, P., and J. F. Stitt (2008), 'Introduction', in P. Rastogi and J. F. Stitt (eds), *Before Windrush: Recovering an Asian and Black Literary Heritage within Britain*, 1–14, Newcastle: Cambridge Scholars Press.

Reay, D., and H. Lucey (2010). 'Identities in Transition: Anxiety and Excitement in the Move to Secondary School', *Oxford Review of Education*, 26 (2): 191–205.

Reay, D., and H. S. Mirza (1997), 'Uncovering Genealogies of the Margins: Black Supplementary Schooling', *British Journal of Sociology*, 18 (4): 477–99.

Sivanandan, A. (1982), *A Different Hunger: Writings on Black Resistance*, Pluto Press.

Solomos, J. (2003), *Race and Racism in Britian* (Third Edit), New York: Palgrave Macmillan.

Spohrer, K. (2011), 'Deconstructing "Aspiration": UK Policy Debates and European Policy Trends', *European Educational Research Journal*, 10 (1): 53–62.

Spohrer, K., G. Stahl and T. Bowers-Brown (2017), 'Constituting Neoliberal Subjects? "Aspiration" as Technology of Government in UK Policy Discourse', *Journal of Education Policy*, online before print 15 June. doi:10.1080/02680939.2017.1336573

Strand, S. (2014). 'Ethnicity, Gender, Social Class and Achievement Gaps at Age 16: Intersectionality and "Getting It" for the White Working Class', *Research Papers in Education*, 29 (2): 131–71. doi:10.1080/02671522.2013.767370

Strand, S., and W. James (2008), 'Educational Aspirations in Inner City Schools', *Educational Studies*, 34 (4): 249–67.

Tomlinson, S. (1981), *Educational Subnormality: A Study in Decision-Making*, London and Boston: Routledge & Kegan Paul.

Tomlinson, S. (1991), 'Ethnicity and Educational Attainment in England: An Overview', *Anthropology & Education*, 22 (2): 121–39.

Trevino, J., M. A. Harris and D. Wallace (2008), 'What's So Critical About Critical Race Theory?', *Contemporary Justice Review: Issues in Criminal, Social and Restorative Justice*, 11 (1): 7–10.

Wallace, D. (2017a), 'Aspiration Anxieties: Developing Middle Class Manhood among Black African Boys in London', in G. Stahl, J. Nelson and D. Wallace (eds), *Masculinity and Aspiration in the Era of Global Neoliberal Education*, 54–77, London and New York: Routledge.

Wallace, D. (2017b), 'Cultural Capital as Whiteness? Examining Logics of Ethno-Racial Representation and Resistance', *British Journal of Sociology of Education*, online before print 2 August.

Wallace, D. (2017c), 'Distinctiveness, Deference and Dominance in Black Caribbean Fathers' Engagement with Public Schools in London and New York City', *Gender and Education*, 29 (5): 594–613.

Wallace, D. (2017d), 'Reading "Race" in Bourdieu? Examining Black Cultural Capital among Black Caribbean Youth in South London', *Sociology*, 51 (5): 907–23.

Warrington, M., and M. Younger (2000), 'The Other Side of the Gender Gap', *Gender and Education*, 12: 493–507.

Waters, M. C., 2008. Comparing Immigrant Integration in Britain and the US, Working Paper: University of Manchester.

Winder, R. (2004), *Bloody Foreigners: The Story of Immigration to Britain*, London: Abacus.

Wright, C., D. Weekes, A. McGlaughlin and D. Webb (1998), 'Masculinised Discourses within Education and the Construction of Black Male Identities amongst African Caribbean Youth', *British Journal of Sociology of Education*, 19 (1): 75–87.

Younger, M., and M. Warrington (1996), 'Differential Achievement of Girls and Boys at GCSE', *British Journal of Sociology of Education*, 17: 299–314.

Younger, M., M. Warrington and R. McLellan (2005), *Raising Boys' Achievement in Secondary Schools: Issues, Dilemmas and Opportunities*, London: Open University Press.

12

Bourdieu in Nigeria: The Colonial Habitus and Elite Nigerian Parents' Aspirations for Their Children

Pere Ayling

Introduction

Sociological studies using Bourdieu's concepts have burgeoned in recent years. The growth of Bourdieuphiles (to use Lamont's (2012: 229) description of Bourdieu's devotees) reflects the increasing popularity of Bourdieu-inspired research and researchers within the field of social science in general, and sociology in particular. Yet, despite their international reach and popularity, Bourdieu's theoretical concepts are rarely utilized in studies in Africa exploring parents' school choices and aspirations for their children. The few Bourdieu-inspired research project in postcolonial contexts have focused on the political (Burawoy and Von Holdt 2012) and literary (Dalleo 2016) fields rather than the micro-social processes of social class reproduction and elite identity formation and/or preservation more specifically. This chapter reflects on a recent research project on Nigerian elite parents which applied Bourdieu's concepts to understand how parents' aspiration of transforming their children into transnational elites, while reproducing their social positioning at the same time, was realized through the consumption of 'white' schooling.

According to Bourdieu, individuals' aspirations cannot be disassociated 'from the objective situation in which they are constituted and from which they are inseparable, a situation that is objectively defined by economic constraints and social norms' (Bourdieu et al. 1990: 16–17). In other words, to understand individuals' or groups' aspirations, one must first look at 'the social conditions [class and racial] within which they are imagined' (Gale and Parker 2015: 81). To put this yet another way, the social field, which is where the habitus is structured and restructured, shapes individuals' aspirations. Studies have shown that the generative principles, capital(s) and rules, in short, the 'intrinsic properties' (Bourdieu 1984: 170), that determine the social field of Nigerian-educated elites are the by-products of colonialism (Smythe and Smythe 1960; Bassey 1999). Consequently, like their African counterparts, Nigerian-educated elites continue to depend on 'colonialism for [their] legitimacy' (Ekeh 1975: 96). This is an important observation because it has major theoretical and methodological implications for studies investigating elite aspirations in postcolonial contexts.

Given that whiteness is a highly valued symbolic capital in former British colonies such as Nigeria (Ayling 2015, 2016, forthcoming), coupled with the fact that we live in a world where social positioning is determined to a large extent by race (Emirbayer and Desmond 2015; Dalleo 2016), it is imperative that race is foregrounded in any analysis of how blacks' aspiration to gain membership of global/transnational elite groups is realized.

The lack of attention to race[1] in Bourdieu's social analysis has been widely acknowledged by several scholars as a major weakness of his theory (Reay 2004; Emirbayer and Desmond 2015; Burawoy and Von Holdt 2012; Dalleo 2016). To be clear, I am not suggesting that Bourdieu did not theorize about colonialism, and by association racism. As Wallace (2016) explains, one only needs to read Bourdieu's earlier works such as *The Algerians* (1962) to see this. Instead, the issue is Bourdieu's reluctance 'to use [race] not only in his analysis of colonialism, but also of French society where he is far more comfortable deploying class as his critical concept' (Burawoy 2012: 79). Furthermore, another equally important point worth mentioning is that Bourdieu focused on the structural rather than the psychic dimensions of colonialism (Go 2013).

To date, there has been no empirical sociological research into how race (and colonialism), along with the pathologizing discourses of blackness, has permeated and reconfigured the habitus of black parents in postcolonial societies, thus shaping *what* and *whom* they aspire for their children to become. This is a lacuna my research attempts to address by extending Bourdieu's social theory through Fanon's psychoanalytic approach to whiteness and colonialism. Utilizing Bourdieu's and Fanon's respective theories in this manner not only ensures a successful deployment of Bourdieu's concepts in postcolonial contexts such as Nigeria, such a convergent approach also bolsters my analysis of elite Nigerian parents' aspirations for their children.

The chapter begins with a description of the research participants before going on to provide a summary of Bourdieu's theorization of elites and elite identity formation, highlighting the two main concepts, namely 'distinction strategies' and 'attributes of excellence', integral to Bourdieu's analysis of elites and elitehood. This is followed by a broad discussion of Fanon's psychoanalytic approach to whiteness and colonialism. The chapter then goes on to reflect on how the coupling of Bourdieu's and Fanon's respective theories provides a stronger conceptual framework within which to understand these parents' aspirations for their children. I argue that both the distinction strategy – which in this case is parents' consumption of predominantly white private boarding schools in the UK – and the resources (the attributes of excellence) that these parents conceive as being the 'ideal weapons' for achieving their aspirations for their children reflect their colonial habitus.[2] The chapter concludes by highlighting some of the methodological and epistemological implications of taking Bourdieu to Nigeria.

Researching elites

The term 'elite' is a fluid concept that is often used to describe individuals and institutions occupying positions of privilege and power in particular countries and/or fields of power. The fluidity of the concept suggests that 'elites are different and differently constituted and understood in different places' and within different fields (Ball 2016: 70). In other words, there is a diversity of elite groups. In my own work, I draw on Boyd's (1973: 16) characteristics of 'elites in modern democratic society', which set out nine key features and values that define these groups. These defining features include holding high occupational positions, a distinctive life style, group consciousness, a sense of exclusiveness, and being seen to hold a functional capability and a positioning of moral responsibility within society. Some of Boyd's characteristics of elites have been supported by other writing which emphasizes minority status and the exclusivity of holding such a positioning (Ellersgaard, Larson and Munk 2012; Keller 1963/1991). I used Boyd's framework to develop a sampling frame for recruiting the elite parents in my study. At the time of carrying out the research, it was estimated that there were only 802 Nigerian children in private boarding schools in the UK (Brooks 2011). This indicated, among other things, that the parents recruited for this study were both a minority and an exclusive group.

Thirty-nine participants took part in the original study. Of the thirty-nine participants, twenty-six were parents and thirteen were gatekeepers, such as head teachers, heads of department, education agents and consultants, and heads of visa sections in the British High Commission, Lagos. Twenty-one of the twenty-six parents had sent their children to private boarding schools in the UK. The fathers in the former group were mostly directors or CEOs of major organizations or owned their own medium or large companies in Nigeria, while two of the mothers held very significant political appointments at federal and state government levels at the time of the fieldwork. The other mothers who had sent their children to UK-based private boarding schools were either running their own businesses and/or were married to senior business or legal executives. At the time of the fieldwork, all the parents were residing in Nigeria. The data and analysis presented in this chapter pertain specifically to this group of parents. Both quantitative (questionnaires) and qualitative (semi-structured interview) data collection methods were used in the research. Pseudonyms will be used when extracts from parents' interview transcripts are presented.

Operationalizing Bourdieu's key concepts in elite identity formation

Manners and style are among the surest signs of nobility. (Bourdieu 1996: 112)

The embodiment of distinction or, to put it more precisely, the 'attributes of excellence' (Bourdieu 1984: 61) and 'distinction strategies' (Bourdieu 1993: 115) are important concepts in Bourdieu's theorization of elite identity formation and reproduction. Bourdieu defines distinction as 'the transfigured, misrecognisable, legitimate form of social class' that 'only exists through *the struggles for the exclusive appropriation of the distinctive signs* which make natural distinction' (1984: 250, original emphasis). According to Bourdieu, refined accents, decorum, dispositions and lifestyles are 'regarded as the attributes of excellence [and] constitutes one of the key markers of "class"' (1984: 66). Elaborating further, Bourdieu contends that these 'attributes of excellence' are 'also the ideal weapon in strategies of distinction' (1984: 66).

Within Bourdieu's framework, membership of an elite group depends not only on economic capital but also on the acquisition of authentic aesthetic taste and distinguishable deportment and dispositions. Crucially, these dispositions and deportments are a form of symbolic boundary employed by the elite classes 'to enforce, maintain, normalize, or rationalize' their advantageous social position (Lamont and Molnar 2002: 186).

While Bourdieu's sociology provides us with 'profound insights into the logic of practical action ... and the importance of symbolic classification struggles'

(Emirbayer and Desmond 2015: 11), a close reading of Bourdieu shows a lack of attention to race in his analysis of elite identity formation. I feel this omission of race in Bourdieu's analysis significantly limits the extent to which his concepts can successfully translate to postcolonial contexts such as Nigeria where race permeates the discourse of aspiration (Ayling 2015). Specifically, by omitting race in his analysis, I observed three significant issues with Bourdieu's thesis on the formation of elite identities. First, he did not consider the role of race in accessing 'attributes of excellence'. Secondly, and related to the first point, Bourdieu did not conceive of a global context where a certain '"Western deportment" is advantageous' and perceived as an attribute of excellence (Ayling 2015: 458). Thirdly, Bourdieu did not consider how race not only shapes the aspirations of elites – or those seeking elite status in postcolonial contexts – but also how white people are the ones whom African elites must aspire to be like if they are to gain entry into transnational/global elite groups. Taken together, I argue that the absence of race in Bourdieu's social analysis has made his framework quite limited and therefore not capable of providing a robust analysis of eliteness and elites' aspirations in postcolonial contexts where whiteness is synonymous with excellence (Hunter and Hachimi 2012).

To ensure that Bourdieu's concepts 'are not rendered useless' (Von Holdt 2012: 27) in postcolonial contexts such as Nigeria, I decided to extend Bourdieu's framework by incorporating it with Fanon's thesis on whiteness. My research interest, among other things, is how eliteness is acquired and reproduced in postcolonial societies such as Nigeria as well as the role of colonialism in shaping aspirations in postcolonial contexts. Concomitantly, my theoretical concern (and contribution) is that, without an extension of Bourdieu's class theory, one could, at best, only have a partial understanding of how elite Nigerian parents pursue their aspiration of reproducing their social position via their children. I also felt that to ignore the significance of colonialism and coloniality (Ndlovu-Gatsheni 2013) in shaping these parents' aspirations as well as their choice of distinction strategy would be to grant theory 'epistemic primacy ... over subjectivist understanding' (Bourdieu and Wacquant 1992: 35, 11). This is something Bourdieu himself vehemently opposed. In the next section, I briefly discuss the (post)colonial context as theorized by Fanon, within which these parents' aspirations for their children are formed, before going on to reflect on how thinking *with* Bourdieu and Fanon in tandem engendered an understanding of aspiration as a complex and rubrical phenomenon in postcolonial contexts.

Frantz Fanon: The 'colonial condition'

Framed within a psychoanalytic perspective and from the perspective of a colonized subject, Fanon (1967/2008) provides a robust and systematic analysis of the long-lasting psychological effects of colonialism on blacks, particularly Africans. In his classic text *Black Skin, White Masks*, Fanon (1967/2008) examines the psychology of colonialism, theorizing that colonization, as perpetuated by the West, has resulted in the gentrification of blacks' minds. Fanon asserts that colonialism shattered the corporeal schema (which he described as 'a definitive structuring of self and the world', and an essential element of any sense of self) of the colonized/black, thus creating 'a real dialectic between the body [of the colonized] and the world' (Fanon 1967/2008: 83). In the place of the normal subjective self, Fanon postulates, a 'racial epidermal schema' (84) arises, which means the colonized can only have 'a relationship to self ... which is scripted by the coloniser', therefore producing in him or her the internally divided condition of 'absolute depersonalisation' (xi).

Furthermore, Fanon contends that colonization has also resulted in whiteness being constructed as the symbol of excellence and virtue. Central to Fanon's postcolonial analysis is how blackness has been historically constructed in ways that reinforce and sustain the superiority of whiteness, mainly through the logic of difference. Fanon writes: '*One is white as one is rich, as one is beautiful, as one is intelligent*' (Sardar 2008, quoted in Fanon 1967/2008: xiii, original emphasis). Conversely, 'the corollary: *he is [black] who is immoral*' (xiii, original emphasis). Fanon asserts that in the 'collective unconscious' – of both whites and blacks – 'the black man [and woman] stands for sin. In Europe, whether concretely or symbolically, the black man stands for the bad side of the character' (145–6).

According to Fanon, these 'postulations [and] propositions slowly and subtly work their way into one's minds and shapes one's view of the world' (1967/2008: xvi) so that, eventually, blacks come to believe in their supposed 'inferiority'. Crucially, Fanon postulates that the residue of colonialism extends into the postcolonial period and can be traced in the life styles, preferences, aspirations, comportment and judgements of black individuals. Within Fanon's framework, entry into transnational elite circles requires the effacement of one's blackness as well as adopting 'ways of speaking associated with educated white society' (Emirbayer and Desmond 2015: 86). To put it another way, though 'black in blood and colour', blacks who aspire to gain membership into a transnational elite class must be 'white' 'in taste, in opinions, in morals, and in intellect' (Macauley

1995: 430, cited in Molande 2008: 186). Of course, as Nayak accurately states, 'Race has no ontological basis but is the tortured result of splintered fantasises projected onto an imaginary Other' (2007: 748).

Notably, while Bourdieu mostly deployed class in his analysis, choosing to reduce all struggles for distinction analytically to the level of class dynamics, race was the salient unit of analysis in Fanon's theoretical framework. However, any analysis that is divorced from either race or class will fall short of providing a nuanced understanding of both the distinction strategy and the (re)sources used by those who aspire to gain or maintain elite status in postcolonial Nigeria. Rather, what is needed to understand elite aspiration in postcolonial societies is an intersectional analysis which draws conceptually from both postcolonial theory/literature and class theory. I found working with Fanon and Bourdieu in tandem useful in this regard.

I found Bourdieu's theorization of elite identity formation and preservation, particularly his notions of the 'attributes of excellence' and 'distinction strategy', to be particularly useful in understanding the social reproduction strategies of Nigerian elite parents. In my research, I demonstrated that Nigerian elite parents' distinction strategies took the form of three key micro-social processes,[3] namely, 'minority status', 'bodily transformation' and 'posh British accent' (see Ayling 2015 for a full analysis). Extending Bourdieu's analysis with Fanon's thesis on whiteness, I theorized white British upper classes' accent, decorum, life style and leisure activities as the 'attributes of excellence', which parents believed would not only help to distinguish their children from the *nouveau riche* but, more importantly, enable them to gain membership of a transnational elite group.

Working *with* Bourdieu and Fanon: 'White' schools as a strategy of distinction for elite Nigerian parents

In this section, I present an overview of my analysis of the data from parents' interview transcripts, utilizing the explanatory powers of both Bourdieu's and Fanon's theoretical frameworks. I reflect on how the consumption of white schooling enabled these parents to pursue their aspiration of transforming their children into national and transnational elites. For the purposes of this chapter, extracts from parents' interview transcripts are used to illustrate and instantiate key concepts in my analysis (cf. Ayling, forthcoming for a more detailed analysis). The analysis of the extracts weaves Bourdieu and Fanon together, demonstrating the complex interplay between race and class and how these influence Nigerian elite parents' aspirations for their children as well as their choice of distinction strategy.

In theorizing with Bourdieu and Fanon, I conceptualized parents' consumption of international schooling as a type of distinction strategy that enables them to achieve their aspirations for their children. Evidence from the data indicated a strong preference for predominately white private boarding schools in the UK. Given the historical constructions of whiteness and white people as having 'the highest possible concentration of values' (Molande 2008: 182), these 'white' schools can be understood as consecration sites for elite membership. That is to say, these schools are the only ones with the power to consecrate elite identity on those seeking membership of elite groups (Bourdieu 1998). They are also the sites where elite habitus and aspirations are constituted and acquired (cf. Forbes and Maxwell, this collection), which has serious implications for the future reproduction of the elite class.

The relatively small numbers of black pupils (and teachers), particularly Nigerians, in these schools invariably confers minority status on these parents' children. Minority status is a form of distinction which allows those who possess it to gain exclusivity. Being 'one of the few Nigerian child[ren]' (Mr Akpan) attending elite boarding schools in the West was considered by parents as a privilege, and it is, since not everyone (especially blacks) who aspire to attend these white elite establishments are admitted into them (Warikoo 2016). Indeed, restriction to an elite group is another important task of elite schools since eliteness is maintained through scarcity and exclusivity (Bourdieu 1996).

Furthermore, I argue that authenticity plays an important role in gaining membership to transnational elite groups or, to be more precise, Western class in Fanon's scheme. Accordingly, the manner and place in which the 'attributes of excellence' are appropriated are as important as the dispositions and deportments themselves (Bourdieu 1984; Forbes and Maxwell, this collection). In analysing the data, I highlight the significance of being in a 'white' boarding school in the UK where these 'attributes of excellence' could be learned not only from 'real British teachers' (Mr Odili) or 'our colonial masters' (Mrs Ola), as another parent put it, but from the *original* source. I concluded that parents' keenness to place their children in predominantly white schools in the UK is an indication that they too are aware that the geographical location of the school and the nationality of the teachers are important if they are to realize their aspiration of transforming their children into national and transnational elites.

The data also highlights how the acquisition of a refined accent, which has been described as a very strong marker of eliteness in contemporary societies (Berghoff 1990; Bourdieu 1996), is another advantage of being with 'real' white British people. Within Bourdieu's framework, a refined accent is analogous to classical music in that it plays a significant role in distinguishing the 'bourgeois world' from that of the 'populace' or, as Bourdieu also suggests, 'inheritors' from 'newcomers' (Bourdieu 1984: 19). Viewed through a Fanonsian lens, acquiring a 'posh British accent' (Mrs Ola) from 'real' British people will not only give their children 'honorary citizenship' (Fanon 1967/2008: 25) into the Whiteworld; it is also one of the ways by which their children can prove that they qualify for the transnational elite groups which they aspire to.

Lastly, evidence from the data shows that these parents were keen to smooth away what they described as the 'ruggedness and brashness' (Mrs Adu) of their children's bodies and dispositions. Consequently, I theorized that given the consecrating powers of white teachers – coupled with the fact that white spaces are 'associated with refinement' – these white elitist schools are perceived by parents as having the capability of 'civilis[ing] [these] otherwise wild bodies' (Puwar 2004: 113), replacing them with Western gentility. The corporal body is an important element in the status game primarily because it is the most indispensable materialization of class and taste (Bourdieu 1977). Given that blacks' bodies are eternally constructed as '"rough" precisely because of the colour of their skin' (Ayling 2015: 466), I contend that these parents' desire to refine their children's bodies and accent is the first step towards them realizing their aspiration of their children gaining membership of a transnational elite class.

Drawing conceptually from both Bourdieu and Fanon, I theorize that, due to the historical context within which the Nigerian-educated elites' social field emerged, these parents have developed a 'colonial habitus', which is a variant of Bourdieu's class-bound habitus (Ayling, forthcoming). I argue that parents' choice of distinction strategy, that is the consumption of 'white' schooling, is a function of their 'colonial habitus'. To put it differently, 'the current configuration of the world [which] is symbolised by the figure of [the West] at the apex and ... Africa at the bottom of the racialized and capitalist hierarchies' (Ndlovu-Gatsheni 2013: xi) has made UK-based British private boarding schools an 'ideal weapon' for non-Westerner aspirants seeking admission into the global elite class.

Lastly, an interesting factor that I observed during the data collection is how the internalization of the colonial habitus has not only provided these parents with the *know-how* of 'the game', it has, more importantly, led to an aspiration to *invest* in the game. In other words, the internalization of the colonial habitus has not only shaped these parents' aspirations for their children (with the Western class being the class to whom their children must aspire to in order to gain membership of transnational elite class), it has also led to the *illusio* or, more specifically, the unfaltering belief in the value of whiteness. Bourdieu describes the illusio as

> the enchanted relation to a game that is a product of a relation of ontological complicity between mental structures and the objectives structures of social space ... games which matter to you are important and interesting because they have been *imposed and introduced in your mind, in your body, in a form called the feel for the game.* (1998: 77, emphasis added)

Fanon's psychoanalytic approach to whiteness and colonialism is important to our understanding of the 'illusio' in postcolonial contexts.

Concluding thoughts

Given that Africa is differently configured to the West, some postcolonial scholars such as Ndlovu-Gatsheni might question the benefits of using Western theories such as Bourdieu's at all in postcolonial contexts, particularly if 'locally produced theories and methods might prove more productive' (2013: 20) (although I perceive that the primacy given to race over class in Fanon's psychoanalysis of distinction in postcolonial contexts is a weakness). There is also a more serious concern, which is that taking Western theories to Africa maintains rather than challenges the dominance of 'white sociology' (Dean 2017: 56). Speaking from a feminist perspective, Harding draws our attention to

> how the development of Western sciences and models of knowledge are embedded in and have advanced the development of Western society and culture but have also led to the simultaneous de-development and continual re-creation of 'other' – third world peoples, women, the poor, nature. (1991: ix)

Therefore, even though Bourdieu's ethnographic experience in Algeria might have 'served as a generative site for his concept of habitus, his relational sociology ... and his reflexive sociology' (Go 2013: 61), his theoretical framework is still perceived, rightly or wrongly, as Euro-centric, or Franco-centric to be more precise, thus considered not useful beyond the global North (Connell 2007).

As a black/African sociologist, I am aware of the epistemological and methodological as well as racial implications of using 'western' theories in postcolonial contexts. I am equally aware of the hegemonic Euro-American epistemologies' tendency to 'assume the character of objective, scientific, neutral, universal and [the] only truthful knowledges' (Escobar 2007, quoted in Ndlovu-Gatsheni 2013: 8). However, my decision to use Bourdieu was motivated by my desire to use the 'right tools' for the job. I was certainly not lured by Bourdieu's popularity within the social sciences but by the usefulness of his concepts as analytical tools. In this regard, what Bourdieu offers, in my view, is not a theory per se but rather 'a toolbox of ideas and approaches to challenge orthodoxy' (Dean 2017: 18).

Seeking the 'right' tools for the job requires that one become reflexive. I found Bourdieu's epistemic reflexivity particularly useful as this approach is 'neither egocentric nor logocentric but quintessentially embedded in, and turned towards, scientific practice' (Bourdieu and Wacquant 1992: 46). Bourdieu also warns against limiting the reflexive gaze to the self which is basically the 'bemoaning [of the sociologist's] class background and location … race or his [or her] gender' (Bourdieu and Wacquant 1992: 69). Rather, Bourdieu urges sociologists to scrutinize our theoretical and ontological positions and the knowledge claims which implicitly underpin them. Ironically, it was the application of Bourdieu's epistemic reflexivity which led me to Fanon.

In this chapter I have argued that 'Bourdieu had little to say in systematic terms about racial fields or [colonial] habitus' (Emirbayer and Desmond 2015: 11). Specifically, I contend that the omission of race from Bourdieu's analysis 'creates a difficulty when applying his theories to colonial and postcolonial contexts in which questions of race and [internal] racism cannot be ignored' (Dalleo 2016: 117). To ensure that Bourdieu's concepts were successfully translated in postcolonial Nigeria, I have demonstrated how I extended Bourdieu's social analysis through capitalizing on Fanon's psychoanalysis of whiteness and colonialism.

I have argued that putting Fanon (race) and Bourdieu (class) into dialogue provides profitable insights into not only the 'distinction strategies' required in elite reproduction in postcolonial contexts, but also the type of capitals (attributes of excellence) needed by elite Nigerian parents who desire for their children to gain membership of transnational elite groups. The elasticity of Bourdieu's concepts of field, capital and the habitus meant they could easily be blended with other conceptual frameworks, with Fanon's being a case in point.

Importantly, the malleability of Bourdieu's concepts allowed me to 'trouble' his concepts, when and if necessary, rather than be beholden to them. Finally, like Burawoy and Von Holdt, I hope that by taking Bourdieu to Nigeria I was

> making him earn his distinction, forcing him to restore the connection of theory to practice [to] see, first whether he can survive the journey, whether he can flourish in the [western] tip of Africa as he did on its Northern [Algeria] coast. (2012: 217)

Notes

1 To be clear, I *do not* subscribe to the reduction of racial categorizations to the bipolar couplet of white(ness) and black(ness). However, like Fanon and more recently Ladson-Billings (1998: 8), I am painfully conscious of the fact that these 'two categories have [unfortunately] remained stable'. That is to say, though racial categorization may have assumed different 'faces and permutations ... in contemporary society' (Ladson-Billings 1998: 8), whiteness and blackness remain the 'two permanent fixtures' on the metaphoric racial ladder; 'with whiteness at the apex, blackness at the base and all other races falling in-between' (Annamma, Connor and Ferri 2013: 14).

2 The colonial habitus, the reverse of the 'white habitus' (Bonilla-Silva 2006: 104), is a 'synthetic' habitus produced by, and reproductive of, internal racism. More specifically, the colonial habitus is a variant of Bourdieu's class-bound habitus in the sense that it is the internalization of racialized schemas or embodied racial history, itself reconfigured and splintered by colonialism and coloniality.

3 Being born into an elite family does not automatically make one an elite. Rather one *becomes* an elite by acquiring certain dispositions and deportments. In other words, 'eliteness' is not only a *process,* but a social construct as well.

Recommended further reading

Ayling, P. (forthcoming), *Distinction, Exclusivity and Whiteness: Elite Nigerian Parents and the International Education Market,* London: Springer.

Burawoy, M., and K. Von Holdt (2012), *Conversations with Bourdieu: The Johannesburg Moment,* Johannesburg: Wits University Press.

Emirbayer, M., and M. Desmond (2015), *The Racial Order,* London: University of Chicago Press.

References

Annamma, S. A., D. Connor and B. Ferri (2013), 'Dis/ability Critical Race Studies (DisCrit): Theorizing at the Intersections of Race and Dis/ability', *Race, Ethnicity and Education*, 16 (1): 1–31.

Ayling, P. (2015), '"Embodying" Britishness: The (Re)making of the Contemporary Nigerian Elite Child', *Curriculum Inquiry*, 45 (5): 455–71.

Ayling, P. (2016), '"Eliteness" and Elite Schooling in Contemporary Nigeria', in C. Maxwell and P. Aggleton (eds), *Elite Education: International Perspectives*, 148–61, London: Routledge.

Ayling, P. (forthcoming), *Distinction, Whiteness and Exclusivity: Educating the Elite Nigerian Child*, London: Springer.

Ball, S. J. (2016), 'The Future of Elite Research in Education', in C. Maxwell and P. Aggleton (eds), *Elite Education: International Perspectives*, 69–75, London: Routledge.

Bassey, M. O. (1999), *Western Education and Political Domination in Africa: A Study in Critical and Dialogical Pedagogy*, London: Bergin & Garvey.

Berghoff, H. (1990), 'Public Schools and the Decline of the British Economy 1870–1914', *Oxford Journals*, 129 (1): 148–67.

Bonilla-Silva, E. (2006) 'Racism without Racists: Color-Blind Racism and the Persistence of Racial Inequality in the United States. Lanham, Maryland: Rowman & Littlefield', in P. Bourdieu (ed.), (1962), *The Algerians*, trans A. C. M. Ross, Boston, MA: Beacon.

Bourdieu, P. (1977), *Outline of a Theory of Practice*, Cambridge: Cambridge University Press.

Bourdieu, P. (1984), *Distinction: A Social Critique of the Judgement of Taste*, Cambridge, MA: Harvard University Press.

Bourdieu, P. (1993) *Sociology In Question*, London: Sage.

Bourdieu, P. (1996), *The State Nobility*, Stanford, CA: Stanford University Press.

Bourdieu, P. (1998), *Practical Reason: On the Theory of Action*, Cambridge: Polity Press.

Bourdieu, P., L. I. Boltanski, R. Castel, J.-C. Chamboredon and D. Schnapper (1990), *Photography: A Middle-Brow Art*, trans. S. Whiteside, Cambridge: Polity Press.

Bourdieu, P., and L. Wacquant (1992), *An Invitation to Reflexive Sociology*, Cambridge: Polity Press.

Boyd, D. (1973), *Elites and Their Education*, Windsor: NFER.

Brooks, M. (2011), *Nigeria: An Analysis of the Market in Nigeria for School-Age Education in the UK*, London: British Council's Education UK Partnership.

Burawoy, M., and K. Von Holdt (2012), *Conversations with Bourdieu: The Johannesburg Moment*, Johannesburg: Wits University Press.

Connell, R. (2007), *Southern Theory*, Cambridge: Polity Press.

Dean, J. (2017), *Doing Reflexivity: An Introduction*, Bristol: Policy Press.

Dalleo, R. (2016) Ed. *Bourdieu and Postcolonial Studies*, Liverpool: Liverpool University press.

Ekeh, P. (1975), 'Colonialism and the Two Publics in Africa: A Theoretical Statement', *Comparative Studies in Society and History*, 17: 91–112.

Ellersgaard, C. H., A. G. Larsen and M. D. Munk (2012), 'A Very Economic Elite: The Case of the Danish Top CEOs', *Sociology*, 47 (6): 1051–71.

Emirbayer, M., and M. Desmond (2015), *The Racial Order*, London: University of Chicago Press.

Fanon, F. (1967/2008), *Black Skin, White Masks*, London: Pluto Press.

Gale, T., and Parker, S. (2015), 'Calculating Student Aspiration: Bourdieu, Spatiality and the Politics of Recognition', *Cambridge Journal of Education*, 45 (1) 81–96.

Go, J. (2013), 'Decolonising Bourdieu: Colonial and Postcolonial Theory in Pierre Bourdieu's Earlier Work', *Sociological Theory*, 31 (1): 49–74.

Harding, S. (1991), *Whose Science? Whose Knowledge? Thinking from Women's Lives*, Milton Keynes: Oxford University Press.

Hunter, M., and A. Hachimi (2012), 'Talking Class, Talking Race: Language, Class, and Race in the Call Centre Industry in South Africa', *Social & Cultural Geography*, 13 (6): 551–66.

Keller, S. (1991) *Beyond the Ruling Class: Strategic Elites in Modern Society*, London: Transaction Publishers.

Ladson-Billings, G. (1998), 'Just What Is Critical Race Theory and What's It Doing in a Nice Field Like Education?', *International Journal of Qualitative Studies in Education*, 11 (1): 7–24.

Lamont, M. (2012), 'How Has Bourdieu Been Good to Think With? The Case of the United States', *Sociological Forum*, 27 (1): 228–37.

Lamont, M., and Molnar, V. (2002) 'The Study of Boundaries in the Social Sciences', *Annual Review of Sociology*, 28: 167–95.

Molande, B. (2008), 'Rewriting Memory: Ideology of Difference in the Desire and Demand for Whiteness', *European Journal of American Culture*, 27 (3): 173–90.

Nayak, A. (2007), 'Critical Whiteness Studies', *Sociology Compass*, 1: 737–55.

Ndlovu-Gatsheni, S. J. (2013), *Coloniality of Power in Postcolonial Africa: Myths of Decolonisation*, Dakar: CODESRIA.

Puwar, N. (2004), *Space Invaders: Race, Gender and Bodies Out of Place*, Oxford: Berg.

Reay, D. (2004), '"It's All Becoming a Habitus": Beyond the Habitual Use of Habitus in Educational Research', *British Journal of Sociology of Education*, 25 (4): 431–44.

Smythe, H. H., and M. M. Smythe (1960), *The New Nigerian Elite*, Stanford, CA: Stanford University Press.

Tarc, P., and A. M. Tarc (2015), 'Elite International Schools in the Global South: Transnational Space, Class Relationalities and the "Middling" International Schoolteacher', *British Journal of Sociology of Education*, 36 (1): 34–52. doi:10.1080/0 1425692.2014.971945

Von Holdt, K. (2012) 'Bourdieu in South Africa', in Burawoy, M. and Von Holdt, K. (2012) *Conversation with Bourdieu: The Johannesburg Moment*, South Africa: Wits University Press.

Wallace, D. (2016), 'Reading "Race" in Bourdieu: Examining Black Cultural Capital among Black Caribbean Youth in South London', *Sociology*, 58 (3): 24–50.

Warikoo, N. (2016), *The Diversity Bargain: And the Other Dilemmas of Race, Admission and Meritocracy at Elite Universities*, Chicago: University of Chicago Press.

13

Bridging the Gap: Using Bourdieu and Critical Race Theory to Understand the Importance of Black Middle-Class Parents' Educational Aspirations for Their Children

Barbara Adewumi

Introduction

Over the last three decades there has been very little research on black middle-class families, in contrast to the many studies exploring the underachievement of black working-class students in urban areas (Gillborn and Mirza 2000; Archer 2003; Platt 2007). As a result, far less is known about the black middle class, and even less about black middle-class parents' aspirations for their children. One of the first pieces of research to cast a more nuanced picture of black middle-class experiences with schooling was conducted by Rollock et al. (2012) on Caribbean-heritage middle-class families. They found five distinct groupings: 'comfortably middle class', 'middle class ambivalent', 'working class with qualifications', 'working class' and, a final group, 'interrogators'. They observed a fluidity between these black middle-class groups due to patterns of identification and dis-identification influenced by limited forms of inclusion based on white middle-class expectations of social mobility. Rollock et al's *The Colour of Class* (2015) further explored how race and class influence the identities of Caribbean parents and their children in a 'dominant white middle-class' society. Rollock et al's research concerning how professional parents managed class advantages and racial disadvantages while supporting their children through school provided the inspiration for my current research.

My qualitative study of twenty-five African and Caribbean parents sought to explore differences in black middle-class parents' strategies and decision-making in regard to their children's futures. Conducted in 2015, the research focused on the growing African and Caribbean middle class in London I call 'the Stayers' and those who had moved out of London to reside in predominantly white Kent, known in the study as 'the Movers'. Thirteen of the twenty-five parents interviewed came from a working-class family background and the other twelve parents came from established middle-class families. Of the twenty-five parents interviewed, fifteen parents had made the decision to move outside of London. As the aim of the study was to understand the strategies and practices adopted by black professional middle-class parents to pursue their aspirations for their children's education, the research explored the extent to which the strategies were linked to parents' perceptions of opportunities, risks and barriers they believed their children were likely to face in British society. Furthermore, the research highlighted that parental practices were commonly influenced by parents' social and economic backgrounds. Specifically, in the data there was evidence that parental aspirations for their children were influenced by the parents' knowledge of the labour market as well as their historical, economic, social and cultural experiences of being black in Britain. However, while Bourdieu's approach to social practices offers a useful tool to understand the dispositions and strategies taken by black middle-class parents, I find that Bourdieu's conceptual toolkit does not always fully explain the interactions between racialized and class experiences (Rollock et al. 2015).

In this chapter, I extend Bourdieu's work on the reproduction of class by incorporating CRT to highlight the influence of race and racism as well as to legitimate class positioning among the black middle classes in what has been a predominantly white middle-class focused area of scholarship (Ball et al. 2011). It should be noted that professed Bourdieusian scholars (in the context of educational research) have only tenuously engaged with the multiple dimensions of ethnically and economically stratified systems linked to radicalized forms of social capital, such as availability of resources, mobilization of family networks, and opportunities to forge connections through social mobility (Vincent et al. 2012a). Therefore, to further explore the extent to which Bourdieu's concepts of capitals are applicable in the analysis of racial identities and aspirations of black middle-class groups in the UK, this investigation required a bridging approach that combined Bourdieu's concept of cultural capital with theories about race.

Throughout my research, I defined parents' aspirations as a culture of hopeful possibilities and outcomes that go beyond their past experiences and present circumstances for the future benefit of their children. Similar to Rollock et al.

(2015), my research highlights how parents' aspirations are formulated through their lived experiences of postcolonial institutional structures and current socio-economic situations. These structures and situations in turn contribute to the way parents navigate a racialized education system for their children. In conducting this research, I relied mainly on Bourdieu's theory of capital to understand how and why parents use these strategies to achieve their aspirations for their children. Capital, for Bourdieu, exists in the forms of economic, social, cultural and symbolic capitals used in the daily lives of individuals. They are used as strategies of reproduction that serve to legitimize structures that confer advantage within society. In understanding Bourdieu's theory of capital, I saw how the parents in my study strategized to ensure the best outcomes for their children. However, a focus on capital alone did not highlight race and the nuanced forms of racism which emerged in the data, and this drew me towards CRT. For example, the parents I labelled the Movers, who possessed high levels of economic capital, chose to leave London and relocate to parts of Kent. Not only did they have the resources and finances to move out, my research showed they found the move meaningful to them in terms of social advancement and securing a good position for their children. The main focus of this chapter is to show how I created a bridge between the social theory of Bourdieu and CRT to analyse how parents' aspirations for their children were formed and *expressed*. Combining these two theories brought to the surface the more salient narratives of parents' everyday classed and raced experiences within the education system.

Bridging Bourdieu and Critical Race Theory (CRT)

Bourdieu's (1983, 1996) theory of class analysis proposed a framework in which social and educational inequalities can be understood as being contextually produced through the interactions of forms of capital within the field of education. Bourdieu's concept of cultural capital has had a particular influence on critiques of the inequalities of white privilege and norms in the British education system. It refers to the general cultural background and skills possessed by an individual, such as linguistic ability, cultural knowledge of art, taste, and shared norms and values. Cultural background is linked with class because (according to Bourdieu) it is influenced by (and influences) economic standing. Based on Bourdieusian logic, if this is the case, how can ethnic groups acquire dominant cultural capital if they do not start on a level playing field with the white majority? For example, Wacquant (2008) found that Americans living in hyper-segregated ghettos have fewer and less dense social ties/networks and have considerably less volume of all forms of capital. Differential distribution of capitals in the United States has been created through the legitimization and naturalization of the hierarchy that elevates white culture at the expense of others (Swartz 1998). The overall premise of this chapter is that researchers who work at the nexus of race and social class should consider engaging Bourdieu's conceptual tools with the particular *social* strengths of CRT.

Within Bourdieu's theoretical approach, social capital refers to forms of social participation and connection such as membership of network groups, communities and families. It has been argued that these forms of social capital are important resources for social mobility and extremely relevant to the discussion of black middle-class aspirations and family support mechanisms that cultivate self-confidence in black middle-class children (Vincent and Maxwell 2016). For example, Bourdieu's conceptual tools have been extended for an analysis of parenting practices that included the investigation of gender, class and race (Reay 2004; Wallace 2016). However, an overwhelming majority of research by Bourdieusian scholars fails to challenge assumptions of white dominant normalcy. That proved to be an inadequate perspective for the analysis of my data on the high expectations and aspirations of the Movers. Yosso (2005: 77) argues that such an application of Bourdieu's tools creates a deficit model of marginalized groups. Therefore, my application of CRT (using CRT's tenets discussed below) as a second lens beside a Bourdieusian schema is an effort to counteract any potential deficit approaches, placing race at the centre of my research, and providing a more nuanced approach to analysing black middle-class parents' aspirations for their children through drawing on the various capitals at their disposal to secure advantage.

Briefly, there are five tenets of CRT. First, CRT regards racism as so deeply entrenched in the social order that it is often taken for granted and viewed as natural (Delgado and Stefancic 2001). Secondly, creating and reinforcing racial subordination and maintaining a normalized position of white privilege is a central focus of the analysis of racial inequality (Crenshaw et al. 1995; Harris 1995). Thirdly, CRT places particular importance on the stories and experiences of racism and marginalization. Fourth is the tenet of interest convergence, where the interest of blacks in achieving racial equality will be accommodated only when it converges with the interests of whites (Bell 1980: 523). The fifth principle in CRT is intersectionality, whereby in complex and multiple ways various systems of subordination synthesize to discriminate against and disadvantage a group of people (Crenshaw 1989). Issues such as historical and sociopolitical context are taken into account while still maintaining awareness of racial inequalities.

Scholars in the UK have adopted CRT to explore the historical black working-class population in Britain, who continue to experience racism, including institutional racism (Gillborn and Mirza 2000). Gillborn et al.'s (2012) findings reveal that, despite their material and cultural capital, many middle-class black Caribbean parents find their high expectations of their children thwarted by racist stereotyping and exclusion. Speaking with both African and Caribbean parents, I found they conversed openly regarding the levels of discrimination, marginalization and subtle forms of misinterpretations of their middle-class identities and these accounts occurred everywhere, from the conversations at the school gates to their work environments.

CRT scholars adopt this theoretical approach to explore how racialized patterns of power through discrimination and oppression feed levels of social power that privilege some while marginalizing others. CRT challenges the traditional interpretation of cultural capital and applies the lens of race to highlight practices of marginalization and discrimination across a range of social institutions (Yosso 2005). In sociological theory, CRT regards race as a social construction and analyses the connections between race, racism, privilege and power that affect both class and gender (Delgado and Stefancic 2001, Solorzano, Ceja and Yosso 2000). Therefore CRT's framework, the tenets, allows for an exploration of the complex dimension of race, which provides a more focused and nuanced interpretation of aspirations and social life among black middle-class families than the single conceptual lens of Bourdieu's analysis (Vincent et al. 2012b). Specifically, CRT's focus on the primacy of race and racism allows us to recognize the structural, socio-economic and historical nature of racial inequality in the education system (Delgado and Stefancic 2001). CRT enables a more critical analysis, enlarging the scope to shed light on the 'images, preconceptions, and myths – that have been propagated by the dominant culture of hegemonic Whiteness as a way of maintaining racial inequality' (Trevino, Harris and Wallace 2012: 8). Interestingly, throughout the research, the Movers uniquely defined themselves outside of the social constructions of 'race' (which thoughtlessly predefined and negated their middle-class existence). They used words such as 'aristocratic', 'diplomat' and 'highly educated and professional heritage' to describe their class realities which, in turn, assisted in constructing a narrative that instilled both social and cultural aspirations for their children.

Black middle-class operationalizing capital

According to Lareau and Horvat (1999), black middle-class parents may experience different sets of acceptable spaces based on white privilege. The concept of acceptance involves an understanding of the complex interplay between race, class and cultural capital. In my study, black middle-class parents in Britain, who possessed high volumes of economic, social and cultural capital, faced a similar struggle for legitimation based on race despite having high aspirations. Bourdieu's theory of social capital allowed me to analyse parents' aspirational aims for their children in order to understand the strategies they use to preserve their social and cultural capital, suggesting that economic capital was only part of a wider strategy when it came to the reproduction of middle-class status (Reay 2010). Wallace (2016) argues that black middle-class Caribbean pupils use their black cultural capital to challenge widespread stigmatization and homogenization of black identities in school by acquiring bodies of knowledge and dispositions to improve their academic performance. Their use of black cultural capital in the classroom, for example (viewed as an 'acceptable space'), ultimately enhanced their relationships with teachers to elevate their class status.

Speaking with the parents, it was clear that high levels of social, cultural and economic capital enabled them to make the move to Kent. Furthermore, the Movers believed that they would enhance their chances of social advancement through moving outside of London. Such a strategic move contributed to shaping aspirations for their children. The main reason the Movers became geographically mobile was to gain access to schools they perceived as better quality, with only two parents of the fifteen moving out of London because of job promotions. In terms of education and opportunity there was a common aspiration and strategizing around time, as over half of the Movers relocated when their children were under the age of 11 with the 'expectation' that their children would pass the 11 plus exam and attend a selective grammar school in Kent. The Movers demonstrate the nuanced navigations around the acquisition and maintenance of cultural capital. At this point Bourdieu's tools do not entirely reveal the social reality of black middle-class aspirations or the intersections of raced and classed experiences. There is a need here for a more engaging and less 'light touch' approach to understanding race and racial experience through a selective appropriation of Bourdieu's tools alongside a CRT perspective.

Applying Bourdieu's tools and CRT to the 'movers'

This section draws on empirical data from the study to show how I created a bridge between Bourdieu and CRT to provide a more extensive analytical framework to uncover the strategies of black middle-class parents and the impediments they experienced in moving outside of London. In the following account, I show how one mother, Mary, a single parent and marketing director, decided to purchase a house in Kent in order to secure the future of her daughter Shelly.

Mary is a highly successful marketing director who was based in London and came from a line of high achievers in her middle-class Nigerian family. As a single mother, she made what she described as a 'calculated decision' to buy a house in Kent in order to get her daughter Shelly, who was mixed race, into a secondary grammar school with the ultimate intention of moving back to London once her daughter started university. Mary recalled that her friends thought that the move was a bold step, as she was going out on her own with Shelly with no support networks, and questioned why she could not just find a reputable school in London and be around 'people like us'. Mary's networks believed that 'out there' (in Kent) there are not enough black families and they were concerned about the level of racism both Mary and Shelly might encounter. However, Mary described her decision as 'an educational investment'. She reflected on the types of conversations she had with Shelly when they first arrived: 'Stick by those children who are in the top sets and get top marks and talk about having aspirations to go to a grammar school. Position yourself amongst that group – you know, like-minded and thinking people.'

The advice given to Shelly to position herself among 'that group' illustrates a traditional Bourdieusian class analysis where class differences are reinforced through the education system, as seen in previous research (Rollock et al. 2012; Archer 2012; Vincent et al. 2012a). Shelly was placed in a position of having to conform to and understand patterns of white middle-class identity within her all-white peer group where her 'feel for the game' was tied closely to knowing the right way of doing things (Bourdieu 1986). In terms of aspirations, Mary had already decided Shelly's career path and believed that being in the 'top sets' and associating with 'like-minded and thinking people' would help preserve their social status. However, early in her time living in Kent, Mary discovered that she had to assert her class position in order to establish her middle-class status and gain a certain level of respect. In an anecdote, Mary described an informal conversation she had with another parent at the school gate:

One day I came straight from work and they were staring with curiosity. One mum asked me where have you been? I said I had a meeting and came after work.

Mum: Oh! What do you do?
Mary: I am a marketing consultant [big smile]
Mum: Oh, so you've been to university then?
Mary: Yeah, sure. I graduated back in 1995, and that sort of thing, so I've
    excelled in the profession.

As a black middle-class professional, Mary felt strongly that she should not have endured that level of scrutiny. Furthermore, she believed that she had to announce her middle classness in a specific way in order to be accepted. Mary, in knowing what was important to other middle-class mothers, operationalized her cultural capital to express her identity as an educated, working professional. Mary's experience illustrates that the state of being black and middle class, and the use of black cultural, economic and social capital, was observed with an element of scepticism. Despite Mary's professional status, she was still subject to the stereotypical perception of the 'black single mother' being a deficient parent. As Mary was born and raised in a middle-class context, she knew what was valued in the field and operationalizing her cultural capital strategically to gain respectability and legitimacy among the white middle-class mothers. By operationalizing Bourdieu's theoretical approach, Mary's narrative connects strongly with how capitals are deployed to secure or heighten one's position. While Bourdieu's tools are useful, they do not necessarily go deep enough to explain the significant impact different levels of dominant social spaces have upon black middle-class parents, where struggles for legitimation of class and power persist. According to CRT, struggles like the one Mary experienced are multiplied within the social context of race and space. This was a recurrent theme with the parents I spoke with: Even though they all defined themselves as high achievers and professionals in their field, their degree of privilege was not perceived to have the same value as that of their white counterparts.

Discussion

The Movers described London as a place of distraction for their children and they felt they needed to move out of London to get away from influential peer groups. Seeking a place in a grammar school was a popular choice for these middle-class parents as they felt it would be a good academic start to support their aspirations for their children's professional career path.

By moving to residential areas in which they form a distinct minority, black pupils and their families face the prospect of isolation and disengagement from predominantly white middle-class communities. As a result of this isolation, support networks of family, friends and churches, both in Kent and in London, were widely used, which highlights another function of social capital that is underexplored in a Bourdieusian approach. There is an increased likelihood that children from these families will experience racism at school, or indeed struggle to find representations of themselves among their peers or teachers; yet these parents were prepared to take a risk in order to secure their children's futures. However, as we see in Mary's story, and as was generally true among other Movers in the study, these black middle-class parents were able to operationalize their various capitals. Through operationalizing such capitals, the parents reinforced their middle class-ness and identity within white middle-class spaces. The participants in this study were highly ambitious parents, many of whom had a clearly defined professional career path for their children. Despite some unfortunate experiences in their move to Kent, the parents I interviewed maintained high aspirations for their children and went out of their way to provide them with the resources and academic support they needed to achieve success.

Many other Movers spoke about occasions where they or their children experienced harassment. Parents felt that their children were initially misrepresented by teachers' assumptions that being black meant you were working class, predominantly from single parent homes and among the weaker students. The participants spoke of black children being more quickly labelled as the 'trouble maker' in the group as well as being more likely to be singled out within their peer group (by teachers and the local police). This also highlights the utility of the CRT tenet that white assumptions and stereotypes become part of black parents' and children's everyday experiences simply based on the colour of their skin. In predominantly white Kent, the parents also talked openly about how as parents they instructed their children not to mix with the wrong crowd and were very particular about whom their children associated with. For example, Roger (a senior social worker) and Mary (featured in this chapter) were very protective for fear of 'contamination' by the behaviour of the white working-class, labelled in the area as 'Chavs', or negative peer influence by other black children labelled as black 'ghetto' types (see Archer 2012 for further discussion). However, intertwined with these negative experiences and safeguarding against risk, some of the parents I interviewed voiced how they often felt a sense of belonging (e.g. 'I wanted them to get to like me': Tayo, a mother of two who moved to a small village community as part of the only black family in the village).

The misrepresentation of black members of society – through stereotyping them as working class – can be interpreted as a way to legitimate the symbolic location of power and class privilege within the white middle class (Archer 2012; Wallace this volume). CRT identifies the taken-for-granted centrality of white assumptions about what constitutes the white middle class. While the professional occupations of these parents in my study symbolize levels of power and class privilege, the abundant mis-perceptions of black middle-class professional status described in the study arguably denies this middle-class group their professional authenticity. Such misrecognition of black cultural capital (Wallace 2016) extends to their children and causes the academic ability of their children to be questioned due to racialized and classed inequalities in education. Given their level of investment, parents expressed concern about the educational and social disadvantage they perceived their children would experience.

Bourdieusian notions of class distinction, the operationalization of capitals and the field of education as a competitive route to preserving social position have indeed been a productive tool in my analysis of black middle-class parents' strategies to secure the success of their children. Parents interviewed felt the need to validate and legitimize their capitals in order to compete in the social field of education. Mary's experience highlights the use of CRT's centring of race, and its reminder that what is valued as resourceful capital should not be judged from a white norm. The incorporation of CRT tenets in experiential knowledge research in a bridge with Bourdieu's tools provides a valuable contribution. With the Movers, the analysis required a more nuanced understanding of (black) racialized middle classness on which the idea of 'people like us' or 'wanting similar things' for their children is constructed alongside white privilege and legitimacy (Rollock et al. 2012).

In thinking critically about the Movers and their experiences in Kent, it should be noted that for Bourdieu inequalities are never static and require an appreciation of complex historical and contemporary intersections of black middle-class groups in the field of education. CRT explicitly explores race, class and gender positionings within black families, linking historical and current injustices that continue to be reflected in education in terms of genuine social mobility (Crenshaw 1989; Delgado and Stefancic 2001). When theorizing about the importance of education through black middle-class experiences, one needs to be mindful of the relational and shifting existence of race, class and gender. Although Bourdieu's approach to education has the capacity to highlight the inequalities of social reproduction of class via structure, agency and the relevant fields, the theoretical tools need to be extended to incorporate those who are racially marginalized irrespective of their middle-class status. The narrow focus of Bourdieusian scholars arguably misses the opportunity to address the issues of genuine struggles over race and racialized barriers to social mobility.

Conclusion

This chapter set out to illustrate the theoretical potential of using a combined approach of Bourdieu's tools and principles of CRT to further our understanding of black middle-class parents' strategic use of economic, social and cultural capital to instil aspirations for their children. Throughout the research, it was clear that the parents wanted a 'better quality of life' and for their children 'to do better' and 'achieve more than they ever had'. Despite levels of difference and displacement in the suburbs of Kent, the Movers felt that geographical mobility was a 'worthy investment' for their children's education. While their friends thought it was a brave decision to leave London and become a 'minority within a minority' and probed their reasoning due to the pervasiveness of racism and the dominant association of middle classness with whiteness in British society, the Movers expressed determination to 'succeed', representing aspirations that are determined by the resourceful use of black cultural capital (Wallace 2016) in the contemporary landscape of Kent. Equipped with degrees and professional occupations, high economic capital and distinct flexible forms of social and cultural capital, it is clear the Movers embody, to varying degrees of success, the ability to strategically calculate their use of capital and find effective ways to 'play the game'. By operationalizing their capitals, they attempt to navigate beyond the social constructions of race, gender and class constructed through *mis*-conceptions of professional identities aligned to white normalcy.

Creating a bridge between Bourdieu's tools and CRT provides a useful theoretical approach to sensitively analysing how black middle-class parents deploy capitals to maintain and secure advantage. The empirical narratives of second-generation Movers and an engagement with Bourdieu's concepts unearthed how class, race and gender intertwine within the context of educational aspirations to influence parents' strategic decisions for their children's futures. My research on the aspirations that black middle-class parents have for their children and the strategies they employ to achieve these aspirations uncovered a more elusive and internalized sense of legitimacy, entitlement and acceptance as well as more hidden forms of class consciousness in relation to being black and middle class in a predominantly white geographical area.

Recommended further reading

Bourdieu, P. (1986), 'The Forms of Capital', in J. Richardson (ed.), *Handbook of Theory and Research for the Sociology of Education*, 241–58, New York: Greenwood Press.

Gillborn, D. (2008), *Racism and Education: Coincidence or Conspiracy?*, London: Routledge.

Rollock, N., D. Gillborn, C. Vincent and S. J. Ball (2015), *The Colour of Class: The Educational Strategies of the Black Middle Classes*, London: Routledge.

References

Archer. L. (2003), Higher Education and Social Class Issues of Exclusion and Inclusion: Routledge.

Archer. L. (2012), '"Between Authenticity and Pretension": Parents', Pupils' and Young Professionals' Negotiations of Minority Ethnic Middle-Class Identity', *Sociological Review*, 60 (1): 129–48.

Ball, S. J., N. Rollock, C. Vincent and D. Gillborn (2011), 'Social Mix, Schooling and Intersectionality: Identity and Risk for Black Middle-Class Families', *Research Papers in Education*, 28 (3): 265–88.

Bell, D. (1980), 'Brown vs. Board of Education and the Interest Convergence Dilemma', *Harvard Law Review*, 98: 518–33.

Bourdieu, P. (1983), 'The Field of Cultural Production, or: The Economic World Reversed', *Poetics*, 12 (4–5): 311–56.

Bourdieu, P. (1986), 'The Forms of Capital', in J. Richardson (ed.), *Handbook of Theory and Research for the Sociology of Education*, 241–58, New York: Greenwood Press.

Bourdieu, P. (1996), *The State Nobility: Elite Schools in the Field of Power*, Oxford: Polity Press.

Crenshaw, K. (1989) *Demarginalizing the Intersection of Race and Sex: A Black Feminist Critique of Antidiscrimination Doctrine, Feminist Theory, and Antiracist Politics, 1989* University of Chicago Legal Forum, 139.

Crenshaw, K., N. Gotanda, G. Peller and K Thomas (eds) (1995), *Critical Race Theory: The Key Writings that Formed the Movement*, New York: New Press.

Delgado, R., and J. Stefancic (2001), *Critical Race Theory: An Introduction*, New York: New York University Press.

Gillborn, D., and H. S. Mirza (2000), *Educational Inequality: Mapping Race, Class and Gender. A Synthesis of Research Evidence*, London: Office for Standards in Education.

Gillborn, D., N. Rollock, C. Vincent and S. J. Ball (2012), '"You Got a Pass, So What More Do You Want?" Race, Class and Gender Intersection in the Educational Experiences of the Black Middle Class', *Race, Ethnicity and Education*, 15 (1): 121–39.

Harris, C. (1995), 'Whiteness as Property', in K. Crenshaw, N. Gotanda, G. Peller and K. Thomas (eds), *Critical Race Theory: The Key Writings that Formed the Movement*, 276–91, New York: New Press.

Lareau, A., and E. M. Horvat (1999), 'Moments of Social Inclusion and Exclusion: Race, Class and Cultural Capital in Family–School Relationships', *Sociology of Education*, 72 (1): 37–53.

Platt, L. (2007), 'Making Education Count: The Effects of Ethnicity and Qualifications on Intergenerational Social Class Mobility', *Sociological Review*, 55 (3): 485–508.

Reay, D. (2004), 'Education and Cultural Capital: The Implications of Changing Trends in Education Policies', *Cultural Trends*, 13 (2): 73–86.

Reay, D. (2010), 'Sociology, Social Class and Education', in M. W. Apple, S. J. Ball and L. A. Gandin (eds), *The Routledge International Handbook of the Sociology of Education*, 396–404, Abingdon: Routledge.

Rollock, N., D. Gillborn, C. Vincent and S. Ball (2012), '"Middle Class by Profession": Class Status and Identification amongst the Black Middle Classes', *Ethnicities*, 13 (3): 253–75.

Rollock, N., D. Gillborn, C. Vincent and S. J. Ball (2015), *The Colour of Class: The Educational Strategies of the Black Middle Classes*, London: Routledge.

Solorzano, D., M. Ceja and T. Yosso (2000), 'CRT, Racial Microaggressions, and Campus Racial Climate: The Experiences of African-American College Students', *Journal of Negro Education*, 69 (1–2): 60–73.

Swartz, D. (1998), *Culture and Power: The Sociology of Pierre Bourdieu*, Chicago: University of Chicago Press.

Trevino, J., M. A. Harris and D. Wallace (2012), 'What's So Critical About Critical Race Theory?', *Contemporary Justice Review: Issues in Criminal, Social and Restorative Justice*, 11 (1): 7–10.

Vincent, C., N. Rollock, S. J. Ball and D. Gillborn (2012a), 'Being Strategic, Being Watchful, Being Determined: Black Middle-Class Parents and Schooling', *British Journal of Sociology of Education*, 33 (3): 337–54.

Vincent, C., N. Rollock, S. J. Ball and D. Gillborn (2012b), 'Intersectional Work and Precarious Positionings: Black Parents and Their Encounters with Schools in England', *International Study in Sociology of Education*, 22 (3): 259–76.

Vincent, C., and Maxwell, C. (2016), 'Parenting Priorities and Pressures: Furthering Understanding of 'Concerted Cultivation'', Discourse: Studies in the Cultural Politics of Education, 37 (2): 269–81.

Wacquant, L. (2008), *Urban Outcasts: A Comparative Sociology of Advanced Marginality*, Cambridge: Polity Press.

Wallace, D. (2016), 'Reading "Race" in Bourdieu? Examining Black Cultural Capital among Black Caribbean Youth in South London', *Sociology*, 51 (5): 907–23.

Yosso, T. J. (2005), 'Whose Culture Has Capital? A Critical Race Theory Discussion of Community Cultural Wealth', *Race, Ethnicity and Education*, 8 (1): 69–91.

Index